RACE POLICY AND M
AMERICA

Edited by
Kathleen Odell Korgen

C000155323

First published in Great Britain in 2016 by

Policy Press
University of Bristol
1-9 Old Park Hill
Bristol
BS2 8BB
UK
t: +44 (0)117 954 5940
pp-info@bristol.ac.uk
www.policypress.co.uk

North America office:
Policy Press
c/o The University of Chicago Press
1427 East 60th Street
Chicago, IL 60637, USA
t: +1 773 702 7700
f: +1 773-702-9756
sales@press.uchicago.edu
www.press.uchicago.edu

British Library Cataloguing in Publication Data
A catalogue record for this book is available from the British Library

Library of Congress Cataloging-in-Publication Data
A catalog record for this book has been requested

ISBN 978-1-4473-1650-3 paperback
ISBN 978-1-4473-1645-9 hardcover
ISBN 978-1-4473-1646-6 ePub
ISBN 978-1-4473-1647-3 Mobi

Cover design by Soapbox Design, London
Printed and bound in Great Britain by CMP, Poole
Policy Press uses environmentally responsible print partners

Contents

List of figures and tables

Figures

Tables

Author biographies

Jessica M. Barron is a postdoctoral fellow in the Social Science Research Institute at Duke University, Durham. Her research focuses on racial inequality and the dynamics of race in multiracial churches. Currently, she is examining multiracial segregation in US cities using newly refined versions of traditional segregation measures.

Tina Fernandes Botts is a Visiting Assistant Professor & Consortium for Faculty Diversity at Liberal Arts Colleges Postdoctoral Fellow at Oberlin College. She is also chair of the American Philosophical Association's (APA's) Committee on the Status of Black Philosophers and the managing editor of the APA's *Newsletter on Philosophy and the Black Experience*. Professor Botts is currently at work on two books: *Philosophy and the mixed race experience* and *Race, Aristotle's proportional equality and the equal protection clause*.

Jenifer L. Bratter is an Associate Professor of Sociology at Rice University and the director of the Program for the Study of Ethnicity Race and Culture. Professor Bratter's research primarily focuses on the ways racial interactions in the realms of families and identities have implications for the ways racial disparities in health and poverty are captured and experienced Her work appears in in peer-reviewed journals and book chapters.

David L. Brunsma is Professor of Sociology at Virginia Tech. He is author and/or editor of *Beyond Black: biracial identity in America* and *Mixed messages: multiracial identities in the "colorblind" era*, among others. He is Founding Co-Editor of the Section of Racial and Ethnic Minorities' new journal *Sociology of Race and Ethnicity* at the American Sociological Association. He lives and loves with his wife Rachel, and his three kids, Karina, Thomas, and Henry in Blacksburg, VA.

Mary E. Campbell is an Associate Professor of Sociology affiliated with the Race and Ethnic Studies Institute at Texas A&M University. Her work on racial identification and racial inequality has been funded by the National Science Foundation and the National Institute on Aging, and has appeared in journals such as the *American Sociological Review*, *Ethnic and Racial Studies*, and *Social Problems*.

E. Namisi Chilungu, PhD, is a Clinical Assistant Professor in the Department of Educational Psychology, Special Education, and Communication Disorders. She has a doctorate and master's degree in Educational Psychology from the University at Buffalo. She is passionate about increasing quality access to education for all students, particularly students from marginalized populations or high-need communities.

Gennifer Furst received her doctorate in Criminal Justice from CUNY Graduate Center/John Jay College. She is an Associate Professor at William Paterson University of New Jersey. Her research interests include incarceration and prison programs, particularly those involving animals.

Marc P. Johnston-Guerrero is an Assistant Professor in the Higher Education and Student Affairs program, Department of Education Studies at The Ohio State University. His research interests focus on racial dynamics in US higher education, with specific attention to issues of multiraciality within understandings of campus climate and college student development.

Andrew Jolivette is Professor and Chair of American Indian Studies at San Francisco State University. He is the author of several books and essays including *Research justice: methodologies for social change* (Policy Press, 2015) and *Obama and the biracial factor: the battle for a new American majority* (Policy Press, 2012).

Nikki Khanna is Associate Professor of Sociology at the University of Vermont. Her areas of specialization are multiracial people and identity and, more recently, the role of race in adoption. She is the author of *Biracial in America: forming and performing racial identity* (Lexington Books, 2011).

Kathleen Odell Korgen is Professor of Sociology at William Paterson University. She received her BA from the College of the Holy Cross and her PhD at Boston College. Kathleen, a public sociologist, specializes in race relations, racial identity, and inequality.

Daniel N. Lipson, PhD, is an Associate Professor of Political Science at SUNY New Paltz. He earned his PhD in Political Science in 2002 at the University of Wisconsin-Madison. His research focuses on the legal and political battles over race-based affirmative action in higher education.

Christa Mason, BA, graduated from Rice University in 2014, majoring in Sociology. She was accepted to The University of Texas at Arlington, where she will earn a Master of Science in Industrial/Organizational Psychology.

Tyrone Nagai is an Assistant Editor at *Asian American Literary Review.* He also served as Art Director of the Mixed-Race Initiative.

Raúl Quiñones-Rosado, PhD, is a social justice educator, antiracism organizer, and Latino leadership coach. His book, *Consciousness-in-action: toward an integral psychology of liberation & transformation,* is used in academic programs in psychology, counseling, social work, and social justice education in the US and Latin America, as well as by political activists, community organizers, anti-oppression trainers, helping professionals, and others. He lives with his family in Cayey, Puerto Rico.

Kristen A. Renn is Professor of Higher, Adult, and Lifelong Education at Michigan State University, where she also serves as Associate Dean of Undergraduate Studies and Director for Student Success Initiatives. Her research focuses on college student identities, development, and success.

Hephzibah V. Strmic-Pawl is an Assistant Professor of Sociology at Manhattanville College. Her teaching and research interests center on race, racism, and social inequality, with a particular focus on multiracialism. Strmic-Pawl's forthcoming book is a comparative analysis of how Asian–White people's and Black–White people's racial identity and opportunities are differentially shaped by the hegemony of the US racial hierarchy.

Rhina Fernandes Williams specializes in critical pedagogy, teacher development, and multicultural education, with a special interest in education for social justice. She is currently a faculty member in the Department of Early Childhood and Elementary Education at Georgia State University in Atlanta.

Introduction

Kathleen Odell Korgen

This is a book about a controversial topic—race policy and multiracial Americans. Simply mentioning the term "multiracial" can draw strong reactions among social commentators and scholars today. As Rainier Spencer (2014: 166) puts it:

> [some] argue that multiracial identity has the potential to undo race in the United States as long as it attends to social justice and does not present itself as a racially superior category, while other scholars contend that multiracial identity is supportive of White supremacy and is a throwback to earlier, simplistic, and racist conceptualizations of the American mulatto.

Many civil rights groups, including the National Association for the Advancement of Colored People (NAACP) and the Urban League, view the creation of a multiracial category (and its support by opponents of civil rights and affirmative action policies such as Newt Gingrich) as a potential threat to race policies established to protect and assist monoracial racial minorities. On the other hand, many multiracial organizations and advocates for a multiracial category within the US Census and other demographic instruments understand the need to address racial discrimination but also "believe in an all-inclusive society, where all individuals are afforded the dignity and autonomy to identify themselves in the ways they believe represent them" (Swirl, no date [a]: para 3). They aim to "create supportive and inclusive communities for all people" (MAVIN, 2014: paras 2, 4) and "have created a home for those who refuse to be boxed into 'choosing just one'" (Swirl, no date[b]: para 2). While acknowledging and working to combat all acts of racism in society, they aim a spotlight on racial issues that impact multiracial persons because of their mixed heritage.

The acknowledgment of persons who identify as multiracial and the issues related to them are the foci of the newly recognized field of critical mixed race (CMR) studies. While building on the work of critical race and ethnic studies, CMR scholars "place mixed race at the critical center of focus" (Daniel, 2014: 1). CMR scholars both stress the social construction of racial categories "that are continuously being created, inhabited, contested, transformed, and destroyed" and challenge "racial essentialism and racial hierarchy" (Daniel et al, 2014: 8). While recognizing "the ambivalence, if not hostility, displayed toward a multiracial identity among traditional communities of color" and some White anti-racists, they maintain that critical multiraciality can serve "as a template for engaging in a transgressive pedagogy and praxis" that can facilitate coalition-building across racial and issue-based groups working for social justice (Daniel et al, 2014: 24). This book is written from and contributes to the CMR perspective.

Regardless of one's perspective on mixed-race Americans and despite the lack of consensus on how this population should or should not be defined and acknowledged, it is clear that the number of people who identify with two or more races is rapidly increasing (US Census Bureau, 2012a, 2012b, 2012c). While some legal scholars have begun to look at the effect of multiraciality on laws dealing with racial discrimination (e.g., Leong, 2010; Botts, 2013; Lucas, 2014), few social scientists have included policy implications in their research on this demographic group. It is time to offer more attention to understanding how existing race policies impact multiracial people and how policies can be shaped to protect and assist this group of racial minorities. This book helps to fill a gap in this area of research on multiracial people in the US.

While there have always been multiracial people in the US, multiracials today live under a system of racial identification and a level of acceptance of interracial relationships much different than in years past (Daniel, 2002). Gallup polls reveal that 87% of Americans now approve of marriages between Black people and White people. This compares to a mere 2% approval rate in 1967, when the Supreme Court declared anti-miscegenation legislation unconstitutional, and a dramatic jump of 22% since just 2002. Today, almost all (96%) of young American adults (18–29) *of all races* approve of such marriages (Newport, 2013).

The very concept of race has become much more fluid since the years when the "one-drop rule" held sway, when racial lines were perceived as largely Black–White and those with any Black ancestry were classified as Black (Davis, 1991; Korgen, 1999; Daniel, 2002; Rockquemore and Brunsma, 2008; Hochschild et al, 2012). Today, the US is much more racially diverse, and multiracial Americans come in many different racial combinations. Some Americans, including growing numbers of those with mixed racial heritage, prefer not to identify racially at all (Rockqemore and Brunsma, 2008; Hochschild et al, 2012; see also Chapter Four, this volume).

Table I.1: Approval for interracial marriage

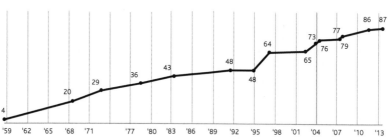

Do you approve or disapprove of marriage between blacks and whites?

● % Approve

1958 wording: "... marriages between white and coloured people"
1968-1978 wording: "... marriages between whites and non-whites"

Source: Retrieved from: http://www.gallup.com/poll/163697/approve-marriage-blacks-whites.aspx

The exact number of Americans with more than one racial heritage is almost impossible to determine, as Harris and Sim (2002) and many of the authors in the forthcoming chapters point out. People can identify themselves differently based on the location, time period, or type of racial identification question posed. Persons who fall under the label of "multiracial" in this text include those who identify, in some way or another, with more than one racial group (on questionnaires, in conversations with others, etc). While the term "multiracial" most often refers to those with parents of different races, it also includes those who are aware of—and embrace—racial mixing in earlier generations

What is beyond doubt is that the percentage of the US population that identifies with more than one race has increased tremendously over the past two decades and, with interracial marriage rates also increasing dramatically, will continue to do so (US Census Bureau, 2012a, 2012b). Almost one in 10 marriages, and one in seven *new* marriages, is now interracial (this statistic includes Hispanics/Latinos), with a 28% increase between 2000 and 2010 (US Census, 2012c; Frey, 2014). Almost 3% of the US population identified with more than one race on the 2010 US Census, a 32% increase from the 2000 Census, the first to allow respondents to check off more than one race (Jones and Bullock, 2012). The US Census Bureau estimates that this demographic group will make up 6.4% of the US population by 2060 (US Census Bureau, 2012a). One Census study that included Hispanics in the multiracial count indicated that 6.8% of the population *now* identifies as multiracial (Frey, 2014).

Race policy has not kept up with this surge in the multiracial population. While many people who oppose a multiracial category also oppose creating policies to protect and support multiracial people *as multiracial people* (believing that those created for monoracial minority racial and ethnic groups suffice), others maintain that multiracial people need and deserve status as a protected minority group. While multiracial people report facing similar amounts of racial discrimination, anti-discrimination laws are still based on monoracial categories (Campbell and Herman, 2010). Moreover, our means for tracking discrimination against the diverse multiracial population have also fallen short due to inadequacies in data collection methods. As the chapters in this book reveal, we must do more to measure the social, economic, educational, and health status of multiracial members of the US population and to establish policies that work to ensure their equitable treatment.

As Strmic-Pawl and Brunsma describe in Chapter Eleven, racial identities comprise doing as well as simply being. They note, as do Brunsma, Delgado, and Rockquemore (2013), that racial identity is multifaceted and involves "formation, maintenance, and navigation." As racial identity becomes more fluid, creating, maintaining, and living with such an identity takes effort and involves decisions based on time and context. Race policies are an important force impacting racial identities.

The authors of the chapters that follow examine race policy from a critical race and CMR perspective. Critical race and CMR scholars recognize racial categories and race policies as social constructions that vary over time and place (Daniel et al, 2014). While socially constructed, these categorizations and policies have very real repercussions that can harm or help minority racial groups (Delgado and Stefancic, 2012). The racial and ethnic labels used today by the US Census were established in 1977 by the Office of Management and Budget (OMB), as part of the overall effort to implement civil rights legislation. The OMB's "Directive No. 15: Standards for the Classification of Federal Data on Race and Ethnicity" defined five main racial and ethnic categories in the US: (1) American Indian or Alaskan Native; (2) Asian or Pacific Islander; (3) Black; (4) Hispanic; and (5) White. In 1997, the OMB separated the Asian or Pacific Islander category into two—Asian and Native Hawaiian or other Pacific Islander—and specified that the one ethnic category "Hispanic" would be changed to "either Hispanic or Latino."[1]

Throughout history, race policies both promoted and prevented racial discrimination and inequality. In the US, such policies have ranged from the legalization of slavery and racial segregation to the abolition of poll taxes and other policies aimed at preventing Black, Native American, Asian, and Hispanic citizens from voting, to banning racial discrimination in workplaces with 15 or more employees, to promoting race-based affirmative action programs. Today, multiracial Americans find themselves caught between existing policies, sometimes benefiting from those targeted towards minority racial groups but with neither protection against nor acknowledgement of discrimination based on their identity as multiracial rather than monoracial.

The chapters that follow focus on this gap in race policy in the US today. In doing so, they gauge the impact of multiracial people on race policy, note where race policy lags behind the growing numbers of multiracial people in US society, and prescribe how race policy can be used to promote racial justice for multiracial Americans in the US. Public policy questions addressed by *Race policy and multiracial Americans* include: do multiracial Americans experience racial discrimination in ways similar to minority monoracial groups? Where do they fall in terms of the current racial hierarchy? Do some multiracial groups face more discrimination than others? What policies aimed at combating racial discrimination should cover multiracial Americans? Should all (or some) multiracial Americans benefit from affirmative action programs? How are educators responding to the growing multiracial population? In an institution organized by race, such as a prison, is it possible to maintain a multiracial identity? Should there be a multiracial category on the US Census?

Part One: The changing racial hierarchy and multiracial Americans

The chapters in Part One examine the history of multiracial Americans and their place(s) in the current racial hierarchy. They offer an overview of the racial demographics of this subsection of the population and of the respective social, political, and economic power of the various multiracial groups within the US. These chapters also take a closer look at two key topics: (1) where the fast-growing, multiracial population of Latino descent fits in relation to the overall racial hierarchy and race policy issues; and (2) the relationships among racial identity, social class, and public policy.

Chapter One, "Multiracial Americans throughout the history of the US," by Tyrone Nagai, provides an overview of the history of multiracial Americans. Nagai indicates how different cultural groups treated multiracial members with varied levels of acceptance and how multiracial persons in the US have been viewed through the lens of the US Census and race policy. In doing so, he gives readers and students the historical knowledge necessary for beginning an examination of the relationship between race policy and multiracial Americans today.

Mary E. Campbell and Jessica M. Barron describe the socio-economic status of multiracial people in the US in Chapter Two, "National and local structures of inequality: multiracial groups' profiles across the US." They make clear the diversity among multiracial Americans and the unique challenges facing each of the many racial combinations that may fall under the umbrella label of "multiracial." Campbell and Barron also point out that experiences vary based on locale and age.

Raúl Quiñones-Rosado vividly describes the rich multiracial history of Latinos in the US in Chapter Three, "Latinos and Multiracial America." He argues that Latinos in the US now confront policies designed to re-racialize many into the White racial category. Quiñones-Rosado demonstrates how this policy encourages the assimilation of many Latinos while deepening the socio-economic disadvantages of Latinos deemed "non-White" and compromising the cohesion of the Latino community in the US.

In Chapter Four, "The connections among racial identity, social class, and public policy?," Nikki Khanna looks at the relationship between social class and racial identity among multiracial Americans. Khanna illustrates the conflation of "Black" culture and social class. She shows how social class impacts the racial groups with which we tend to interact most and the racial identity of multiracial persons. The higher multiracial people are on the socio-economic ladder, the more likely they are to identify as White or multiracial—or as no race at all. Khanna discusses the repercussions of this trend on social support for race-based public policies in the US.

Part Two: Race policy and multiracial Americans

The chapters in Part Two focus on the impact of multiracial Americans on various racial policy questions, including affirmative action programs, racial categorizations, educational programs and pedagogy, prison procedures, and health policy. These chapters also examine the influence of race policies on racial identity. Each chapter reveals that how multiracial people categorize themselves and are categorized by policymakers affects policy implementation and evaluation.

Multiracial Americans often face racial discrimination from monoracial Americans across the racial spectrum. However, without the existence of an official multiracial category, their experiences of racial discrimination are often ignored or not even noticed. In Chapter Five, "Multiracial Americans and racial discrimination," Tina Fernandes

Botts looks at how current race policies do not adequately protect multiracial Americans from racial discrimination. She describes the prevalence of the racial discrimination they face and suggests policies that could address such discrimination.

While, as Botts describes, multiracial Americans encounter racial discrimination often overlooked because of a lack of a multiracial category, many people believe that they benefit more than they should from affirmative action programs. Should affirmative action policies include all—or some—multiracial Americans? This is one of the questions addressed in Chapter Six, "Should all (or some) multiracial Americans benefit from affirmative action programs?" Daniel N. Lipson describes how rationales for affirmative action have changed over the years and discusses the place of multiracial Americans in current and possible future versions of affirmative action programs.

In Chapter Seven, "Multiracial students and educational policy," Rhina Fernandes Williams and E. Namisi Chilungu delve into issues related to multiracial Americans in K-12 (kindergarten through 12th grade) schools. These students have largely been ignored in discussions of educational policy and have even been left out of multicultural educational curricula. This chapter brings into focus the experience of multiracial schoolchildren in an educational system that now overlooks them. Williams and Chilungu conclude with suggestions for policymakers and teachers about how to create optimal learning environments in schools to make them more inclusive of and welcoming towards multiracial students.

After graduating from the K-12 system and entering college, questions of identity come to the forefront for most young people. Multiracial students face particular pressures to define themselves on college campuses, where they are often pressured to "choose sides." Complicating this dilemma enormously is the prevailing ideology of color-blindness, which discourages open discussions about racial issues (Bonilla-Silva, 2003). Campus faculty and staff must find ways to foster interracial interaction and discussions of race that enable students to become aware of racial injustice and empowered to address it.

In Chapter Eight, "Multiracial Americans in college," Marc P. Johnston-Guerrero and Kristen A. Renn focus on the impact of the growing multiracial college student population on college campuses and how campus environments influence them. They note that "before multiraciality can become fully integrated into the higher education landscape ... higher education policies must come to terms with some of the complexities associated with the diversity of students and institutions." In this chapter, Johnston-Guerrero and Renn highlight and unpack some of those complexities and make suggestions about how to improve higher education policies that effect multiracial college students.

In Chapter Nine, "Multiracial Americans, health patterns, and health policy: assessment and recommendations for ways forward," Jenifer L. Bratter and Christa Mason explore the influence of multiracial Americans on race-based health policy and the effects of existing policies on multiracial Americans. They answer the following questions: how can we better understand the health needs of multiracial Americans? Where do they stand in the racial health-care hierarchy? How does the lack of reliable racial data on multiracial Americans complicate health-care policy and services for multiracial people? They conclude with specific suggestions on how to improve health care for multiracial persons.

In Chapter Ten, we move from the institution of health care to the "total" institution of prisons (Goffman, 1961). In "Racial identity among multiracial prisoners in the color-blind era," Gennifer Furst and Kathleen Odell Korgen provide a qualitative analysis of the influence of the hyper-racialized prison environment on the racial identity of multiracial prisoners. They examine whether it is possible to identify as multiracial while incarcerated and whether the prison experience influences how prisoners from multiracial backgrounds racially identify. They also consider whether the color-blind ideology—so dominant in the larger society—has permeated prison walls.

Part Three: Multiracial Americans, the color-blind ideology, and the future of race relations

The last section of the book looks at how the growing numbers and recognition of multiracial Americans impact Americans' perceptions of race and race policy in the US. These chapters focus on the effect of multiracial Americans on the color-blind ideology, divisions among racial minority groups in the US, and race policy in the US.

Chapter Eleven, "Multiraciality and the racial order: the good, the bad, and the ugly," authored by Hephzibah V. Strmic-Pawl and David L. Brunsma, looks at the present and potential influence of multiracial Americans on the racial hierarchy in the US. In particular, they address the possibilities of multiraciality creating "a positive window for racial reconciliation and bridge-building" or working "to reproduce or strengthen White dominance." They conclude with some suggestions for steering multiraciality in a positive direction.

In Chapter Twelve, "Multiracial identity and monoracial conflict: toward a new social justice framework," Andrew Jolivette looks at how multiracial Americans can affect efforts to organize for racial justice. He argues that multiracial activists have prompted many monoracial organizations to embrace multi-issue organizing that is both more inclusive and more effective in promoting social change. Jolivette concludes with an outline of a "new social justice framework" to ensure "ongoing cross-ethnic coalition-building and policy reform among mixed-race and monoracial groups."

In the Conclusion, "Policies for a racially just society," I describe the connection between race policies and a racially just society and outlines the policies that the authors in this book have put forward toward that goal. While race relations have improved over the past few decades, and the increasing numbers of interracial marriages and those who identify as multiracial indicate greater fluidity in race relations and flexibility in racial identification, evidence of racial discrimination remains abundant. The color-blind ideology must be put to rest as we create new race policies that promote racial justice for people of mixed racial heritage in an increasingly diverse and unequal society.

Note

[1] Hispanics and Latinos tend to be viewed as a racial, rather than an ethnic, group and thus face racial discrimination. They are also usually treated (though not yet on the Census) as a racial category in terms of interracial marriage rates and the offspring of interracial relationships.

References

Bonilla-Silva, E.. (2003) *Racism without racists: Color-blind racism and the persistence of racial inequality in the United States.* Lanham, MD.

Botts, T.F. (2013) Antidiscrimination law and the multiracial experience: a reply to Nancy Leong. *Hastings Race and Poverty Law Journal* 10: 191–218.

Brunsma, D.L., Delgado, D. and Rockquemore, K.A. (2013) 'Liminality in the multiracial experience: Towards a concept of identity matrix', *Identities: Global Studies in Culture and Power*, 20(5): 481–502.

Campbell, M.E. and Herman, M. (2010) Politics and policies: attitudes toward multiracial people and political candidates. *Ethnic and Racial Studies* 33(9): 1511–36.

Daniel, G.R. (2002) *More than black: multiracial identity and the new racial order.* Philadelphia, PA: Temple University Press.

Daniel, G.R. (2014) Editor's note, *Journal of Critical Mixed Race Studies*, 1(1):1-5.

Daniel, G. R., Kina, L., Dariotis, W.M.. and Fojas, C. (2014) 'Emerging paradigms in critical mixed race studies', *Journal of Critical Mixed Race Studies*, 1(1):6-65

Davis, F.J. (1991) *Who is Black*. University Park, PA: The Pennsylvania State University Press.

Delgado, R. and Stefancic, J. (2012) *Critical race theory: an introduction* (2nd edn). New York, NY: New York University Press.

Frey, W.H. (2014) *Diversity explosion: how new racial demographics are remaking America*. New York, NY: Brookings Institution Press.

Goffman, E. (1961) *Asylums: essays on the social situation of mental patients and other inmates*. Garden City, NY: Anchor Books.

Harris, D.R. and Sim, J.J. (2002) Who is multiracial? Assessing the complexity of lived race. *American Sociological Review* 67: 614–27.

Hochschild, J., Weaver, V., and Burch, T. (2012) *Creating a new racial order: how immigration, multiracialism, genomics, and the young can remake race in America*. Princeton, NJ: Princeton University Press.

Jones, N.A. and Bullock, J. (2012) The two or more races population: 2010. United States Census Bureau, US Department of Commerce. Available at: http://www.census.gov/prod/cen2010/briefs/c2010br-13.pdf

Korgen, K.O. (1999) *From Black to biracial*, Westport, CT: Praeger.

Leong, N. (2010) Judicial erasure of mixed-race discrimination, *American University Law Review*, 59(3): 469–555.

Lucas, L.S. (2014) Undoing race? Reconciling multiracial identity with equal protection. *California Law Review* 102(5): 1243.

MAVIN (2014) MAVIN builds healthier communities by providing educational resources about mixed heritage experiences. Available at: http://www.mavinfoundation.org/new/purpose/

Newport, F. (2013) In U.S., 87% approve of Black-White marriage, vs. 4% in 1958. Gallup, 25 July. Available at: http://www.gallup.com/poll/163697/approve-marriage-blacks-whites.aspx

Rockquemore, K. A. and Brunsma, D.L. (2008) *Beyond Black: Biracial identity in America*, 2nd edn. Lanham, MD: Rowman & Littlefield.

Root, M.P.P. (1992) *Racially mixed people in America*. Thousand Oaks, CA: Sage.

Spencer, R. (2014) "Only the news they want to print": mainstream media and critical mixed-race studies. *Journal of Critical Mixed Race Studies* 1(1): 162–82.

Swirl (no date[a]) Our values. Available at: http://www.swirlinc.org/

Swirl (no date[b]) Philosophy of work. Available at: http://www.swirlinc.org/

US Census Bureau (2012a) U.S. Census Bureau projections show a slower growing, older, more diverse nation a half century from now. 12 December. Available at: https://www.census.gov/newsroom/releases/archives/population/cb12-243.html

US Census Bureau (2012b) 2010 Census shows multiple-race population grew faster than single-race population. 27 September. Available at: https://www.census.gov/newsroom/releases/archives/race/cb12-182.html

US Census Bureau (2012c) 2010 Census shows interracial and interethnic married couples grew by 28 percent over decade. 25 April. Available at: http://www.census.gov/newsroom/releases/archives/2010_census/cb12-68.html

ONE

Multiracial Americans throughout the history of the US

Tyrone Nagai

While there are many places that could be used as starting points for a history of multiracial people in the US, perhaps none is better than acknowledging the fact that the presence of multiracial people in what we now call North America pre-dates the formation of the US by at least three centuries (Forbes, 1993). These diverse societies and peoples once found in what is now the US had very divergent attitudes and practices for handling racial mixture. This chapter illuminates the ways in which different cultures responded to multiracial people in what is now the US by examining: (1) the 17th-century legal decrees concerning miscegenation between Africans and Europeans and the children born to such unions in Colonial Virginia; (2) traditional practices regarding membership and identity among the Seminole in Florida and the Navajo (or Diné) in the Four Corners region of the Southwest; (3) the ambiguous status of Mestizos in 16th- to 18th-century New Spain; and (4) the intermarriage of Chinese men and Hawaiian women in the 19th century.

This chapter will describe how a dominant ideology concerning racial mixing developed in the US, beginning in the colonial period and accelerating with the founding of the nation. This ideology, based on White supremacy and racial hierarchy (Daniel, 2002), was enforced through anti-miscegenation laws and the "one-drop rule," which was a restrictive form of hypodescent that classified everyone with African ancestry as Black (i.e., "one drop of blood") (Davis, 1991; Jordan, 2014). Racial categorizations were a key means for enforcing this racial hierarchy. The chapter will also include a discussion of the evolution of different systems of categorization and enumeration for multiracial people, as stipulated in the US Constitution, US Census, and Supreme Court cases.

African slavery, anti-miscegenation laws, and the one-drop rule

The history of multiracial people in the US largely follows the nation's racialized history as a whole and parallels the history of African-Americans in particular. By the mid-1600s, the use of African slaves to provide inexpensive labor for tobacco plantations began to take root, and an elite group of wealthy European planters "created the legal and institutional structures needed to guarantee property rights regarding slaves" in colonial America (Menard, 2013: 380). These new "legal and institutional structures" defined what constituted a slave—a form of property or chattel that could be bought, sold, traded, and owned (Fisher, 1992: 1055). A significant aspect of these property laws included explanations of how sexual relations between Europeans and Africans, and the children that resulted, would be governed.

The prevailing colonial patterns of settlement, such as the ratio of European males to females and Europeans to African slaves, also catalyzed the development of slavery and a binary racial order (Jordan, 2014). For example, in 1620, the Virginia Company wrote about the need for more European women in the colony to facilitate the development of families who would tend to the land (Spruill, 1998). By the time of the 1790 US Census, there were still just 95 free White women for every 100 free White men in Virginia (US Bureau of the Census, 1790; Moller, 1945). The proportion of Africans living among Europeans in Colonial Virginia was initially very small, but it increased from 2% in the mid-17th century to nearly 40% by the late 18th century (Jordan, 2014). Thus, the desire among European men for more women in Virginia, along with the steady increase of the African population, produced social conditions ripe for interracial sexual encounters involving Africans and Europeans.

In 1662, the Virginia legislature was forced to prescribe how children born of enslaved African mothers and free European fathers would be considered under the law. The judgment went against traditional English common law, which generally accorded children the status of their fathers. Instead, the Virginia legislature decided that all children born to a slave mother would also be slaves regardless of the father's race or station in life (Hening, 1823). The effect and legacy of this law and others like it was to codify and institutionalize what came to be known as the one-drop rule (Davis, 1991; Daniel, 2002; Hollinger, 2003; Jordan, 2014). In practical terms, the one-drop rule meant that any person having any trace of African ancestry was categorized as Black, no matter the amount of European ancestry in their background.

In 1691, the Virginia Assembly went further to create legal boundaries between Africans and Europeans by outlawing miscegenation or interracial sexual relationships (Higginbotham and Kopytoff, 1989). Enforcement fell especially hard on European women with mixed or "mulatto" children (Higginbotham and Kopytoff, 1989). The punishment for the European mother was a fine of 15 pounds and the requirement that the mixed child work in servitude for 30 years (Takaki, 1993). The effect of this law was not only to discourage interracial unions, but also to further enforce the subjugation of mixed or "mulatto" children and their European mothers. European men would never have to legally recognize any child they fathered with a slave.

The legacy of the one-drop rule and anti-miscegenation laws originating in Colonial Virginia spread to other colonies, especially those in the South, where slavery was particularly profitable. The one-drop rule and anti-miscegenation laws continued to dominate US social customs, legal statutes, political discourse, and cultural norms for the next 300 years, continuing long after the abolition of slavery in 1865. Some would argue that the specters of the one-drop rule and anti-miscegenation laws still influence US views on multiraciality, and this thread will be taken up in other chapters of this book.

Seminole views of multiraciality

Even though the one-drop rule and anti-miscegenation laws formed the cornerstone of popular attitudes and legal thinking about racial mixing in the US, these were not the only ways to conceptualize the status of multiracial people. After all, places like Colonial Virginia were inhabited by more than just Europeans and Africans. Native groups also played an important role in the racial hierarchy being established and negotiated in colonial America. For example, because of the harsh conditions of plantation life in the South, some African slaves ran away in the hope of finding freedom. Starting in the late 1600s and continuing for about 150 years, slaves who fled the Southern colonies for freedom in the Florida Everglades could find refuge among the Seminoles, who often invited runaway slaves to join their ranks (Ogunleye, 2006; Hatch and Still, 2012). The Black Seminole population was estimated at 1,400 individuals by the mid-1800s (Thybony, 1991). Many of these ex-slaves lived alongside and intermarried with the Seminoles, and they and their children were accepted and protected by the tribe (Claudio, 1998; Soodalter, 2012). In fact, many Seminoles with some African ancestry were born into freedom and lived to an old age without ever having to endure a day of bondage (Ogunleye, 2006). Thus, while in Colonial Virginia, a law was put in place to force all mixed children born with even "one drop" of African blood into slavery, in the Florida Everglades during the same time period (and even later in some remote parts of the Everglades), a mixed child of African, European, and/or Native descent would be born and live free among the Seminoles.

Navajo views of multi-ethnicity and multiraciality

Over two thousand miles west of the Seminole lands, in what is now known as the Four Corners region—lands where the corners of Utah, Colorado, Arizona, and New Mexico meet—the Navajo developed another way of integrating other tribes and nationalities into their nation. Instead of using race, the Navajo drew on a combination of clanship, language, worldview, and land to accept Zunis, Utes, Tewas, and Mexicans within their ranks, including children of mixed parentage. In the Navajo clanship system, Navajo individuals simultaneously identify themselves through their mother's clan, father's clan, maternal grandfather's clan, and paternal grandfather's clan (Lee, 2006). Over time, new clans were created and adopted in order to accommodate new groups into Navajo society (Lee, 2006). As long as a Navajo individual knew their clanship, spoke Navajo, and followed the traditional belief system of the Navajo, they could be considered a part of the nation even if their Navajo ancestry was quite distant (Aronilth, 1985; Yazzie, 1994; Lee, 2006).

This system of identity, belonging, and membership among the Navajo developed organically as a result of intra-tribal relations over the years, including colonization and wars (Emerson, 2014). The obvious implication is that cultural affinity superseded "blood quantum" or hypodescent as a way of defining tribal identity among the Navajo. So, the Navajo did not have a notion of race or racial membership that was analogous to the European model. As a result, a Navajo's "race" was not part of the criteria for defining tribal membership. In contrast, the "blood quantum" system, which European legislators first used in Virginia in 1705, defines tribal membership by meeting a certain threshold of tribal ancestry or "blood" regardless of one's cultural affinity, tribal involvement, or residential location (Spruhan, 2006). The Indian Reorganization Act of 1934 imposed the blood quantum system on all Native tribes, including the Navajo and Seminole, to demarcate membership and the level of racial purity (Spruhan, 2007/2008).

Mestizos of New Spain

While the Navajo adapted their traditional system of tribal membership to include groups, such as Mexicans, within and adjacent to their traditional homeland, the case of mestizos in 16th- to 18th-century New Spain (which included the lands of US states such as California, Texas, Colorado, Arizona, New Mexico, Nevada, Utah, and Louisiana, as well as what is now the country of Mexico) illustrates yet another type of classifying multiracial people in the "New World." The word "mestizo"became common in New Spain to refer to a person of mixed Spanish, Native, and/or African ancestry. The word "mulatto" was also used to refer to a mixed person with African ancestry.

When the Spanish began to colonize New Spain in the 1520s, among their ranks were Africans, Moors, and "mulattos"who served as soldiers and settlers (Forbes, 1966). Thus, the very colonization of New Spain introduced not only Europeans and Africans to the Native population, but also racially mixed persons of African and European descent. Within a short time, authorities in New Spain became concerned about the increasing numbers of mestizos, their perceived idleness, and "mestizo vagrancy" (Garr, 1975). King Phillip II proposed shipping mestizos to the Philippines and Chile, which were also under Spanish colonial rule (Garr, 1975). Although it seems unlikely that this specific plan was actually implemented, there is evidence of mestizos and "mulattos," as well as convicts, vagabonds, and orphans, being sent to the frontier areas of New Spain, such as California, to supplement flagging populations in those regions (Forbes, 1966; Garr, 1975).

The unreliability of colonial censuses in New Spain makes it difficult to enumerate the number and proportion of Natives, mestizos, "mulattos,"Spaniards, and Africans in the population, especially because the labels for different types of racial mixing became quite subjective and fluid (Restall, 2009). Nevertheless, a census conducted in 1794 suggests that the approximately 1,000,000 residents of New Spain were a racially diverse population that was 71% Native, 16% mestizo or "mulatto," and 13% Spanish (Valdés, 1978). Among more urban areas, such as Mexico City, mestizos and "mulattos" made up over 25% of the population (Valdés, 1978).

Several racialized patterns concerning mestizos in New Spain emerged regarding the ratio of men to women, sexual relations, and social status. For example, in 1773, Friar Junipero Serra pointed out the shortage of Spanish women in California and the difficulty of preventing Spanish soldiers from lusting after Indian women (Garr, 1975). One year later, a military officer remarked that the population of

Northern New Spain (Northern Mexico) was so racially mixed among Africans, Natives, and Spaniards that it was difficult to trace anyone's ancestry (Forbes, 1966). In the 1790s, California Governor Diego de Borica requested *mujeres blancas* ("White women") from the viceroy of Mexico City to supplement the "women of quality" in the state (Garr, 1975). Thus, the shortage of Spanish women led to high rates of interracial relationships, high birth rates for mestizo and "mulatto" children, and concern from the colonial government.

Despite mestizos and "mulattos" outnumbering Spaniards, New Spain's European rulers viewed them as inferior to those of "pure blood" Spanish heritage (Garr, 1975; Forbes, 1983). At the same time, mestizos, often fluent in both Spanish and an indigenous language, served as intercultural mediators and translators (Schwaller, 2012). Mestizos tended to maintain ties to both sides of their families because connection to the Spanish side offered social, economic, and political opportunities while connection to the indigenous side provided sanctuary when problems or tensions arose with Spanish authorities (Schwaller, 2012). As a result, being mestizo meant that one was simultaneously unwanted because of perceived inferiority while desperately needed in order to enable communication between different sectors of society and to help populate outlying territories.

Perhaps what best illustrates the ambiguity and fluidity of mestizo identity was the practice of purchasing *cédulas de gracias al sacar* ("thanks for getting out of it"), which were certificates of "whiteness" issued by King Charles III of Spain (Daniel, 2010). These certificates enabled mestizos to legally erase their Native and/or African origins. Possessing a certificate gave mestizos both legal status as *Españoles* and greater opportunity for vertical social mobility. It also reflected the comparatively more fluid racial demarcations between "pure" Spaniards, mestizos and "mulattos," and Natives (Daniel, 2010).

The Chinese-Hawaiians

While the treatment of the mestizos of New Spain in the 16th to 18th centuries seemed to vacillate between acceptance and rejection depending on social, political, and economic considerations, the experiences of Chinese-Hawaiians in the 19th and early 20th centuries offer a still different picture of the treatment of multiracial people. In 1835, William Hooper of Boston established the first sugar cane plantation in Hawaii and other planters soon followed (Avakian, 2002). To procure a more cooperative, and less ethnically united, labor force for the growing plantation economy, the Royal Hawaiian Agricultural

Society brought the first group of 293 Chinese workers to the islands in 1852 (Avakian, 2002). One year later, the racial composition of Hawaii was still less than 1% Chinese and over 95% Native Hawaiian (Nordyke, 1989). By some estimates, Chinese men outnumbered Chinese women in Hawaii by a 10 to 1 margin at this time (Lorden, 1935). As a result of the limited number of Chinese women available, some Chinese men married Hawaiian women (Reece, 1914). In 1871, the Hawaiian Board Mission reported that 121 of 1,201 Chinese men in Hawaii had married Hawaiian women, and estimated that 167 multiracial children had come from these interracial relationships (Takaki, 1989).

What makes the Chinese-Hawaiian example particularly illustrative of different levels of acceptance and treatment of multiracial people is that some of the Chinese men married to Hawaiian women simultaneously maintained pre-existing marriages to women in China (Takaki, 1989). In other words, some Chinese men who came to Hawaii had left their wives and children in the old country, married Hawaiian women and started families with them, but continued to travel back to China to maintain relationships with their family there. In addition, the wives and children of these Chinese men sometimes travelled between Hawaii and China as well. For example, a Chinese-born son might immigrate to Hawaii to live with his Chinese father, adoptive Hawaiian mother, and Chinese-Hawaiian siblings. Alternatively, a mixed Chinese-Hawaiian son might immigrate to China to live with his father's Chinese wife. No matter the situation, the personal testimonies from these families indicate that the multiracial children were treated well and accepted by mothers in both Hawaii and China, with little regard to their biological race, and there was often a fusion or blending of Chinese and Hawaiian cultures (Lorden, 1935; Takaki, 1989).

Beyond the scope of family, Chinese-Hawaiians lived in a society and culture that, by the early 20th century, became a symbol of the "melting pot" ideology that celebrated immigrant assimilation into a homogenized US culture (Griffiths, 1916). Chinese-Hawaiians not only assimilated into the dominant culture in Hawaii, but attained a high level of social status and success, even above that of multiracial White-Hawaiians (Reece, 1914; Smith, 1934). As more Chinese men fulfilled their labor contracts on the plantations, started their own rice farms or family stores, and married Native Hawaiian women, they started to form whole, distinct, and segregated Chinese-Hawaiian communities, such as in Kau, Hilo, and Honolulu (Lorden, 1935; Takaki, 1989). The economic prosperity achieved by the Chinese paired with the political connections of the Hawaiians made Chinese-Hawaiians especially well-positioned to ascend the socio-economic ladder (Smith, 1934).

Over time, the numbers of Chinese-Hawaiians began to stabilize and then wane as more Chinese women became available for marriage in the islands and as Chinese-Hawaiians married into other multiracial groups (Smith, 1934; Lorden, 1935).

Multiraciality in the US Constitution, Census, and social policy

As the examples of the African slaves in Colonial Virginia, Seminoles in Florida, Navajo in the Four Corners, mestizos in New Spain, and Chinese-Hawaiians demonstrate, contact among Native, European, African, and Asian populations between the 1500s and 1800s was geographically widespread. However, societal reactions to racial mixing, intermarriage, and the birth of multiracial children varied on a spectrum from complete subjugation and enslavement to complete freedom and equality. When attempting to describe the accelerated process of racial mixing he witnessed in early 20th-century Hawaii, Reece (1914: 104) wrote: "When two races meet, the normal course of their association is through introduction, hostility, tolerance, indifference, co-operation, friendship, fusion." While Reece's model might be seen as too linear, optimistic, or naive, it does raise some important questions. Is it a natural tendency for different racial groups to blend together if they live in close proximity to one another? If so, what happens to this natural tendency when a government attempts to legally enforce racial segregation in a society composed of multiple races and ethnicities? The following discussion of the Constitution, Census, and race policy in the US helps to answer that question.

After Virginia and the other English colonies declared their independence in 1776 and formed the United States of America, a series of governmental actions attempted to standardize the enumeration and status of all racial groups, including multiracial people, through constitutional means. The first such action consisted of a 1787 agreement between Northern and Southern states known as the "three-fifths clause," whereby three fifths of the population of slaves would be counted in the official population of the US. Northern states were largely comprised of free White persons, while Southern states had higher numbers of slaves in their populations. The Southern states wanted to include them and the Northern states did not as the number of representatives per state in Congress is based on each state's population. In the end, the compromise became part of Article 1, Section 2, Paragraph 3 of the United States Constitution.

The sentence in the Constitution immediately following the three fifths clause is particularly relevant to the history of multiracial people in the US. It mandates that the US government conduct a "decennial" census (every 10 years). Thus, beginning as far back as 1787, we can see the importance of using the US Census to collect data on race, that is, "free persons" and "slaves." Over the next 200 years, the US Census questions and categories changed in various ways to suit the political, economic, and social needs of the nation. One thing, however, stayed the same. People were always counted as belonging to one racial category, even if they were racially mixed.

Special categories for multiracial people became common in the 1800s. Categories such as "mulatto," "quadroon," "octoroon," "hexadecaroon," and "quintroon" were used to indicate varying levels of mixture between White and Black (Hochschild and Powell, 2008). "Mulatto" described persons of mixed race, part Black and part White; "quadroon" meant one quarter Black ancestry; "octoroon" meant one eighth Black; "hexadecaroon" meant one sixteenth Black; "quintroon" was a person who had one parent who was an octoroon and one White parent. Thus, people who were mixed were categorized in a single, independent (non-White) racial group rather than multiple racial groups simultaneously.

After the Civil War ended in 1865 and slavery was abolished with the passage of the 13th Amendment, Black and multiracial Americans in traditional slave states were no longer destined to a life of servitude. This freedom, while constitutionally guaranteed, was short-lived. Ideologies of White supremacy, the economic need for cheap labor in the cotton industry, and the social acceptance of racial segregation—all of which accompanied the culture and legacy of slavery—became dominant forces once again after federal troops withdrew from the South in 1877 (Steinberg, 1989). Wealthy Southern White people started to regain political power by dividing poor White and Black Americans from one another through laws enforcing racial segregation. These laws were referred to as Jim Crow laws, after the name given to Black characters played by White people in blackface in stage shows during the 1800s.

In 1896, Homer Plessy, a man who was one eighth Black, challenged a Jim Crow law in Louisiana that separated railroad passengers by race. Plessy's case made it all the way to the US Supreme Court, which ruled that the "separate but equal" treatment of Black people ("coloreds") and White people was legal in public places. This ruling reaffirmed racial segregation in schools, hospitals, trains, and many other public places.

While activists worked to overturn racial segregation and challenge racist policies and attitudes in the late 19th century, eugenicists believed that they could prove the superiority of one racial group over another through scientific investigation. Comparing differences in the average volume of the human skull was one method used in the attempt to rank racial groups by intelligence. These so-called biological differences were found to have originated from researcher bias once blind testing became the scientific standard (Gould, 1981).

Efforts to avoid "contaminating" the purity of so-called "supreme" races by discouraging or preventing sexual relations between persons of different racial groups were also part of the eugenicist agenda, even in the US (Sandall, 2008). Eugenicists thought that the White race was weakened through mixing with other races but other races were strengthened by being mixed with White (Park, 1928).

In 1954, the US Supreme Court effectively reversed the Plessy decision when it ended "separate but equal" racial segregation in public schools with the *Brown v. Board of Education* decision. Just over a decade later, in 1967, the last legal prohibitions against interracial marriage were overturned with the US Supreme Court's unanimous ruling in *Loving v. Virginia* (Moran, 2001). Richard and Mildred Loving were residents of Virginia, which had banned marriage between White and "non-White" partners, so they married in Washington, DC, in 1958. Richard was White and Mildred was Black and Native American. The police in Virginia arrested and jailed Richard and Mildred in 1959 for violating a law that criminalized interracial couples who married out of state and returned to Virginia to live (Newbeck, 2008). The Lovings were eventually forced to move out of Virginia with their three children, and they sought additional legal help. The American Civil Liberties Union filed a lawsuit on behalf of the Lovings, which eventually led to the legalization of all interracial marriages, and this finally put an end to anti-miscegenation laws.

As the Loving case made its way through the court system, the US government continued to develop its methods for counting and categorizing people by race. The Civil Rights Act of 1964 led to Executive Order 11185, which aimed to deliver better public education to minority ethnic and racial groups. The Federal Interagency Committee on Education (FICE), established to carry out this order, recommended that "compatible" and "non-duplicative" racial and ethnic categories be used by all federal agencies in order to collect more accurate data on race. In 1977, the Office of Management and Budget's (OMB) "Directive no. 15: standards for the classification of federal data on race and ethnicity" defined five main mutually exclusive racial and ethnic categories in the US: (1) American Indian or Alaskan Native; (2) Asian or Pacific Islander; (3) Black; (4) Hispanic; and (5) White.

This system reinforced a long-standing tradition whereby multiracial people were forced to identify with only one race.

The 1983 case of Susie Guillory Phipps illustrated the continued influence of the one-drop rule and the notion of static, immutable racial categories. It also showcased the way in which racial identification depends on social construction and legal precedent more than biology or genetics (Omi and Winant, 1986). In the course of preparing for a trip she and her husband planned to take, Phipps applied for a passport, and she was informed that she was not, as she thought she was, White. It turned out that she was 3/32nds Black, and the state of Louisiana classified anyone 1/32nd or more Black to be Black. Her birth certificate, which she had not previously seen, also indicated that she was Black. Phipps sued the Louisiana Bureau of Vital Records to change her racial classification from Black to White.

Phipps's attorney argued that the assignment of racial categories on birth certificates was unconstitutional and that the classification of all those with 1/32nd or more Black ancestry as Black was inaccurate. He asked for expert testimony from a retired Tulane University professor who cited research indicating that most White people have 1/20th "Negro" ancestry. Assistant Attorney General Ron Davis defended the law by pointing out that some type of racial classification was necessary to comply with federal record-keeping requirements and to facilitate programs for the prevention of genetic diseases. In the end, Phipps lost. Despite being 91% "White," the one-drop rule prevented her from legally changing her race on her birth certificate, so she remained "Black."

The growing acceptance of multiraciality

By the 1990s, growth in the numbers of interracial marriages, multiracial people, and multiracial organizations began to challenge and complicate the government's use of single, mutually exclusive racial categories. The number of interracial marriages tripled from 321,000 in 1970 to 964,000 in 1990 (US Bureau of the Census, 1994, 2011). Likewise, the number of multiracial children quadrupled from 500,000 in 1970 to 2,000,000 in 1990 (US Bureau of the Census, 1997). With the increasing number of interracial marriages and multiracial children, a number of advocacy organizations—such as Project RACE (Reclassify All Children Equally), A Place for Us (APFU), and MultiEthnic Americans (AMEA)—emerged to serve this growing population.

The year 1997 marked a significant tipping point in public attitudes toward multiraciality. That year, 21-year-old golfer Tiger Woods made headlines on the *Oprah Winfrey Show* when he described his racial background as "Cablinasian," an abbreviation representing his "Caucasian," "Black," "American Indian," and "Asian" heritage. Woods explained how he felt uncomfortable being labeled "African-American," and was reluctant to check only one box for his racial background on school forms. Woods' declaration of a multiracial identity on national television challenged the one-drop rule and the idea that racial categories are mutually exclusive and homogeneous.

That same year, the US Census announced that it would allow individuals to choose more than one racial identity beginning in 2000. This decision resulted from pressure applied from organizations like Project RACE, APFU, and AMEA (Spencer, 1999; Daniel, 2002; Farley, 2002; Williams, 2005; DaCosta, 2007). White women married to middle-class Black men spearheaded petitions at the state and local level because they felt that their children were being forced to choose one parent over the other on government forms (Williams, 2006). Moreover, close to 500,000 people had identified as multiracial by checking off more than one race or writing in more than one race in the "other" category on the 1990 US Census (Williams, 2005). Former Census Bureau director Kenneth Prewitt remarked that people who marked two or more racial categories on the 1990 US Census were assigned to a single race based on which box had the darkest pen mark (Williams, 2005). For people who used the "other" category to write in "Black–White" or "White–Black" as their race, the census counted the former as "Black" and the latter as "White" and ignored the second race listed (Lee, 1993).

With the change in the US Census rules and the influence of multiracial celebrities like Tiger Woods, it was clear that, 30 years after *Loving v. Virginia* legalized interracial marriage across the US, the movement to grant multiracial people the freedom to create and define their own identities on government forms was well underway (Weisman, 1996). The publication of Maria P.P. Root's groundbreaking books—*Racially mixed people in America* (Root, 1992) and *The multiracial experience: racial borders as the new frontier* (Root, 1996)—also reflected this social change. A flood of other books and articles on multiracial Americans has appeared since then. Few, if any, though, discuss race policy issues that accompany changes in the racial categorization of people with multiracial backgrounds.

Closing thoughts

As other chapters in this book will discuss, the paradigmatic shift that occurred in 2000 in response to the growing number of multiracial people in the US and pressure from multiracial advocacy groups raises many new policy questions concerning racial identity, boundaries, and hierarchy that need to be answered. For example, what are the implications of treating multiracial people as a separate racial group or alternative racial category when it comes to discrimination, affirmative action, and educational and health policy? How can multiracial people be counted, tracked, and classified in places like colleges and prisons, where achieving racial parity still poses significant challenges? How do multiracial identities complicate arguments for or against a color-blind society, analyses of social class and race, and movements for social justice? Understanding the tension between the centuries-long history of anti-miscegenation, racial segregation, and hypodescent, on the one hand, and the alternative possibilities offered by intermarriage, racial integration, and unconditional acceptance of multiracial people, on the other, creates a useful framework for such an endeavor.

References

Aronilth, W., Jr (1985) *Foundations of Navajo culture*. Tsaile, AZ: Navajo Community College.

Avakian, M. (2002) *Atlas of Asian-American history*. New York, NY: Checkmark Books.

Claudio, S. (1998) The English has now a mind to make slaves of them all. *American Indian Quarterly* 22(1/2): 157–81.

DaCosta, K. (2007) *Making multiracials: state, family, and market in the redrawing of the color line*. Redwood City, CA: Stanford University Press.

Daniel, G.R. (2002) *More than Black? Multiracial identity and the new racial order*. Philadelphia, PA: Temple University Press.

Daniel, G.R. (2010) *Race and multiraciality in Brazil and the United States: converging paths?* University Park, PA: Penn State University Press.

Davis, F.J. (1991) *Who is Black? One nation's definition*. University Park, PA: The Pennsylvania State University Press.

Emerson, L. (2014) Interview conducted on 10 January in San Diego, CA.

Farley, R. (2002) Racial identities in 2000: the response to the multiple-race response option. In: J. Perlmann and M.C. Waters (eds) *The new race question*. New York, NY: Russell Sage, pp 33–61.

Fisher, W.W. (1992) Ideology and imagery in the law of slavery—symposium on the law of slavery: theories of democracy and the law of slavery. *Chicago–Kent Law Review* 68(3): 1051–83.

Forbes, J.D. (1966) Black pioneers: the Spanish-speaking Afro-Americans of the Southwest. *Phylon* 7(3): 233–46.

Forbes, J.D. (1983) Hispano-Mexican pioneers of the San Francisco Bay region: an analysis of racial origins. *Aztlan: A Journal of Chicano Studies* 14(1): 175–89.

Forbes, J.D. (1993) *Africans and Native Americans: the language of race and the evolution of Red-Black peoples*, Champaign, IL: University of Illinois.

Garr, D. (1975) A rare and desolate land: population and race in Hispanic California. *Western History Quarterly* 2: 133–48.

Gould, S.J. (1981) *The mismeasure of man*. New York, NY: W.W. Norton & Company.

Griffiths, A.F. (1916) The Japanese race question in Hawaii. *The Journal of Race Development* 6(4): 422–40.

Hatch, T. and Still, C. (2012) Osceola fights to save the Seminole. *American Heritage* 62(2): 34–39.

Hening, W.W. (1823) *The statutes at large: being a collection of all the laws of Virginia, from the first session of the legislature in the year 1619*. New York, NY: R & W & G. Bartow.

Higginbotham, A.L. and Kopytoff, B.K. (1989) Racial purity and interracial sex in the law of Colonial and Antebellum Virginia. *Georgetown Law Journal* 77(6): 1967–2029.

Hochschild, J.L. and Powell, B.M. (2008) Racial reorganization and the United States Census 1850–1930: mulattoes, half-breeds, mixed parentage, hindoos, and the Mexican race. *Studies in American Political Development* 22(1): 59–96.

Hollinger, D.A. (2003) Amalgamation and hypodescent: the question of ethnoracial mixture in the history of the United States. *The American Historical Review* 108(5): 1363–90.

Jordan, W.D. (2014) Historical origins of the one-drop racial rule in the United States. *Journal of Critical Mixed Race Studies* 1(1): 99–132.

Lee, L.L. (2006) Navajo cultural identity: what can the Navajo Nation bring to the American Indian identity discussion table? *Wicazo Sa Review* 21(2): 79–103.

Lee, S.M. (1993) Racial classifications in the US Census: 1890–1990. *Ethnic and Racial Studies* 16(1): 75–94.

Lorden, D.M. (1935) The Chinese-Hawaiian family. *American Journal of Sociology* 40(4): 453–63.

Menard, R. (2013) Making a "popular slave society" in colonial British America. *Journal of Interdisciplinary History* 43(3): 377–95.

Moller, H. (1945) Sex composition and correlated cultural patterns in colonial America. *William and Mary Quarterly* 3(2): 128.

Moran, R.F. (2001) *Interracial intimacy: the regulation of race and romance.* Chicago, IL: University of Chicago Press.

Newbeck, P. (2008) *Virginia hasn't always been for lovers: interracial marriage bans and the case of Richard and Mildred Loving.* Carbondale, IL: Southern Illinois University Press.

Nordyke, E.C. (1989) *The peopling of Hawaii* (2nd edn). Honolulu, HI: University of Hawai'i Press.

Ogunleye, T.M. (2006) Àrokò, *Mmomomme Twe, Nsibidi, Ogede,* and *Tusona*: Africanisms in Florida's self-emancipated Africans' resistance to enslavement and war stratagems. *Journal of Black Studies* 36(3): 396–414.

Omi, M. and Winant, H. (1986) *Racial formation in the United States: from the 1960s to the 1980s.* New York, NY: Routledge & Kegan Paul Inc.

Park, R.E. (1928) Human migration and the marginal man. *American Journal of Sociology* 33(6): 881–93.

Reece, E.J. (1914) Race mingling in Hawaii. *American Journal of Sociology* 20(1): 104–16.

Restall, M. (2009) *The Black middle: Africans, Mayas, and Spaniards in colonial Yucatan.* Redwood City, CA: Stanford University Press.

Root, M.P.P. (1992) *Racially mixed people in America.* Thousand Oaks, CA: Sage.

Root, M.P.P. (1996) *The multiracial experience: racial borders as the new frontier.* Thousand Oaks, CA: Sage.

Sandall, R. (2008) Sir Francis Galton and the roots of eugenics. *Society* 45(2): 170–76.

Schwaller, R.C. (2012) The importance of mestizos and mulatos as bilingual intermediaries in sixteenth-century New Spain. *Ethnohistory* 59(4): 714–38.

Smith, W.C. (1934) The hybrid in Hawaii as a marginal man. *American Journal of Sociology* 39(4): 459–68.

Soodalter, R. (2012) On removing Seminoles. *Military History* 29(2): 62–9.

Spencer, R. (1999) *Spurious issues: race and multiracial identity politics in the United States.* Boulder, CO: Westview.

Spruhan, P. (2006) A legal history of blood quantum in federal Indian Law to 1935. *South Dakota Law Review* 51(6): 1–50.

Spruhan, P. (2007/08) The origins, current status, and future prospects of blood quantum as the definition of membership in the Navajo Nation. *Tribal Law Journal* 8: 1–17.

Spruill, J.C. (1998) *Women's life and work in the Southern Colonies*. New York, NY, and London: W.W. Norton & Company.

Steinberg, S. (1989) *The ethnic myth: race, ethnicity and class in America*. Boston, MA: Beacon Press.

Takaki, R. (1989) *Strangers from a different shore: a history of Asian Americans* (2nd edn). New York, NY: Penguin Books.

Takaki, R. (1993) *A different mirror: a history of multicultural America*. Boston, MA: Little, Brown, and Co.

Thybony, S. (1991) Against all odds, Black Seminole won their freedom. *Smithsonian* 22(5): 90–9.

US Bureau of the Census (1790) Heads of Families at the First Census 1790. Available at: http://www2.census.gov/prod2/decennial/documents/1790m-02.pdf.

US Bureau of the Census (1994) Table 1. Race of wife by race of husband: 1960, 1970, 1980, 1991, and 1992. Washington, DC. Available at: http://www.census.gov/population/socdemo/race/interractab1.txt US Bureau of the Census (1997) Results of the 1996 race and ethnic targeted test. Population Division Working Paper no 18, Washington, DC.

US Bureau of the Census (2011) The 2011 statistical abstract of the United States. Washington, DC.

Valdés, D.M. (1978) The decline of the Sociedad de castas in Mexico City. PhD thesis, University of Michigan.

Weisman, J.R. (1996) An "other" way of life: the empowerment of alterity in the interracial individual. In: M.P.P. Root (ed) *The multiracial experience*. Thousand Oaks, CA: Sage, pp 152–64.

Williams, K.M. (2005) Multiracialism & the future of civil rights. *Daedalus* 134(1): 53–60.

Williams, K.M. (2006) *Mark one or more: civil rights in multiracial America*. Ann Arbor, MI: University of Michigan Press.

Yazzie, R. (1994) "Life comes from it": Navajo justice concepts. *New Mexico Law Review* 24: 175–90.

TWO

National and local structures of inequality: multiracial groups' profiles across the US

Mary E. Campbell and Jessica M. Barron

Why compare multiracial groups?

This chapter describes the income and education profiles of the 10 largest multiracial groups in the US. Our goal is to better understand how these groups are positioned within the racial inequality system in the US. Racial inequality and discrimination is long-established in the US, with White people experiencing significantly more privileged positions along many different axes (e.g., educational, occupational, income, health, etc) than Black people and Native Americans. Some have argued, however, that as we become an increasingly multiracial society, some of the ways in which racial inequality is organized might change (e.g., Yancey, 2003; Bonilla-Silva, 2004; O'Brien, 2008; Lee and Bean, 2010), and the rapidly growing multiracial groups (along with Latino/as and Asians, rapidly growing immigrant groups) might be at the forefront of these changes because their position in the system of racial inequality may be shifting (as discussed by Quiñones-Rosado in Chapter Three and Strmic-Pawl and Brunsma in Chapter Eleven).

What kinds of outcomes might we predict for groups of individuals who identify with more than one race? One prediction might be that because multiracial individuals have family or ancestral connections to more than one racial group, and these racial groups have different average socio-economic characteristics, multiracial groups will fall (on average) in between the characteristics of those two specific racial groups. These many group-specific differences may result in multiracial groups experiencing different kinds of oppression and/or privilege, and therefore result in their occupying different positions in the US "racial hierarchy." This assumes, however, that there are no other forces affecting their outcomes. If, in fact, multiracial groups face more or less discrimination than single-race groups, their outcomes may not be a simple averaging of the single-race group outcomes. One goal here, then, is to gain some leverage on the question of whether the outcomes of multiracial groups appear to be shaped by the specific histories and outcomes of their single-race origin groups, or whether multiracial groups also share some commonalities (because of their shared ties to multiple racial groups) that distinguish them from groups who only claim a single racial background. Also, all of these groups are spread unevenly across the US, and the experiences of these groups might depend heavily on the region in which they live and the particular history of that area. We might hypothesize that groups may face more discrimination in some local contexts compared to others (e.g., the experience of part-Black groups being different in the South compared to the West) or experience other geographic variation because of differences in the local history, size, or composition of the group. We therefore ask three main questions in this chapter in order to capture some of the important facets of this variation:

1. What are the inequality patterns for multiracial groups?
2. Are those inequality patterns the same for children and adults?
3. How do those patterns vary across major cities in the US?

One thing that is important to keep in mind throughout this chapter is that we are examining groups based only on their self-identification, and past research makes it clear that different groups experience different influences on their identification. For example, individuals with both Black and White heritage are often used as the prime example of a group that has historically faced significant pressure to identify as Black alone, rather than claim a multiracial identification (e.g., Korgen, 1998; Spencer, 1999; Daniel, 2002; DaCosta, 2007; Rockquemore and Brunsma, 2008; Khanna, 2011), while Asian–White individuals are often used as an example of a group who have historically had the flexibility to choose their identification more freely (e.g., Xie and Goyette, 1997; Khanna, 2004). Although many argue that these historical pressures are weaker today and multiracial identification is accepted much more broadly, allowing individuals to claim multiracial identification more freely, we must still remember that self-identification is a choice, and therefore that not everyone aware of a multiracial background will claim a multiracial identification, and not everyone who identifies as multiracial has parents of two different races (see, e.g., Harris and Sim, 2002; Brunsma, 2005; Campbell, 2007). As Harris and Sim (2002) famously put it, what we are describing are the characteristics of *"a"* multiracial population rather than *"the"* multiracial population. We would be including different individuals if we, for example, changed the format of the question used to measure "race" or used the self-identification of parents to identify multiracial people rather than focusing on the self-identification of the individual.

Why use survey data?

Although national survey data have significant limitations for understanding the experiences of multiracial people, including the limitations imposed by the structure of the racial identification questions and the lack of information on the meaning of those categories to the individuals, we argue that large-scale survey data are very useful for the questions we wish to answer in this chapter. Survey data allow us to take a national approach to answering these questions and to systematically compare the cities with the largest self-identified multiracial populations. Still, we acknowledge the limitations of these data. One significant limitation is that the two-question format (separating Latina/o "ethnicity" or origin from all of the "racial" categories; see Figure 1) limits our understanding of whether individuals who claim both a Latina/o identification and a single racial identification are actually claiming a multiracial identification. Thus, although someone who identifies as Mexican-American and White *might* be doing so because they have one Mexican-American parent and one Anglo parent or feel connected to both Anglo and Mexican ancestry, there is no way to separate those who are doing so from those who are simply answering "White" in the race question because they are being forced to choose a box (see, e.g., Rodriguez, 2000). Thus, for Latinas/os and non-Latinas/os, we only consider individuals who chose two or more groups in the "race" question (question 6 in Figure 1) as multiracial because those individuals are clearly identifying with more than one category in the same question. A second significant limitation is that because the survey is taken at home and then mailed in, there is no way to be sure that the individuals we analyze actually filled out these two questions for themselves. It is likely that in most households, one person fills out the survey for everyone in the household. Thus, while we would prefer to use each individual adult's and child's self-identification, in many cases (especially for children), we have a proxy response filled out by another member of the household.

Using the five-year American Community Survey (ACS) data from 2007 to 2011, we compare the 10 largest non-Latina/o and Latina/o multiracial groups (non-Latina/o groups: White–Black, White–Asian, White–American Indian, Black–American Indian, Asian–Some Other

Figure 2.1: American Community Survey questionnaire, 2011

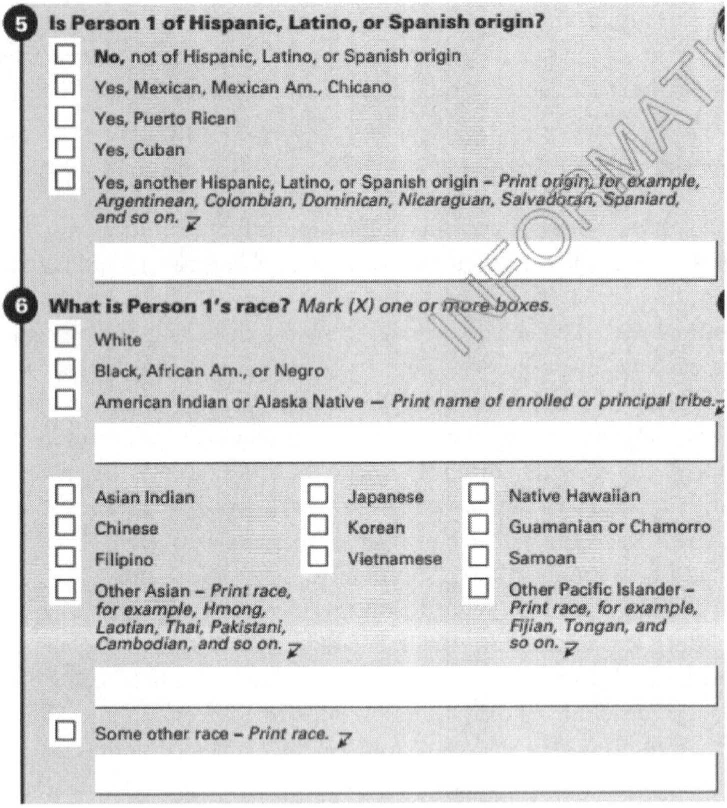

5 Is Person 1 of Hispanic, Latino, or Spanish origin?

- ☐ **No,** not of Hispanic, Latino, or Spanish origin
- ☐ Yes, Mexican, Mexican Am., Chicano
- ☐ Yes, Puerto Rican
- ☐ Yes, Cuban
- ☐ Yes, another Hispanic, Latino, or Spanish origin – *Print origin, for example, Argentinean, Colombian, Dominican, Nicaraguan, Salvadoran, Spaniard, and so on.*

6 What is Person 1's race? *Mark (X) one or more boxes.*

- ☐ White
- ☐ Black, African Am., or Negro
- ☐ American Indian or Alaska Native — *Print name of enrolled or principal tribe.*
- ☐ Asian Indian
- ☐ Chinese
- ☐ Filipino
- ☐ Other Asian – *Print race, for example, Hmong, Laotian, Thai, Pakistani, Cambodian, and so on.*
- ☐ Japanese
- ☐ Korean
- ☐ Vietnamese
- ☐ Native Hawaiian
- ☐ Guamanian or Chamorro
- ☐ Samoan
- ☐ Other Pacific Islander – *Print race, for example, Fijian, Tongan, and so on.*
- ☐ Some other race – *Print race.*

Race, White–Black–American Indian, and Black Asian; Latina/o groups: Latina/o–White–Some Other Race, Latina/o–Black–Some Other Race, and Latina/o–Asian–Some Other Race). We compare both children and adults from each of these groups, because much of the literature on multiracial groups has focused on the experiences of children or adolescents and their socio-economic and demographic outcomes (see, e.g., Campbell, 2009; Cheng and Lively, 2009; Herman, 2009; Bratter and Kimbro 2013). Less work has been done on adults who identify as multiracial, so it is less clear whether adults' experiences in the racial hierarchy in the US tend to fall "in between" the different racial groups that they claim as part of their identification.

Where do the multiracial groups "fit" in the racial hierarchy in the US?

Adults

There is a tremendous amount of socio-economic diversity among the 10 largest multiracial groups in the US. Table 2.1 includes weighted sociodemographics for multiracial and single-race groups. Looking at the descriptive results for multiracial adults in the US in Table 2.1 shows us that the median household income (in 2011 dollars) for the groups ranges from under $40,000 for Black–American Indian adults to over $70,000 for Asian–Some Other Race adults. This wide range of income relates to the many demographic differences between the groups, such as the sizable variation in family structure (percentage of the group who are married or never married), nativity (percentage of the group who were born outside and inside the US) and education (percentage of the group who have earned at least a high school degree or at least a bachelor's degree).

The most educated multiracial groups on average are White–Asian and Asian–Some Other Race adults. More than 40% of both groups have earned a bachelor's degree or more. Adults who identify as Asian–Some Other Race are as highly educated as those who identify as only Asian, the most educated of the single-race groups. The groups with the lowest levels of college attainment are Latina/o–White–Some Other Race and Latina/o–Black–Some Other Race, both with less than 20% of the group having achieved at least a bachelor's degree. Comparing these numbers to Latinas/os overall, whose rate of earning a bachelor's degree or more is 14%, the multiracial Latina/o groups all have similar or slightly higher educational attainment. This shows us that like the national numbers for other Latinas/os, these numbers are likely influenced by the bimodal nature of immigration to the US today (where many immigrants are very highly educated, and many have very little education; see, e.g., Bean et al, 2004). On the one hand, more than one third of each of these groups was born outside of the US, and many of these individuals have low levels of education. For example, 11% of foreign-born Latinas/os have at least a college degree, significantly lower than the average for the group overall. Foreign-born individuals in the multiracial Latina/o groups are also less likely to have a college degree than the group overall, with the notable exception of Latina/o–Asian–Some Other Race adults. On the other hand, the Asian–Some Other Race group has by far the largest proportion who are foreign-born (83%), and they also have the highest percentage of

Table 2.1: Average socio-economic characteristics of the 10 largest multiracial groups: adults, 2007–2011 ACS, weighted

Multiracial groups	White–Black	Latino/a White–SOR	White–Asian	White–AIAN	Latino/a Black SOR	Black–AIAN	Asian–SOR	White–Black–AIAN	Black–Asian	Latino/a Asian–SOR
Group size	475,500	450,000	688,600	1,020,400	63,300	191,000	62,000	99,100	84,700	38,400
Average age	32	39	36	45	36	44	43	41	37	39
Median household income ($)	42,486	49,666	64,524	43,145	41,480	39,008	72,820	41,019	52,243	55,902
High school degree or more[a] (%)	92	73	94	87	82	89	88	93	91	83
Bachelors or more[a] (%)	28	17	42	20	18	21	50	28	30	24
Married (%)	27	45	43	44	30	30	63	30	35	43
Never married (%)	60	38	46	28	54	43	26	46	48	42
Foreign-born (%)	9	42	29	1	36	2	83	3	43	37
US citizen (%)	94	83	78	99	84	98	51	98	69	81
Bilingual (%)	8	57	21	5	52	6	69	7	21	49

Single-race groups	White	Black	Asian	AIAN	Latino/a
Group size	156,774,600	27,024,000	11,511,100	1,473,500	32,449,500
Average age	49	43	43	43	40
Median income household ($)	58,742	38,180	70,000	37,473	41,388
High school degree or more[a] (%)	92	84	88	82	64
Bachelors or more[a] (%)	32	18	51	14	14
Married (%)	56	32	61	41	49
Never married (%)	23	44	28	23	35
Foreign-born (%)	5	11	81	2	58
US citizen (%)	97	94	53	99	83
Bilingual (%)	6	7	74	23	69

Notes

SOR = Some other race

AIAN = American Indian, Alaska Native

[a] Educational attainment rates for adults 25 and older, all other statistics refer to adults 18 and older

college-educated group members, showing that many of the foreign-born in the US are highly educated.

One of the important and often overlooked demographic characteristics of a group is the percentage who are functionally bilingual (in both English and a heritage language). Bilingualism has some significant advantages, including the ability to maintain strong intergenerational ties with relatives who do not speak English while still being able to easily navigate US social institutions that rely almost exclusively on English-speaking ability. Table 2.1 shows that bilingualism varies widely among multiracial groups as well, with more than 50% of the sample of some groups reporting that they are bilingual. Two of these groups are Latina/o (Latina/o–White–Some Other Race and Latina/o–Black–Some Other Race), while one is not (Asian–Some Other Race). For these groups, connection to two or more racial and ethnic backgrounds is also often tied to strong connections to two or more languages. For others, however, like White–American Indian and Black–American Indian respondents, very few speak a language other than English, suggesting that Native American language ability is not a strong characteristic of these multiracial groups. The other two part-Asian multiracial groups (White–Asian and Black–Asian) fall in between, with about one fifth of the group reporting that they are bilingual.

Children

We see similar diverse patterns of outcomes for children in Table 2.2. It is important to note that these demographic characteristics do not follow exactly the same pattern we see if we look at multiracial adults. First, let us consider group size. If we examine children only, we would find that the largest multiracial groups in the US are White–Black and White–Asian children. If we examine adults only, we would conclude that White–American Indians are the largest group by far, followed by White–Asians. This difference is important for our thinking about the diversity of multiracial groups, and likely reflects differences in: (1) the history of interracial relationships among racial groups; (2) patterns of self-identification compared to identification by someone else in the household (i.e, few children are self-identifying—someone else, such as a parent, is likely filling out the form for them); and (3) the meaning of the categories for the individuals who claim a multiracial identity (e.g., many have argued that adults who formerly called themselves White make up a large portion of the White–American Indian category among adults; see, e.g., Nagel, 1997; Snipp, 2003).

Table 2.2: Average socio-economic characteristics of the 10 largest multiracial groups: children, 2007–2011 ACS, weighted

Multiracial groups	White–Black	Latino/a White-SOR	White–Asian	White–AIAN	Latino/a Black SOR	Black–AIAN	Asian–SOR	White–Black–AIAN	Black–Asian	Latino/a Asian–SOR
Group size	1,105,500	418,100	777,800	420,800	101,900	73,000	23,200	78,300	84,200	40,000
Median household income ($)	38,623	51,430	88,881	47,596	36,871	34,435	80,711	37,249	56,000	62,610
Foreign-born (%)	1	5	6	1	3	1	21	1	6	4
US citizen (%)	99	98	96	99	99	99	93	99	96	98
Bilingual (%)	3	37	15	4	30	7	48	6	15	33

Single-race groups	White	Black	Asian	AIAN	Latino/a
Group size	42,756,300	11,125,800	3,474,800	620,400	17,651,200
Median income household ($)	89,960	45,308	98,239	36,215	51,105
Foreign-born (%)	2	3	25	1	11
US citizen (%)	99	98	90	100	98
Bilingual (%)	6	6	62	15	65

Notes

SOR = Some other race

AIAN = American Indian, Alaska Native

[a] Educational attainment rates for adults 25 and older, all other statistics refer to adults 18 and older

The demographic data for multiracial children also reveal different patterns than we find for multiracial adults. There are greater household income disparities among the groups of children identified as multiracial, with household incomes of multiracial youth ranging from an average of $34,000 for Black–American Indians to an average of $89,000 for children with a White–Asian identification. This is a higher average household income for the richest group of youth, White–Asians, and a lower average income for Black–American Indians, the poorest group, than we see among adults. Children identified as multiracial are also more likely to be born in the US and to speak only one language than adults. Asian–Some Other Race children are the only multiracial youth group to have a significant number of foreign-born group members, and rates of bilingualism are far lower for children than for adults identified as Asian–Some Other Race. Almost all children identified as multiracial in this survey were born in the US, and most speak only one language fluently. As Table 2.2 indicates, the most bilingual group of children is Asian–Some Other Race youth, 48% of whom are bilingual, followed by Latina/o–White–Some Other Race youth at 37%, Latina/o–Asian–Some Other Race youth at 33%, and Latina/o–Black–Some Other Race youth at 30%. All of the other groups are below 20% in their rates of bilingualism, whereas six of the 10 adult groups had bilingualism rates above 20%.

These patterns of inequality, for both adults and children, show that the same structures of racial inequality that affect single-race groups also affect multiracial groups (as Botts points out in Chapter Five). African-Americans, Native Americans and Latinas/os face high levels of discrimination in the US, and we see that multiracial groups with some Black or Latina/o background also have lower levels of income than, for example, multiracial groups with Asian and White heritage. If we look at median household income for adults, of the five groups with incomes below $45,000, four are part-Black, and the fifth is part-Native American. The three groups with the highest incomes (over $55,000) all are part-Asian. Of course, multiracial groups do complicate these questions; for example, the groups that are part-White are expressing a connection to a racialized minority *and* the majority group, while the other groups are expressing connections to multiple racialized minority groups with different histories and experiences in the US. Still, the outcomes of multiracial groups do often follow patterns that resemble the racial inequality experiences of the single-race groups to which they are connected.

Does it matter where you live?

In addition to comparing the national averages for group outcomes, we include a comparison of a few important socio-economic outcomes for multiracial groups living in the 10 cities in the US with the greatest number of multiracial people (New York, Los Angeles, Chicago, Houston, San Diego, Honolulu, Phoenix, San Jose, San Antonio, and Philadelphia) in order to test whether the racial stratification system for multiracial people is similar across the US or varies by local context. We began our investigation by looking at all 10 groups for all 10 cities, but in many cases, the sample sizes were too small to result in reliable estimates. Thus, we show selected results for the four largest multiracial groups in the 10 cities, excluding any estimates that are based on a sample of fewer than 100 respondents in that city.

Figure 2.2: Median household income for multiracial adults, divided by city median household income, 2007–2011 ACS

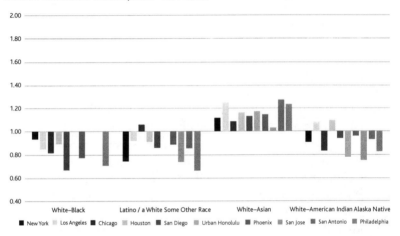

As an example of why this local variation is important, consider Figure 2.2, in which we examine the median household income of each multiracial group divided by the median household income in the city in which they live (in 2011 dollars) for adults who identify as multiracial. We divide the group's income by the median value for the city because some cities have higher median incomes overall than others; incomes appear high for all groups in San Jose, for example, if you do not control for this variation across cities. If the group's value is greater than 1, their median household income is above the city average. This figure shows us that only White–Asian adults have household incomes that are consistently above the median for their city, but that there is also considerable variation by place for some of the groups, though many of these differences are not significant when we examine statistical models of family income divided by city median income.[1] For example, White–Black adults who live in the cities shown in Figure 2.2 do not have relative incomes that differ significantly from White–Black adults who live in Honolulu, and, similarly, there is little significant variation by city for White–Asian adults. If we compare the incomes (relative to their city medians) for Latino/a–White–Some Other Race adults across cities, however, there are variations that are statistically significant ($p < .01$). For example, Latino/a–White–Some Other Race adults who live in Honolulu earn significantly more relative to the city median than those who live in Los Angeles, New York, or Philadelphia, among other cities. White–American Indian adults who live in Houston are also earning significantly more relative to their city average than their peers in Honolulu ($p < .01$). These variations are important because they show us that even with a basic adjustment for variation across cities in the overall level of economic well-being in the city, the experience of these groups varies considerably across places. Equally important, if we are only comparing groups in New York or Philadelphia, we would conclude that Latina/o–White–Some Other Race individuals come from the most disadvantaged group, but in Los Angeles, Chicago, San Diego, or Phoenix, we would conclude that the most disadvantaged group is White–Black adults. These disparities mean that our conclusions about the structure of racial oppression and privilege in the US depend at least in part on *where* in the US we are examining those disparities.

We also see sizable local variation if we consider the household incomes of children identified as multiracial, though these differences are again not all statistically significant. In Figure 2.3, we see the median household incomes for children identified as multiracial (with only those cases where at least 100 respondents under the age of 18 from that group live in that city, and again divided by the median household income in the city), and these patterns also show large disparities in the experiences of the same group across multiple cities. White–Asian children who live in Honolulu are significantly ($p < .05$) disadvantaged relative to their peers in every other city listed here. Note that the median household income for children identified as White–Asian is significantly ($p < .001$) greater than the median household incomes for adults who identify as White–Asian; this remains true even if you control for differences between the cities in which the children live. Interestingly, this is true for all four of the largest multiracial groups; the

Figure 2.3: Median household income for multiracial children, divided by city median household income, 2007–2011 ACS

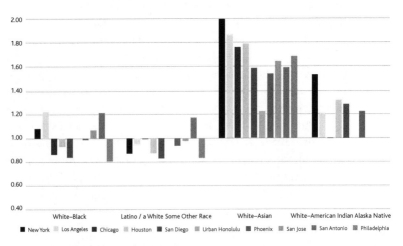

children identified with that group come from significantly ($p < .01$) higher-income families than the adults identified with that group, controlling for differences between cities. This serves as an important reminder of our earlier point that multiracial children and multiracial adults are in some ways quite different from each other, and the lessons we learn from one population should not be applied uncritically to the other population. Perhaps this is because of differences in how adults self-identify compared to how parents identify their children (e.g., there could be a relationship between parental income and the likelihood that you identify your child as multiracial, but a different relationship between income and self-identification), or perhaps this relates to other differences between the groups.

We created figures similar to Figures 2.2 and 2.3 for the percentage of the adults in each group who were married, born outside the US, bilingual, high school graduates, and college graduates. Some of the patterns vary little across cities; for example, the marital status of the groups is very similar across contexts (although most of the groups are slightly more likely to be married if they are living in Houston, Texas, than in the other cities), and high school graduation rates are quite consistent for most of the groups as well (although Latina/o–White–Some Other Race adults are a little more likely to have completed high school if they are living in Honolulu rather than elsewhere). These results are available from the authors on request, and for the remainder of this section, we focus on the outcomes that have more variation across cities.

When we consider patterns of foreign birth among multiracial adult groups in Figure 2.4, we see very large variations across urban contexts. More than 20% of adults identifying as White–Black in New York City were born outside the US, while only 5% of the same group in Chicago were born abroad. Similarly, the majority of New York's Latina/o–White–Some Other Race population was born abroad, while that is not true of that population in any of the other cities. Another dramatic comparison emerges for White–Asian adults, the majority of whom in Houston were born outside the US, but in Honolulu, less than 10% of this group were born outside the US These wide disparities highlight the fact that in different areas, these groups are truly different populations. This is not surprising because these contexts are very different. Honolulu has a long history of Asian immigration and acceptance of intermarriage, for example, neither of which is typical of Houston's history. Still, it means that when we are thinking about these groups in a national setting, we need to remember that local contexts may influence who identifies with the group, as well as what they experience in their daily lives.

Figure 2.4: Foreign-born adults by multiracial groups and city, 2007–2011 ACS

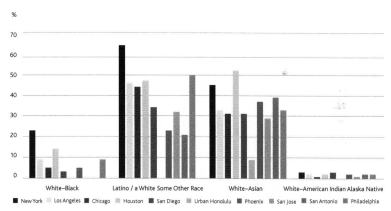

Figure 2.4's findings help to explain the large differences in bilingualism between the groups, which we see in Figure 2.5. The relationship between place of birth and bilingualism is not necessarily direct because bilingualism for the first generation often requires learning English, while bilingualism for second and higher generations generally requires the ability and desire to maintain the heritage language of earlier generations. Both of these patterns can vary by place because of differences in the support systems available for each requirement. Adults

who identify as White–Black or White–American Indian are relatively unlikely to report that they speak two languages well. Latina/o–White–Some Other Race and White–Asian adults, on the other hand, often speak two languages well, though the bilingualism rates are highest in New York and Houston. Again, these rates vary substantially, with the lowest bilingualism rates for Latina/o–White–Some Other Race adults in San Jose and Phoenix, and the lowest for White–Asians in Honolulu, all places with a long history of immigration.

Figure 2.5: Bilingual adults by multiracial groups and city, 2007–2011 ACS

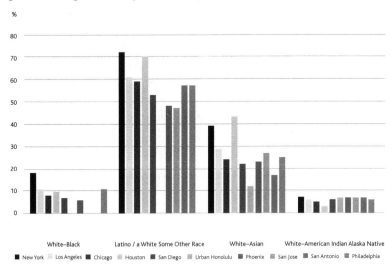

Figures 2.6 and 2.7 show the same outcomes for children. Again, we see that White–Black and White–American Indian children are very unlikely to be foreign-born or bilingual, and that there is a large amount of variation in these outcomes for Latina/o–White–Some Other Race and White–Asian children. Foreign birth rates for both Latina/o–White–Some Other Race and White–Asian groups are significantly higher in Houston than in other cities.

Overall, far fewer children than adults in these groups are bilingual, with the highest bilingualism rates found in New York (though still only 39% of Latina/o–White–Some Other Race and 16% of White–Asian children). Almost all of the multiracial children who speak only one language speak only English. In New York, 7% of Latina/o–White–Some Other Race children speak only a language other than English—the highest rate found for any city. Again, the most common outcome for these multiracial children is speaking only English, followed by relatively small numbers of bilingual children.

Figure 2.6: Foreign-born children by multiracial groups and city, 2007–2011 ACS

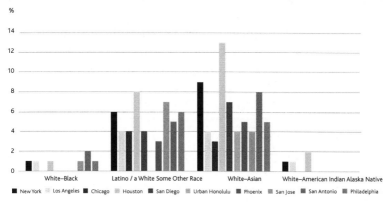

Figure 2.7: Bilingual children by multiracial groups and city, 2007–2011 ACS

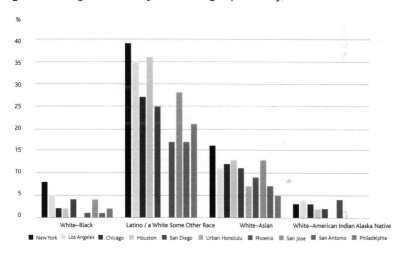

Our final socio-economic outcome of interest is college graduation for adults aged 25 years or older, found in Figure 2.8. Here, we see a 20% gap between the most advantaged group of White–Black adults (in New York City) and the most disadvantaged group (in San Antonio). Similarly, we see a gap of more than 30% between the most advantaged group of White–Asians (in New York) and the least advantaged (in Honolulu). As education is a good predictor not only of income, but also of other positive life outcomes like stable employment, good health, and longer life expectancy (Hout, 2012), we can view this as one of our most important outcomes. The wide variation we see here means that these groups, on average, have quite dissimilar experiences across cities. For example, note that in nine of the 10 cities, we would conclude that White–Asians are the most privileged group, but in Honolulu, the (relatively small) White–American Indian population has a greater proportion of college graduates than the (relatively large) White–Asian population. Hawaii is often mentioned in studies of multiracial groups as an outlier or exception to the patterns in the mainland US because of its long history of immigration, intermarriage, and acceptance of multiracial identities (e.g., Rosa, 2001; Lee and Bean, 2004). These data show that one of the consequences of these different histories is a very different socio-economic profile for those adults who identify as multiracial in Honolulu.

Figure 2.8: Adult college graduates (age 25+) by multiracial groups and city, 2007–2011 ACS

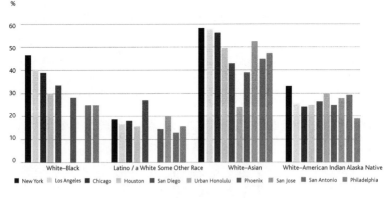

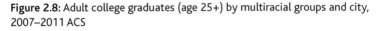

The differences among these cities go deeper than the simple gaps in socio-economic indicators we have been describing here. For example, racial residential segregation research makes it abundantly clear that where groups live has profound consequences for their life chances and social position in the US (Alba and Logan, 1993; Jargowsky, 1996; Charles, 2006). A recent aggregate study of 49 US metropolitan areas, using the 2010 US Census and refined measures of unevenness, exposure, neighborhood composition, and diversity, reported the differences in spatial patterns of White–Black, White–Asian and Black–Asian multiracial adults (Barron, 2013). Black–White adults occupy an intermediate space where they are not considerably segregated from White people or Black people even though White people and Black people continue to be highly segregated from one another. For example, in the average city, only 4% of White–Black adults would have to move to another neighborhood in order to achieve even distribution with White people, whereas 42% of Black people would have to move in order to achieve even distribution with White people. Yet, as we see with socio-economic indicators, cities vary in important ways. For example, in New York, a city where segregation between Black people and White people is high, at least 40% of White–Black adults live in neighborhoods that are less than 20% White.

In contrast, White–Asian adults live in much more contact with White people than all of the other multiracial groups in the study. White–Asian adults, on average, live in neighborhoods that are at least 60% White. However, in Los Angeles and Honolulu, cities with substantial "non-White" populations, White–Asian adults do not reside in predominately White neighborhoods. In fact, in Honolulu, White–Asians experience their highest levels of segregation from White people, where 10% of White–Asian adults would have to move to a different neighborhood to achieve even distribution with White people. Honolulu is the only city where segregation between White people and White–Asian adults reaches double digits.

In comparison, Black–Asian adults, as a dual-minority group, experience remarkably different neighborhood outcomes. Black–Asian adults have the lowest contact with White people of any multiracial group, living in neighborhoods less than 20% White. This is most pronounced in New York, where 71% of Black–Asian multiracial people live in "non-White" neighborhoods. Conversely, Black–Asian adults live in the most racially diverse neighborhoods, which may signal a connection between dual-minority status and the preference for diverse residential settings. The study concludes that there may be desirability or stigma attached to certain racial identities that result in different residential experiences among multiracial groups (Barron, 2013).

Concluding thoughts

Over the last 20 years, research has consistently shown that it is important not to think of the multiracial population as monolithic, but rather to acknowledge the different experiences of different multiracial groups. This chapter demonstrates that it is also important to remember that even if we examine just one multiracial group, their experiences will vary significantly depending on the local context. It is also important to remember the ways in which multiracial children and adults are not the same, and to understand that, often, our discussion of multiracial people tends to focus on the young (e.g., Streeter, 2002). Our results show that children and adults identified as multiracial are not experiencing the same outcomes, and these differences can be important. Remember, for example, the much greater socio-economic advantage of White–Asian children in the largest US cities (in Figure 2.3) compared to the incomes of White–Asian adults (in Figure 2.2). Comparisons like this remind us that if we just think of the experiences of children, we are likely to exaggerate some of the privileges and oppressions experienced by these groups, which could lead us to erroneous conclusions about the future of the groups or the meaning of their demographic changes. Similarly, we see from these results that if we focus only on national averages, we miss considerable differences in the make-up of the groups across local areas. As each city and region has its own history, integrating these differences into research and policy development is complex, but our findings here suggest that there are several pieces of information that could be important first steps, including data about the length of time the immigrant group has had a strong representation in the city (i.e, mostly recent immigration versus a long history of that immigrant group in the area) and the average age of the group in the area.

The US racial landscape has always been complex (e.g., there have always been multiracial people, immigration, interracial relationships, etc), but the rhetoric of racial inequality in the US has not always acknowledged that diversity. For many years, most discussions of racial inequality and racial policy in the US focused on the disparities between just Black people and White people, but as US society comes to acknowledge the diversity that exists, it becomes more difficult for the average person to think about the US racial terrain as a Black–White binary. Many authors, such as Bonilla-Silva (2004), Daniel (2002, 2006), O'Brien (2008), and Lee and Bean (2010), have argued that the growing recognition of the diversity in the US is creating new forms of racial hierarchy—ones that emphasize the importance of skin tone, or a "racial middle," or that are based on evolving rules about whether or not one is classified as Black.

The empirical results in this chapter do not, of course, tell us how the US is changing or what the future holds for these groups because they focus only on one point in time. What they do tell us is the importance of considering the local experiences of groups when developing policy, and the importance of considering how the experiences of multiracial groups are related to the experiences of single-race groups. For example, multiracial groups connected to Black people or Latinos/as are generally disadvantaged compared to those connected to White people and Asians, and those connected to both (i.e. Black–Asians) tend to have intermediate outcomes. When we contrast White–Asian individuals with Black–Asian individuals, we find that connection to whiteness and a minority group has had different implications than connection to two different racialized minority groups (e.g., Williams and Thornton, 1998). Multiracial Americans thus complicate our understanding of racial and ethnic stratification in the US because of the complexity of the groups' relationships to the hierarchies of oppression and privilege. The findings also remind us that when we are developing policy to reduce racial inequality, it is important to consider how differences in the local environment affect the experiences of those groups.

Note

[1] The models we ran are slightly different than the descriptives shown here because relative income is right-skewed, so our dependent variable was the natural log of family income divided by median city income, and our independent variables were dummy variables indicating the city in which the individual lived. Models for adults and children are available from the authors on request.

References

Alba, R.D. and Logan, J.R. (1993) Minority proximity to whites in suburbs: An individual level analysis of segregation. *American Journal of Sociology* 98(6): 1388–427.

Barron, J.M. (2013) Living life in the middle? Multiracials, residential segregation and the fate of the U.S. color-line. Unpublished dissertation, College Station, Texas A&M University.

Bean, F.D., Leach, M., and Lowell, B.L. (2004) Immigrant job quality and mobility in the United States. *Work and Occupations* 31: 499–518.

Bonilla-Silva, E. (2004) From bi-racial to tri-racial: towards a new system of racial stratification in the USA. *Ethnic and Racial Studies* 27: 931–50.

Bratter, J.L. and Kimbro, R.T. (2013) Multiracial children and poverty: Evidence from the early childhood longitudinal study of kindergartners. *Family Relations* 62: 175–89.

Brunsma, D.L. (2005) Interracial families and the racial identification of mixed-race children: evidence from the early childhood longitudinal study. *Social Forces* 84: 1131–57.

Campbell, M.E. (2007) Thinking outside the (black) box: measuring black and multiracial identification on surveys. *Social Science Research* 36: 921–44.

Campbell, M.E. (2009) Multiracial groups and educational inequality: a rainbow or a divide? *Social Problems* 56: 425–46.

Charles, C.Z. (2006) *Won't you be my neighbor? Race, class and residence in Los Angeles.* New York, NY: Russell Sage Foundation.

Cheng, S. and Lively, K.J. (2009) Multiracial self-identification and adolescent outcomes: a social psychological approach to the marginal man theory. *Social Forces* 88: 61–98.

DaCosta, K. (2007) *Making multiracials: state, family and market in the redrawing of the color line.* Stanford, CA: Stanford University Press.

Daniel, G.R. (2002) *More than Black? Multiracial identity and the new racial order.* Philadelphia, PA: Temple University Press.

Daniel, G.R. (2006) *Race and multiraciality in Brazil and the United States: converging paths?* University Park, PA: The Pennsylvania State University Press.

Harris, D.R. and Sim, J.J. (2002) Who is multiracial? Assessing the complexity of lived race. *American Sociological Review* 67: 614–27.

Herman, M.R. (2009) The Black–White–other achievement gap: testing theories of academic performance among multiracial and monoracial adolescents. *Sociology of Education* 82: 20–46.

Hout, M. (2012) Social and economic returns to college education in the United States. *Annual Review of Sociology* 38: 379–400.

Jargowsky, P.A. (1996) *Poverty and place: ghettos, barrios, and the American city.* New York, NY: Russell Sage.

Khanna, N. (2004) The role of reflected appraisals in racial identity: the case of multiracial Asians. *Social Psychology Quarterly* 67: 115–31.

Khanna, N. (2011) *Biracial in America: forming and performing racial identity.* Lanham, MD: Lexington Books.

Korgen, K.O. (1998) *From Black to biracial: transforming racial identity among Americans.* Westport, CT: Praeger.

Lee, J. and Bean, F.D. (2004) America's changing color lines: immigration, race/ethnicity, and multiracial identification. *Annual Review of Sociology* 30: 221–42.

Lee, J. and Bean, F.D. (2010) *The diversity paradox: immigration and the color line in twenty-first century America.* New York, NY: Russell Sage Foundation.

Nagel, J. (1997) *American Indian ethnic renewal: Red Power and the resurgence of identity and culture.* Oxford: Oxford University Press.

O'Brien, E. (2008) *The racial middle: Latinos and Asian Americans living beyond the racial divide.* New York, NY: NYU Press.

Rockquemore, K.A. and Brunsma, D.L. (2008) *Beyond Black: biracial identity in America* (2nd edn). Lanham, MD: Rowman & Littlefield.

Rodríguez, C.E. (2000) *Changing race: Latinos, the Census, and the history of ethnicity in the United States.* Critical America Series. New York: New York University Press.

Rosa, J.C. (2001) The coming of the neo-Hawaiian American race: nationalism and metaphors of the melting pot in popular accounts of mixed-race individuals. In: T. Williams-León and C.L. Nakashima (eds) *The sum of our parts: mixed-heritage Asian Americans*. Philadelphia, PA: Temple University Press, pp 49–56.

Snipp, C.M. (2003) Racial measurement in the American census: past practices and implications for the future. *Annual Review of Sociology* 29: 563–588.

Spencer, R. (1999) *Spurious issues: race and multiracial identity politics in the United States*. Boulder, CO: Westview Press.

Streeter, C.A. (2002) The hazards of visibility: "biracial" women, media images, and narratives of identity. In: L.I. Winters and H.L. DeBose (eds) *New faces in a changing America: multiracial identity in the 21st century*. Thousand Oaks, CA: Sage Publications, pp 301–22.

Williams, T.K. and Thornton, M.C. (1998) Social construction of ethnicity versus personal experience: the case of Afro-Amerasians. *Journal of Comparative Family Studies* 29(2): 255–67.

Xie, Y. and Goyette, K. (1997) The racial identification of biracial children with one Asian parent: evidence from the 1990 Census. *Social Forces* 76: 547–70.

Yancey, G.A. (2003) *Who is White? Latinos, Asians, and the new Black/nonblack divide*. Boulder, CO: Lynne Rienner Publishers.

THREE

Latinos and multiracial America

Raúl Quiñones-Rosado

Reframing Latino identity for the 21st century

"Multiracial Americans" is not a term I commonly use to refer to Latinos in my social justice education and antiracism organizing work. In the community and institutional settings where this work most often takes place, it is hard enough to get people, whether in education, human services, law enforcement, the judicial system, religion, philanthropy, non-profits, or government, to examine how they think about race and racism or to explore the powerful personal feelings and challenging social behaviors that these ideas generate. It is much harder to get these community and institutional leaders, policymakers, and enforcers to consider how racism—race prejudice plus institutional power, or, as journalist Bill Moyers more poignantly declares, "White supremacy enforced through state control" (*Moyer's & Company*, 2014)—continues to operate within their own organizations and institutions, disproportionately and negatively impacting the Latino and Black American communities being served. In these racially diverse educational and organizing contexts designed to promote fundamental changes in institutional practices in order to foster racial equity, the conversation about Latinos mostly revolves around how "Latino" (or "Hispanic") should be considered a "race," a distinct racialized ethnicity, counted separately from White people, Black Americans, Native Americans, Asians, and others, in order to account for and counter persisting racial inequities.

Even when working solely with Latino and Latina leaders, the main emphasis of the work is on how we, as Latinos—that is, people of Latin American origin in the US—have historically come to be collectively racialized as a separate and distinct "non-White" racial group. This emphasis, deliberately aimed at challenging racism and creating racial equity, is focused on strengthening our collective identity as Latinos as a racial group in the context of the US. Toward such strategic purpose, to refer to Latinos as "multiracial" at the outset typically only adds confusion to an already conceptually complex, emotionally charged, and politically challenging process.

It must also be noted that use of the term "Americans" to refer to the people, historically or currently, of the US can be a source of irritation to many Latinos, particularly to many of us who have lived in Latin America. Many of us tend to affirm—often adamantly so—that "American" refers not specifically or uniquely to *estadounidenses*, that is, "United Statesians." "American," we insist, more accurately refers to *all* the peoples of The Americas, from La Patagonia all the way north to Canada and Alaska, and many of us resist the appropriation of the term by those who, herein, I shall refer to as US Americans.

Having clarified these points, I do find it very appropriate, and quite opportune, to examine layers of greater complexity concerning Latinos as "multiracial Americans" and Latino racial identity within the context of a book on multiracial peoples of the US and critical perspectives on race policy. This exploration is particularly opportune at a time when antiracism organizers, institutional leaders, and policymakers alike may be wondering, or perhaps worrying, what will be the impact of the rate and scope of Latino population growth over the coming decades—especially given the anticipation that Latinos, together with other "People of Color," will become a racial "majority" in the US within the next 30 years (Quiñones-Rosado, 1998, 2010; Passel and Cohn, 2008; US Census Bureau, 2014a).

Exploration of some of the many complexities regarding Latinos is also timely as this demographic shift coincides with a process, already decades long, of reframing racial categories or, more precisely, a redefining of who is White in the US. Once again in its history, the US's race policy is in a process of being re-crafted by policymakers and implemented by institutional gatekeepers. A process of racial realignment is already being entertained by the media, the workplace, the marketplace, the body politic, and the general population, impacting perceptions, conceptions, and judgments about who Latinos are and, more importantly, what will be their (New?) place in this racially stratified society in the 21st century.

The pluri-national, pan-ethnic, and racially mixed peoples of Latin American origin in the US, historically racialized as "non-White," are being redefined, reclassified, and reconfigured, resulting in the re-racialization of a significant portion of the Latino population as "White." Facilitated by current race policy, this process, if left unchallenged, may well result in maintaining, if only on paper, a "White majority" throughout the century ahead. This racial reframing undermines ongoing and hard-fought efforts to recognize and correct racial disparities in educational, health-care, human services, law enforcement, and criminal justice systems. It is a process that would help to maintain White supremacy—in our institutions and throughout our culture—for the foreseeable future.

As a social psychologist and member of the Latino community, I wonder—and often worry—not only how Latinos and Latinas will continue to collectively identify ourselves, but also, and in some ways even more importantly, how we will be seen and related to by other racial groups in the US by the mid-21st century—particularly as driven by officially sanctioned, state-controlled, race policy. More specifically, I wonder if Latinos, historically racialized as "non-White," will still be considered, referred to, and treated as "People of Color" in the decades ahead. Or, like other previously racialized ethnic groups—Irish, Italians, Jews, and others—will Latinos, currently categorized by policymakers as Hispanic/Latino/Spanish ethnics *of any race* (Office of Management and Budget, 1997), also be collectively reassigned out of the racial middle (O'Brien, 2008) to a new place and status, within the historical binary of White and Black upon which race and racism have been constructed (Bonilla-Silva, 2010). In this chapter, then, I describe the current policy of re-racialization of Latinos and the effort to assimilate light-skinned Latinos into the White collective. I also argue for a race policy that supports a collective Latino identity.

Racializing and re-racializing Latinos

Until very recently, Latinos have been the fastest-growing segment of the US population and, at over 53 million people, they now comprise the country's largest so-called "minority" group (US Census Bureau, 2011). What may not be commonly known, except to US Commerce Department demographers and planners in both the public and private sectors, is that Latinos are an economic force, with purchasing power of over $1 trillion annually. Latinos are, and have always been, a vital part of the US labor force, as well as of the US military. Of particular interest to political operatives in both major parties, Latinos also help win elections. In 2012, there were over 23 million eligible Latino voters; with an additional 800,000 Latinos turning age 18 each year, Latinos are increasingly becoming a formidable political force (García, 2013).

As peoples of Latin American origin who live in the US, Latinos are not members of any singular national, ethnic, or racial group. We are pluri-national: we originate from the 20 different sovereign Latin American nations, plus Puerto Rico, an unincorporated US territory. We are pan-ethnic: even within these individual nations, there are often many ethnicities or cultural groups. We are multi-racial, but not only at a macro-level in terms of the racial diversity within each nation and across the continent; we are also what I refer to as *multizo*[1] in terms of the large number of persons who are racially mixed.

Contrary to perceptions that Latinos constitute a body of voluntary immigrants to the US, much like Europeans, though markedly unlike kidnapped and enslaved Africans, the fact is that people of Latin American origin are here as a result of the US's centuries-long policies and strategies of territorial and economic expansion (González, 2011). The vast majority of Latinos are of Mexican origin and, as an oft-repeated statement reminds us: Mexicans did not cross the border; the border crossed Mexicans. The US war on Mexico (1846–48) resulted in the transfer to the antebellum US and its slave-based economy of almost half of Mexico's national territory. With the signing of the Treaty of Guadalupe Hidalgo, the United States of America gained possession over the northernmost part of the United Mexican States: Texas, Colorado, Oklahoma and Kansas, New Mexico, Utah, Nevada, Arizona, and California (Acuña, 1988). Of course, with possession of the lands, the US also gained control of its Mexican and Native American populations. In the case of Mexicans, the treaty granted US citizenship—a major concession to Mexico given that, as per the US Naturalization Act of 1790, citizenship was a status strictly reserved for White people, that is, people of European descent, which Mexicans were clearly not (Acuña, 1998; Rodríguez, 2000).

Like the northern Mexican territories, Puerto Rico is also land obtained through US military intervention in Latin America. In 1898, during the Spanish–American War, US armed forces invaded Cuba and Puerto Rico, Spain's last remaining colonies in The Americas, taking both islands as treasure of war.[2] Nineteen years later, for geopolitical purposes and against the will of Puerto Rico's local civilian legislative body, the US imposed its citizenship upon its new subjects, conveniently allowing Puerto Rican men to be drafted into active duty in the US armed forces in the First World War (González, 2011; Rodríguez, 2005). While the former Mexican states were eventually incorporated as states of the Union, Puerto Rico remains an unincorporated territory to this day —a *de facto* colony—of the US.[3]

Beyond the addition of Mexicans and Puerto Ricans to the country's population over these past 160-plus years, millions of other Latin Americans have since immigrated to the US. Most significantly, the US Latino community has also come to include people from Cuba, El Salvador, the Dominican Republic, and other parts of Central America and South America's Caribbean nations, the regions of Latin America closest to and, historically, of greatest economic and geopolitical interest to the US. This steady flow of political and economic refugees from Latin America has continued as a consequence of US policy toward Latin America (González, 2011; US Census Bureau, 2011).

After its wars on Mexico's and Spain's colonies in the Caribbean, the US government directed its military might towards supporting US American economic interests throughout Latin America. To date, there have been over 76 US military interventions and countless covert actions in the region (Global Policy Forum, 2005). These interventions, together with US business and trade agreements with Latin American governments, have resulted in what journalist/historian Juan González refers to as the "harvest of empire": ongoing waves of immigrants, documented and otherwise, from Latin America to the US, forced out of their homelands by economic and political conditions created by US geopolitical and economic interests beyond its own national borders. These geopolitical strategies were implemented in addition to other specific immigration policies established by the US in cooperation with Latin American governments and local business interests in order to actively recruit laborers to supplement labor shortages in US farms, factories, and mines (González, 2011).

Of the 53 million Latinos in the US today, about 35% are foreign-born (Brown and Patten, 2014). The majority of Latinos are US citizens, born and raised in the country, most over multiple generations. The growth of the Latino population, currently driven more by domestic births than by immigration, is a trend that is expected to continue throughout the 21st century (Krogstad and López, 2014). Already having surpassed the African-American population in 2000, the US Census Bureau projects that by 2060, Latinos will comprise just under 30% of the population (US Census Bureau, 2014a). "By the end of this century, a majority of the people living in the United States will trace their origins, not to Europe, but to Latin America," suggests Juan González in the documentary based on his book (*Harvest of empire*, 2012).

In considering race policy, what must remain clear is that throughout this entire history, from pre-Civil War times to the present, people of Latin American origin in the US, collectively, were neither perceived nor treated as White people. Latinos, as a group, even when officially counted as White by virtue of treaty, law, or policy, have suffered discrimination based on their perceived "non-White" racial backgrounds.[4]

Three important legal cases provide evidence of this race policy in regards to Mexicans. In 1897, Ricardo Rodríguez, a Mexican citizen of indigenous ancestry, petitioned the US Federal Court in San Antonio, Texas, to become a US citizen, which was granted "despite the court's belief he was not White," (Haney-López 1996: 44) a legal prerequisite for becoming a naturalized citizen until 1952. This rare exception was granted on the basis of US treaties with Spain and Mexico conferring citizenship to Mexicans in territories now belonging to the US (Haney-Lopez, 1996). In *Hernández v. Texas* (1954), the US Supreme Court found that Mexican-Americans were "a class apart" or "other White," while in *Cisneros v. Corpus Christi Independent School District* (1970), the US Federal Court found that "Mexican Americans, as an identifiable minority group based on physical, cultural, religious, and linguistic distinctions," warranted protections against discrimination such as those extended to African-Americans, as per *Brown v. Board of Education* (1954) (Allsup, 2010a, 2010b, para 2).

The segregation of Mexican and Puerto Rican military personnel in the US armed forces from the First World War through the Korean War, like that of Black people and Asians, also stands as evidence of the *de facto* racialization of Latinos as "People of Color" (Oropeza, 2012). Moreover, the documented and undocumented stories of Latinos and Latinas segregated into urban *barrios* or bordertown *colonias*, exploited in factories, farm labor camps, hotel rooms, or restaurants, mistreated and miseducated in English-only schools across the nation, stand as unimpeachable testimony to the daily reality of being identified as a racialized "other": other than White.

Yet, in spite of this long history of racialization, race policy of the past decades has sought to de-racialize Latinos: to assert that Latinos are not to be viewed as members of a distinct *racial* group, but, rather, should be considered members of an *ethnic* group who can be of any race. That is, as "Hispanic/Latino/Spanish," we can be: White; Black/African American/Negro; American Indian/Alaska Native; Asian; and Native Hawaiian/Pacific Islander. Or, at least, we can be *counted* as one of these racial categorizations.

Racial assimilation through race policy

The racial assimilation of "People of Color" has always been a concern in efforts to end racial oppression, to mitigate its negative impacts, and to create racial equity in US society. In contrast to *integration*, a group's process of gaining admission into and occupying a legitimate place within society while maintaining their own group identity, *assimilation* is the process by which "People of Color" psychologically internalize the patterns of thought and behavior of White culture while largely *replacing* their own cultural and racial identity. In a racist society such as the US's, assimilation, whether that of individuals or of entire groups, requires that the distinct identity of those previously racialized as "non-White" is absorbed into whiteness. At the individual level, a "Person of Color" who assimilates *passes* for White. At the collective level, a "People of Color" who assimilate lose their distinct identity and their unique existence as the group *dissolves* into the White collective.

The assimilation of Latino/a individuals, and potentially their various collectivities, is another negative outcome of living within a culture of racial oppression and yet another challenge for antiracism and racial equity efforts. As a manifestation of internalized racial oppression, assimilation functions as a disruption within the process of racial identity development. This disruption can occur to a person born and raised within a Latino-identified family or, as is increasingly the case, to a child of mixed Latino and White parents (Vargas, 2015). Assimilation is a psychosocial phenomenon that occurs mostly beyond the conscious awareness of the individual, someone who is, to some degree, distanced from their cultural heritage, unaware of their people's history, disconnected from family roots, or disassociated from community. At this individual level, assimilation may be mitigated or prevented through any number of liberating and transformative psycho-educational strategies—a topic beyond the scope of this chapter. Yet, beyond efforts to mitigate or avoid the negative impact of assimilation on Latinos individually, it is fundamentally important and urgently necessary that we examine the impact, if not question the purpose, of race policy on a larger scale and its role in assimilating many Latinos into the White collective, rather than integrating all Latinos into US society.

As antiracism organizers and racial equity advocates work in Latino communities and build multiracial alliances to transform institutional practices and change race policy, there are multiple layers of cultural complexity to consider. Many involve how the dynamics of internalized racial oppression of Latinos in the US may interact with historical patterns of structural racism in Latin American contexts—cultural, sociological, and psychological backdrops of Latino identity. For example, the cultural legacy of Spain's racist caste system[5] throughout Latin America, which, like the historical racial paradigm of the US, also privileges people deemed to be White, is an issue that needs to be acknowledged and examined among Latinos. Addressing light-skin privilege, colorism, and Eurocentrism and their intersections with classism, sexism, and nationalism within Latin American cultures of origin and, then, how these, in turn, may relate to Latino assimilation and collusion with White supremacy in the US remains a primary task of antiracism. Meanwhile, we must also examine the extent to which race policy supports or undermines efforts toward racial equity and the potential for true integration without racial assimilation into whiteness of all "Peoples of Color."

Undoubtedly, an ambivalent national race policy that insists on dividing Latinos among multiple races and, then, re-racializing more than half of this segment of the population as White would surely appear to foster the process of Latino assimilation. On the one hand, current race policy ensures that Latinos are counted as a specific demographic separate from White people, African-Americans, and other racial groups for the purpose of monitoring shifts in the economic, political, cultural, and social patterns of this group relative to other groups and for the purpose of establishing other relevant public policy. Implemented through institutions' use of "Hispanic" and "non-Hispanic" labels, this policy simultaneously tracks persons by the official "races": White; Black; American Indian/Alaska Native; Asian; and Native Hawaiian/ Pacific Islander. Census reports, for example, typically show complex population tables with three data sets: (1) total population; (2) "non-Hispanic" population; and (3) Hispanic population. An additional layer of complexity, and difficulty in using the information, is that numbers for people of "two or more races" also appear in each set. Yet, on the other hand, when presenting total population by race in simplified form, the Census Bureau aggregates much of the "Hispanic" population to the "White" totals (US Census Bureau, 2014b). Such application of current race policy, intentionally or unintentionally, would maintain a numerical White majority well beyond 2042, when the demographic shift has been projected to occur. Besides ensuring that White people remain the racial majority and retain the "majority rules" rationale for their continued cultural dominance, privileged social status, and political-economic control,[6] the ambivalent nature of current race policy would certainly serve to perpetuate structural racism and its corollary, racial inequities.

"Hispanic" as a policy of racial assimilation

The term "Hispanic" was adopted in the 1980s, a time when Latinos were identified as the fastest-growing segment of the population and were, within a mere two decades, projected to numerically surpass the African-American population. The adoption of this term also followed on the heels of the US Census Bureau moving away from a door-to-door census-taking process to using the national postal service to collect the raw data, starting with the 1960 Census. A term more politically convenient, if not also seemingly more culturally fitting, than those previously used (such as Spanish, Spanish-language, and Spanish-surnamed) was deemed necessary as household occupants themselves, and no longer Census enumerators, would be the ones to identify and report the race(s) of household members and return completed forms by mail (González, 2011; Mora, 2014).

In *Making Hispanics*, G. Cristina Mora (2014) convincingly argues that government bureaucrats adopted the term "Hispanic" with the active involvement of Latino activists and corporate media. Each of these three sectors, Mora posits, needed a simple label that could potentially reconcile the many different national identities combined under it, distinct groups often at odds with one another. Each of them needed a term that could serve their particular interests: race policy in the case of government bureaucrats; regional and national politics for Latino activists; and demographically targeted marketing for the media and their corporate clients.

To be clear, the adoption of a term that sought to create a unifying identity for peoples of Latin American origin in the US, groups often at odds with each other, was indeed a political achievement. In large measure, it reflected a major shift of critical consciousness spurred by decades—from the mid-1950s into the early 1980s—of African-American civil rights and Black Power movements, then expanding into the liberation struggles of women, of Native Americans, and of Latinos: the United Farm Workers, the Brown Berets, the Young Lords, and the Puerto Rican pro-independence movements, among others (Mora, 2014).

While "Hispanic" ostensibly served to unify Latinos, or, at least, generate a greater sense of shared identity across Latino groups, it also advertently or inadvertently had other results in the general public psyche. To many other US Americans, the term gave people an acceptable way to collectivize Latinos, as well as a way to avoid calling them "Mexican" or "Puerto Rican," identifiers that, in the context of post-civil rights racial narratives and emerging multicultural sensitivities of the 1980s and 1990s, could have been considered "politically incorrect." To many, while still proudly Mexican, Puerto Rican, or, increasingly, Cuban, Dominican, Salvadoran, and other Latin American heritages, widespread adoption of the term "Hispanic" in popular and official discourse meant that they were finally acknowledged as part of the fabric of US American society.

Yet, in the 30-plus years since its ubiquitous adoption by public, private, and non-profit sectors alike, the term "Hispanic" has also, in effect, reoriented the shared language of race throughout the general public. "Hispanic" seems to have redefined the ways in which Latino identity has historically been collectively perceived and conceived, both by Latinos and by other groups. Although still resisted or outright rejected by many Latinos, widespread acceptance of the "Hispanic" label has, for all intents and purposes, functioned as a sociolinguistic reframe that has shifted US Americans' collective subjective referents of this social identity group away from our actual origin—Latin America—stereotypically characterized as economically poor, politically unstable, ethically questionable, culturally backward, racially hybrid, and, thus, decidedly, "non-White." Instead, "Hispanic" has redirected our collective thinking toward Spain: European, cultured, and, ostensibly, White. In effect, the pervasive use of the term "Hispanic" has not only reoriented the racial narrative of US society, but misled it, placing it at the service of White supremacy (Acuña, 1988; Quiñones-Rosado, 1998).

It is important to consider the role of the US government in advancing the misleading reframing of Latino identity.[7] For the 2000 Census, the US Department of Commerce, through its Census Bureau, would remind us that, according to official race policy as established by the US Office of Management and Budget (1997), "Hispanic/Latino/ Spanish" was not to be considered a *race*, but, rather, an *ethnicity*.[8] In order to reduce the high percentage of Latinos that would typically choose "Some Other Race" in the absence of a Latino category (Rodríguez, 2000), Census responders would first indicate if they were "Hispanic/Latino/Spanish," and if they answered "Yes," they would then specify their national origin: Mexico, Puerto Rico, Cuba, etc. Clearly stating that "people who identify their origin as Hispanic, Latino, or Spanish may be of any race" (US Census Bureau, 2013), the next questionnaire item directed members of this *ethnic* group to identify their *race* based on one of five categories: White; Black/African American/Negro; American Indian/Alaska Native; Asian; and Native Hawaiian/Pacific Islander.

To be sure, in both the 2000 and 2010 Census processes, Latinos were, indeed, counted as a separate group, albeit not a racial one. Then, like today, the federal government and its agencies needed data sets specific to this growing demographic sector, information that, in turn, can be used by policymakers and implementers in health, education, public welfare, housing, transportation, industry, retail, banking and finance, and every social, cultural, political, and economic institution and system. This information is presumably gathered in order to track health, income, wealth, and other indicators of well-being in our communities. Furthermore, this data continues to be collected, in large measure, because of the activism of Latino advocacy groups and, more recently, the lobbying of Hispanic for-profit interest groups.

Yet, this counting and tracking of Hispanics/Latinos—still necessary because of the legacy and persistence of structural racism—is done in a way that invisibilizes the reality that Latinos have always been and still are a racialized ethnicity, a group perceived and conceived in the collective US consciousness as "non-White," as "People of Color." This data collection is done in a way that, in effect, steers many Latinos into being counted as White. By separating race from ethnicity as distinct categories, and asking Latinos to identify *both* their Latino ethnicity and their race, the percentage of Hispanics/Latinos who were counted as White by the Census increased from just under 48% in 2000 to 53% in 2010.[9]

Conclusion

The US Census Bureau and numerous systems and institutions, public and private, will surely continue to count Latinos and track our outcomes in education, health, law enforcement, judicial and penal systems, employment, income, and wealth for the immediate and, perhaps, for the foreseeable future. However, the historic ambivalence of race policy toward Latinos and the apparent attempt to racially assimilate large segments of the Latino population through current policy do not serve the well-being and development of this community, nor that of US society overall. A standard and uniform policy-based practice to classify/categorize Latinos as a racial group, albeit a racialized ethnicity, is important and still necessary in order to clearly and accurately document and track the real outcomes of institutional practices over time. Such a new policy across states and across agencies by federal mandate would ensure a more accurate count of Latinos and racial disparities in the treatment and outcomes of Latinos and all "People of Color" relative to White people.

The current historical moment of multiracial identity inquiry could provide an excellent opportunity to develop a common identity and a greater sense of solidarity among Latinos across national and ethnic identities. For example, while issues concerning immigration impact Mexican and Central American communities differently than South American or Caribbean immigrant communities, there appears to be pan-Latino activism, leadership, and solidarity in the national movement for immigration reform.

Of course, we cannot assume that broadly shared historical and cultural paradigms of pan-ethnic multiracial Latinos are sufficient to organize us to struggle for greater racial equity. Indeed, acknowledgment of our particular national, cultural identities is often a prerequisite to deeper conversations about racial identity and our experiences with racism, whether within our own communities or relative to others in the larger US context. Knowledge and familiarity with the layered complexities of national, cultural, and race identity—further textured by class, educational level, citizenship or immigration status, geography, age, generation, time in the US, marriage with US Americans, and children—help facilitate the trust-building necessary for movement-building. Our experiences of racial oppression, whether through interpersonal micro-aggressions or institutional exclusion, exploitation, or other negative outcomes, are not necessarily the starting point of organizing among Latinos. Often, it is finding common ground within or between our culture(s) that can lead to reminding people—or informing them for the first time—of a long history of shared struggle against racism and bring us together.

This is also an opportune moment to revitalize a once strong sense of common cause with Black Americans and other communities of color in the US, including those who identify as multiracial, as we together develop antiracist social policy and liberating practice for cultural transformation. An ongoing challenge faced by antiracism educators and organizers, particularly in the context of the US, is the persistent fragmentation of our antiracism analyses, efforts, and strategies. In many places we observe, Latinos rarely participate in antiracism efforts that they may perceive as only pertaining or relevant to African-Americans, while relatively few African-Americans seem to express much interest in efforts perceived to be geared toward Latinos. This fragmentation, a clear expression of internalized racism and lateral distrust resulting from generations of racism, is evident even within our own national antiracism networks, which have yet to articulate a multiracial vision or strategy that directly addresses attempts to reconfigure—once again—White racial identity and assimilate large segments of the Latino population into the White collective.

Antiracism educators and organizers, Latino or otherwise, cannot and should not assume that the process of assimilation into the White racial collective of at least 50 million people—half of the projected 100 million multiracial Latinos in the US by mid-century—is an inevitable, or even a likely, outcome. From where we stand, among members and leaders within this multiracial national movement against racism, we cannot and should not assume that we, collectively, are destined to repeat what has happened to other racialized ethnic groups re-racialized into whiteness. They did not have the benefit of knowing what we now know. Our participation in the articulation and promotion of an antiracist race policy is crucial. Promoting a combined racial and national origin category on the US Census is an important part of that effort.

Notes

[1] From "*mulato*" (Spanish–White/Black) and *mestizo* (Spanish–White/Indigenous), yet inferring our multiraciality—the presence of multiple races and history of racial mixing—beyond White (Spanish, other Europeans, and Mid-Easterners), Black (African), and Amerindian (Taíno, Azteca, Maya, etc) of the early colonial period, to include more recent immigrations to Latin America of Chinese, Japanese, Koreans, and others from around the globe.

[2] In this war, Spain's colonies in the Pacific, Guam, and The Philippines were also invaded and occupied by US military forces, and transferred in the Treaty of Paris of 1898.

[3] The 3.6 million citizens living in the colony cannot vote for the US president and do not have congressional representation other than a non-voting "Resident Commissioner." Puerto Ricans that join their 4 million compatriots of the diaspora on the US "mainland" do gain these basic civil rights, though only while officially resident of one the 50 states or the District of Columbia.

[4] In each census since the Mexican–American War until 1980, except for the 1930 Census, people of Latin American origin were to be counted as White unless deemed of another race by census enumerators during in-person interviews (Rodríguez, 2000).

[5] Early in its colonization of The Americas, Spain created a system of *castas* that classified people not only as Spanish, "*indio*" (indigenous), and "*negro*" (African), but also according to their "racial" mix: Spanish–"*indio*" were "*mestizo*"; Spanish–"*negro*" were "*mulato*"; "*negro*"–"*indio*" were "*sambo*"; and so on. "Racial nomenclature was variable and dozens of labels existed," according to Wade (2010: 27).

[6] Clearly, the South African apartheid experience serves as a reminder that a numeric majority is not required for White cultural dominance, privileged socio-economic status, and state control.

[7] In *Making Hispanics*, Mora (2014) narrates how the media and Latino advocacy organizations also played a key role in advancing this reframing process.

[8] I would argue that *Hispanic/Latino/Spanish* is a racialized pan-ethnic category, a sociopolitical construct, in effect, no different than *White* (racialized pan-ethnics of European origin), *Black* (racialized pan-ethnics of African origin), *Native American* (racialized pan-ethnics of indigenous peoples), *Asian*, and other identity groups commonly referred to as *races* in US society.

[9] Please bear in mind that what I am saying is that many Latinos are being added to the "White population count," not that Latinos *count*, *matter*, or *have value* in the same way that White people do in order to actually be considered White in US society.

References

Acuña, R. (1988) *Occupied America: a history of Chicanos*. New York, NY: Harper Collins.

Allsup, V.C. (2010a) *Hernandez V. State of Texas*. Handbook of Texas Online, published by the Texas State Historical Association. Available at: http://www.tshaonline.org/handbook/online/articles/jrh01 (accessed 16 September 2014).

Allsup, V.C. (2010b) *Cisneros V. Corpus Christi ISD*. Handbook of Texas Online, published by the Texas State Historical Association. Available at: http://www.tshaonline.org/handbook/online/articles/jrc02 (accessed 16 September 2014).

Bonilla-Silva, E. (2010) *Racism without racists: color-blind racism & racial inequality in contemporary America* (3rd edn). Lanham, MD: Rowman & Littlefield Publishers.

Brown, A. and Patten, E. (2014) Statistical portrait of Hispanics in the United States, 2012. Pew Research Center Report, 29 April. Available at: http://www.pewhispanic.org/2014/04/29/statistical-portrait-of-hispanics-in-the-united-states-2012/

García, A. (2013) The facts on immigration today. Center for American Progress Report, August. Available at: http://cdn.americanprogress.org/wp-content/uploads/2013/04/081213_ImmigrationFastFacts-1.pdf (accessed 4 June 2014).

Global Policy Forum (2005) US military and clandestine operations in foreign countries: 1798–present. Global Policy Forum Report, December. Available at: https://www.globalpolicy.org/us-military-expansion-and-intervention/26024.html

González, J. (2011) *Harvest of empire: a history of Latinos in America* (rev edn). New York, NY: Penguin Books.

Haney-López, I. (1996) *White by law: the legal construction of race*. New York, NY: New York University Press.

Harvest of empire (2012) *Harvest of empire: the untold story of Latinos in America*. Documentary film, Onyx Films/EVS Communications, Washington, DC.

Krogstad, J.M. and López, M.H. (2014) Hispanic nativity shift: US births drive population growth as immigration stalls. Pew Research Center Report, 29 April. Available at: http://www.pewhispanic.org/2014/04/29/hispanic-nativity-shift/

Mora, G.C. (2014) *Making Hispanics: how activists, bureaucrats, and media constructed a new American*. Chicago, IL: the University of Chicago Press.

Moyer's & Company (2014) *Facing the truth—the case for reparations*. Television program, published by Public Affairs Television, Inc., broadcast by Public Broadcasting Service, date of broadcast, 21 May. Available at: http://billmoyers.com/episode/facing-the-truth-the-case-for-reparations

O'Brien, E. (2008) *The middle race: Latinos and Asian Americans living beyond the racial divide*. New York, NY: New York University.

Office of Management and Budget (1997) Revisions to the standards for the classification of federal data on race and ethnicity. Federal Register Notice, 30 October. Available at: http://www.whitehouse.gov/omb/fedreg_1997standards

Oropeza, L. (2012) Fighting on two fronts: Latinos in the military. American Latino Theme Study, published by the National Park Service, US Department of the Interior. Available at: http://www.nps.gov/latino/latinothemestudy/military.htm (accessed 26 September 2014).

Passel, J.S. and Cohn, D. (2008) U.S. population projections: 2005–2050. Pew Research Center Report, Washington, DC.

Quiñones-Rosado, R. (1998) Hispanic or Latino? The struggle for identity in a race-based society. *The Diversity Factor* 6(4): 20-24.

Quiñones-Rosado, R. (2010) Where are Latinos in a future multiracial society? *Yes! Magazine*, Positive Futures Network, posted 22 March. Available at: http://www.yesmagazine.org/people-power/where-are-latinos-in-a-future-multiracial-society

Rodríguez, C.E. (2000) *Changing race: Latinos, the Census, and the history of ethnicity in the United States*. New York, NY: New York University Press.

Rodríguez, V.M. (2005) *Latino politics in the United States: race, ethnicity, class and gender in the Mexican American and Puerto Rican experience.* Dubuque: Kendall/Hunt Publishing Company.US Census Bureau (2011) Overview of race and Hispanic origin: 2010. US Department of Commerce Census Brief. Available at: http://www.census.gov/prod/cen2010/briefs/c2010br-02.pdf

US Census Bureau (2013) About race. Available at: http://www.census.gov/topics/population/race/about.html

US Census Bureau (2014a) Population projections. Available at: http://www.census.gov/population/projections

US Census Bureau (2014b) USA QuickFacts website. Updated 3 December. Available at: http://quickfacts.census.gov/qfd/states/00000.html

Vargas, N. (2015) Latina/o Whitening: which Latina/os self-classify as White and report being perceived as White by other Americans. *Du Bois Review: Social Science Research on Race* 12(1): 119–36 . Available at: https://www.academia.edu/6062669/Vargas_Nicholas._Forthcoming._Latina_o_Whitening_Which_Latina_os_Self-Classify_as_White_and_Report_Being_Perceived_as_White_by_Other_Americans._Du_Bois_Review_Social_Science_Research_on_Race

Wade, P. (2010) *Race and ethnicity in Latin America* (2nd edn). New York, NY: Pluto Press.

FOUR

The connections among racial identity, social class, and public policy?

Nikki Khanna

In 2010, over nine million Americans (2.9% of the population) identified as multiracial on the US Census—a 32% increase in the last decade (Jones and Bullock, 2012). Harris and Sim (2002: 625, emphases added), however, noting the fluidity of racial identity among multiracial people, claim that the Census likely failed to fully capture the number of Americans with ancestors from two or more racial groups, arguing that these numbers merely reflect a "count of *a* multiracial population, not *the* multiracial population."[1]

Put simply, multiracial ancestry does not necessarily translate into multiracial identity. Someone other than the multiracial person may fill out the Census questionnaire—often parents fill out the Census for their multiracial children—and how multiracial children self-identify and how their parents identify them may not match (Harris and Sim, 2002; Campbell and Eggerling-Boeck, 2006). Studies also show that identity is fluid and inconsistent—multiracial people may change their identification over time (Hitlin et al, 2006) and/or self-identify differently in different contexts (Burke and Kao, 2010). Harris and Sim (2002), for instance, found that some multiracial adolescents identified as multiracial in some contexts but not in others (e.g., some identified as multiracial at school, but not at home). Further, racial identity is shaped by a multitude of factors, including (but not limited to): knowledge of one's ancestry (Morning, 2000); racial appearance (Brunsma and Rockquemore, 2001; Khanna, 2004); cultural exposure (Stephan, 1992; Khanna, 2004); family structural variables (Dalmage, 2000; Harris and Sim, 2002; Herman, 2004; Rockquemore and Laszloffy, 2005); family and peer socialization (Rockquemore and Brunsma, 2002; Rockquemore et al, 2006); regionality (Brunsma, 2005); age (Morning, 2000; Harris and Sim, 2002); social norms (e.g., the one-drop rule) (Davis, 1991; Daniel, 2002; Harris and Sim, 2002; Roth, 2005; Herman, 2010; Khanna, 2010a, 2010b); social networks (Hall,

1980; Root, 1990; Saenz et al, 1995; Xie and Goyette, 1997; Harris and Sim, 2002; Rockquemore and Brunsma, 2002; Herman, 2004); and social class (Daniel, 2002; Rockquemore and Brunsma, 2002; Herman, 2004; Khanna, 2010; see also Korgen, 2010).

The influence of social class on racial identity

Studies on multiracial Americans reveal a link between social class and racial identity. A handful of studies, for instance, have found that higher social class is linked to minority identification. Studies show that higher education among Asian parents leads to a greater tendency to label their Asian–white multiracial children as Asian (Saenz et al, 1995; Xie and Goyette, 1997)—possibly because education produces heightened racial awareness (Portes, 1984). Qian (2004) similarly finds that black–white couples with graduate degrees are more likely to label their children as black than couples with a high school education or less. Admittedly, though, these studies are contradicted by a growing body of work that suggests the opposite. According to Brunsma (2005: 1133), "researchers have found that ... the higher one's social class, the less likely he/she is to relate to minority status or identify with the 'lower status' racial identity" (see also Daniel, 2002; Rockquemore and Brunsma, 2002; Yancey, 2003—all cited in Brunsma, 2005). Although these findings appear inconsistent, it is important to keep in mind that the aforementioned Census studies look at how parents identified their multiracial children, not how multiracial people self-identified, which likely explains the contradiction.

Moreover, studies also reveal a relationship between socio-economic status and claiming a multiracial identity. Middle-class multiracial Americans are more likely to identify as multiracial than those from lower social classes (Korgen, 1998, 2010; Morning, 2000; Harris, 2002). Higher education and affluence are correlated with multiracial identities (Morning, 2000; Harris, 2002; Roth, 2005; Masuoka, 2011), and for black–white multiracial Americans, a rejection of traditional social classification norms (e.g., the one-drop rule, which historically defined anyone with black ancestry as black) (Roth, 2005). Brunsma (2005) argues, however, that while there is a positive relationship between socio-economic status and multiracial identity among Asian–white Americans, there was no effect for black–white Americans, suggesting that the one-drop rule may affect this group regardless of socio-economic status—though, again, the contradictory findings may best be explained by the fact that his study looked at how parents identified their multiracial children, not at how multiracial people self-identified.

Hence, if we look solely at patterns of *self*-identification, higher socio-economic status is clearly correlated with a lowered likelihood of identifying with the minority or "lower status" group and an increased likelihood of identifying as multiracial. Further, Rockquemore and Brunsma (2002: 71) find that some multiracial people have "transcendent" identities, meaning that they "do not use race as a construct to understand the social world or their place in it." Put simply, they have a non-racial identity, and in an earlier study (Khanna, 2011), I found that some middle-class multiracial respondents (at times) identified in non-racial terms when asked about their racial identity— for example, as "human," "American," or a "girl." Although more work is needed to understand how social class is linked to transcendent identities, Rockquemore and Brunsma (2002; see also Daniel, 2002) find that those with transcendent identities had the whitest networks of all respondents in their sample, suggesting that those who choose not to identify with any race may, in fact, come from middle-class backgrounds.

How does social class influence racial identity?

Although we know that social class and racial identity are linked, we are just beginning to understand *how* social class influences racial identity. To begin, scholars recognize that socio-economic status affects people's access to different types of social networks—for instance, poorer individuals have a greater chance of living in neighborhoods with higher percentages of black people (Korgen, 1998), while wealthier individuals are more likely to have contact with white people (Rockquemore, 1998). Social networks have been shown to influence identity and empirical research suggests that the racial composition of local areas and neighborhoods affects racial identities, illustrating the importance of social context on identity. Multiracial Americans with black ancestry are more likely to adopt a black identity where there is a predominance of black neighbors (Hall, 1980, 1992; Roth, 2005) and less likely to identify as black if they have ties to "non-black" communities (Campbell, 2007). Asian-American–white couples are more likely to identify their children as Asian the presence in a neighborhood of Asians increases (Saenz et al, 1995; Xie and Goyette, 1997), and Asian–white adolescents are more likely to identify as white as the proportion of white neighbors increases. Similar trends have been found for other groups: Native Americans living on or near reservations or in areas with high concentrations of Native Americans are more likely to identify as Native American (Eschbach, 1995;

Liebler, 2001; Qian, 2004); multiracial Hawaiians living in areas with high concentrations of Native Hawaiians are more likely to identify as Native Hawaiian (Kana'iaupuni and Liebler, 2005); and multiracial Hispanics living in white neighborhoods are more likely to identify as white (Herman, 2004).

Social class also influences the diversity (or lack thereof) of racial socializing agents (in our neighborhoods, but also in our schools and places of worship), which can impact racial identity. For instance, studies show that one's cultural exposure to different ethnic/racial groups may shape one's identity (Hall, 1992; Johnson, 1992; Khanna, 2004), and according to Stephan (1992: 56), cultural exposure takes place in the family, but also "in the schools and through neighborhoods and friends." Hall (1992), for instance, found that the more her multiracial black respondents knew about black culture, the more likely they were to choose a black identity, and other studies found that those raised in predominantly white areas that were isolated from communities of color often see themselves culturally as white (Twine, 1996; Kilson, 2001). Twine (1996), for instance, argues that social class is linked with social networks and culture, and finds that multiracial black girls developed white cultural identities within the context of their middle-class white communities. In an earlier study (Khanna, 2010a, 2010b, 2011), I found that middle-class black–white biracial respondents who grew up in white spaces often conflated black "culture" with social class—they self-identified as white and differentiated themselves from the negative stereotypes they associated with blackness (e.g., black people do not value education, black people do not speak "proper English"). The images they associated with blackness, however, arguably have less to do with black "culture" and more to do with social class.

Finally, according to Fhagen-Smith (2010), middle-class culture itself is linked to multiracial identity, which may explain why middle-class Americans are more likely to identify as multiracial than those in lower social classes. While those from lower classes may feel limited in their identity options, middle-class Americans are socialized to expect more choices and freedom in how they self-identify. They expect more choices in identity because the culture of the middle class expects more choices in general. Our social class structures our lives and determines what resources and opportunities are available to us and, according to Fhagen-Smith (2010: 35), "a major middle-class value is having choices, options, and control over one's life." Thus, it may not be a coincidence that many multiracial activists and leaders often come from middle-class backgrounds; they were socialized to expect choices and fought back when larger society attempted to limit their racial identity options (i.e, expected them to identify with one race). Further, it is plausible that expectation of choice among middle-class Americans not only made "multiracial" a viable identity option, but also made a "transcendent" identity possible (Rockquemore and Brunsma, 2002). Middle-class multiracial Americans expect more racial options, which arguably may also include the option of not identifying with any race at all.

Implications for the US Census and for race policy

Middle-class multiracial Americans are more likely than those in lower social classes to identify as multiracial and are less likely to identify with their "lower status" group. This is because social class often shapes our social networks, the racial composition of our communities, our exposure to various racial "cultures," and our expectations for choice in how we identify ourselves. As such, middle-class multiracial Americans are more likely to live in predominantly white areas, are less likely to be exposed to "cultures" of color, and are more likely to expect choices in how they self-identify, which distinguishes them from those in lower social classes.

As social class has an influence on racial identity, this has important implications for Census statistics and, hence, the subsequent race policy borne from those numbers. Census figures regarding race provide more than a snapshot portrait of racial groups in American society; they serve a functional purpose given that race figures are tied to race-based public policy. According to Wright (1994), racial statistics serve "an important purpose in the monitoring and enforcement of civil rights laws," and Census numbers are used to monitor racial disparities in areas such as education, health care, housing, income, and wealth. These numbers are then used to shape public policy designed to narrow racial gaps and ensure fair treatment.

Census measures are imperfect, however, and how racial groups are defined in the Census is socially constructed and shaped by political decisions. For instance, "white" is defined as anyone "having origins in any of the original peoples of Europe, North Africa, or the Middle East" (Humes et al, 2011). Within this so-called racial category is wide physical, historical, and socio-economic variation, though these groups are lumped together for political purposes. "Asian/Pacific Islander" is also widely defined, joining diverse ethnic groups, such as Indians, Japanese, and Cambodians, with their distinctive physical characteristics, unique histories, and varied social class backgrounds. Native Hawaiians have their own category, though they could arguably be grouped with Native Americans—though political decisions have prevented it because that might make them eligible for some federal programs aimed at indigenous groups on the mainland.

Admittedly, none of the race categories are ideal, and these flawed measures are only compounded by the relatively new opportunity for Americans to self-identify as multiracial on the Census. The 2000 Census was the first to give Americans the opportunity to self-identify as multiracial by checking two or more boxes, though the fluidity of racial identity, especially among multiracial Americans, raises the question: what do Census figures on the multiracial population actually tell us? As described earlier, Harris and Sim (2002: 625) claim that in 2000, we got a count of "a" multiracial population, but not "the" multiracial population. If multiracial identity is, according to Campbell and Eggerling-Boeck (2006: 155), "socially constructed, quite varied across individuals, and often fluid across time and situation for a particular individual," what do these numbers mean and what are the implications for race policy in the US?

To be sure, a "skewed" portrait of race in American society could potentially have real consequences for race policy in the US. If middle-class white–minority multiracial Americans are choosing not to identify with their minority race (as research suggests), this may affect public policy aimed at minority groups—for example, those policies designed to combat racial discrimination. Indeed, early critics of adding a "multiracial" category to the Census (which would exist as a standalone category alongside other racial categories) argued that it might adversely affect minority numbers as multiracial Americans identify as "multiracial" in lieu of checking traditional minority categories (e.g., "black," "Asian," "Native American"). Given that the "numbers drive the dollars" (Wright, 1994), this was especially worrisome for minority groups who could benefit from federal programs designed to level the playing field. This was addressed in a compromise that allowed Americans to check multiple racial boxes rather than a single "multiracial" category. Using this format, Census data could then be re-aggregated—for example, someone who checks both the "black" and "white" boxes would be counted as multiracial, but in terms of numbers and federal programs, would also be counted as "black" for the purposes of civil rights enforcement (Williams, 2006). However, admittedly, data cannot be re-aggregated for those with white–minority backgrounds who simply check the "white" box (maybe because he/she is middle-class, grew up in white spaces, and had little connection to their minority culture and people).

Moreover, the effects of social class and identity on race policy go well beyond how Americans self-identify on the Census. Looking beyond Census figures, how multiracial people identify in their day-to-day lives also has real implications for minority groups and social support for race-based public policy. If higher income multiracial Americans distance themselves from minority groups (1) identity-wise (how they racially self-identify) and (2) physically (in terms of where they live and raise their families), this could also have repercussions for their respective minority groups. For instance, it could lead to less power for those groups—numerically, socially, and politically. Those in the lower social classes with less money and resources are less likely to hold political office, vote, or be politically organized. Hence, those who make race policy may feel less pressure to advocate for their interests. Harris and Khanna (2010: 667), who look at the effects of the growing heterogeneity within the black community on the broader black community (including class diversity and the rise in the number of people with black–white multiracial ancestry), recognize the "high degree of privilege" that some of these groups often hold as compared to other black people. It is important for them to identify with other black people because it:

> may determine how (or if) they advocate for causes important to the [black] community at large like Head Start programs, affirmative action in education and employment, non-punitive welfare policy, or sensible drug laws. Divestiture of the most privileged people in the community may translate into the loss of important allies in the black community. (Harris and Khanna, 2010: 667)

Further, those in the middle class are less likely to identify with their minority race—or with any race for that matter—and, hence, may be more likely to adopt a color-blind attitude than those in lower social classes. According to Bonilla-Silva (2010), this color-blind attitude (also termed color-blind racism) is the dominant post-Civil Rights Era racial ideology, in which people (usually white people) claim that "they don't see any color, just people" (Bonilla-Silva, 2010: 1). Those who espouse the color-blind ideology perceive discrimination as a thing of the past, and argue that if "people of color" would only just work harder, they too (like white people) could be successful in American society. If middle-class multiracial people do not identify with "people of color," they, like many white people, may be more likely to adopt this color-blind ideology, which ignores the realities of racial inequality and racial discrimination in today's society. As a consequence, they may be less likely to support race-based public policy, such as welfare programs and affirmative action in hiring and education, which are designed to level the playing field and help those most in need.

Relatedly, while some politicians interested in ending race-based public policy may garner support from some middle-class multiracial Americans because of a shared color-blind ideology, they have also pointed to multiracial people (often middle-class) as a sign that we are now living in a post-racial world, where race has little meaning and race-based public policies are no longer necessary. Squires (2007), who looks at how multiracial people are framed in the media, argues that Barack Obama, with his biracial ancestry, immigrant family history, and middle-class background, is typically seen as rising above race. She writes: "Emphasizing his parents' interracial marriage, his father's status as an immigrant from Kenya, and Obama's elite education at Harvard, journalists and interviewees surmised that Obama is not 'stereotypically black,' but rather 'transcends race'" (Squires, 2007, p 195). Certainly, his class background has advantaged him in ways that make his race less salient than it would be for others, but not all multiracial Americans are middle-class and not all multiracial Americans have the so-called ability to "transcend" race.

Like journalists, some politicians also have characterized multiracial people as transcending race and have used them as a sign and symbol of this new color-blind era. For instance, conservative Ward Connerly, who is himself multiracial, is one of the nation's leading opponents of affirmative action and has challenged the collection of ethnic/racial data in the state of California. In earlier work (Khanna, 2004: 19), I argued that:

> Connerly used his multiracial background to argue against counting race—as intermarriage rises and the multiracial population grows, he argued that America's "silly little boxes" are increasingly irrelevant, outdated, and destructive. Arguing for a color-blind society, he claimed that the only way to defeat racism was to end the very classifications that we use to divide and separate ourselves.

While his opponents have argued that eliminating racial classifications would only eliminate our ability to track discrimination, other conservative politicians share Connerly's view and have even drawn on multiracial support. Newt Gingrich, for example, once teamed up with Project RACE (Reclassify All Children Equally), an activist multiracial organization, in the effort to add a multiracial category to the US Census—though it is no secret that the once Speaker of the US House of Representative's broader goals have been to rid the Census of *any* racial categories (which he called "outdated, divisive, and rigid") and eventually end programs such as affirmative action (Holmes, 1997).[2] According to Gingrich:

> We must make America a country with equal opportunity for all and special privilege for none by treating all individuals as equals before the law and doing away with quotas, preferences and set-asides in Government contract, hiring and university admissions. (Holmes, 1997)

A coalition with multiracial organization Project RACE and the addition of a catch-all multiracial category to the Census was arguably one promising step in that direction. Although a compromise was eventually reached that allowed multiracial Americans to check multiple race boxes (and allowed for the re-aggregation of data, as described earlier), consolidating all multiracial people together in a "multiracial" box would have been useful to those advocating for an end to race-based public policies. A catch-all box would have functioned to mask multiracial diversity, dilute minority numbers, and, above all, obstruct the collection of race data. Although, arguably, most multiracial people (and certainly most multiracial organizations) did not support Gingrich's efforts and that of Project RACE, we cannot overlook the alliances that politicians create with some middle-class multiracial people and organizations to further their own goals to end or curb race-based policy in the US.

Conclusion

Racial identity is very much linked to social class given that middle-class multiracial Americans are: (1) more likely to identify as multiracial; (2) less likely to identify with their minority or "lower status" race group; and, perhaps, (3) more likely to identify in non-racial terms than those in lower social classes. Moreover, middle-class Americans are comparatively more likely to live in white spaces, less likely to have contact with black people and other "people of color," and more likely to expect choices in how they self-identify. If they identify as multiracial on the Census (by checking multiple racial boxes), their data will be re-aggregated in ways to preserve minority numbers— though if white–minority multiracial Americans simply check "white," this could have implications for federal programs, funding, and social policies aimed at minority racial groups.

Most importantly, if middle-class multiracial Americans physically and psychologically distance themselves from "people of color," this will no doubt have real implications for social and political support for race-based public policy if they take their money, resources, and power with them. To the extent that they support the color-blind ideology held by many of their white middle-class counterparts, they may also be less inclined to support social policies and programs aimed at "people of color" that are premised on the idea that discrimination and racism persist. Some politicians, indeed, have pointed to the very existence of multiracial Americans as a sign that we are today living in a color-blind era, and some have successfully created alliances with multiracial people and/or organizations to further their goals to end race-based policies, though it is important to note that the majority of multiracial organizations have distanced themselves from these efforts. As the population of multiracial Americans continues to grow, however, only time will tell if and how this segment of the American population will impact their respective communities of color and, hence, how they may directly and indirectly affect race-based public policies aimed at combating persistent racial inequality in American society.

Notes

[1] It must be noted that there is, in reality, no such thing as "the" multiracial population given that race is socially constructed. According to Harris and Sim (2002: 625): "This does not mean that the Census Bureau erred in its enumeration of the multiracial population. Rather ... the census, like every other data set, captures an individual's 'true' race for a particular purpose, in a particular context, at a particular point in time (Telles and Lim 1998)."

[2] Like Gingrich, Connerly would later shift from advocating for the elimination of racial categories to recommending the addition of a stand-alone multiracial identifier to University of California admissions and other university forms that report data on race and ethnicity, though the measure was rejected by University of California Regents in 2004 (see Daniel, 2006).

References

Bonilla-Silva, E. (2010) *Racism without racists: color-blind racism & racial inequality in contemporary America*. Lanham, MD: Rowmman & Littlefield.

Brunsma, D.L. (2005) Interracial families and the racial identification of mixed-race children: evidence from the early childhood longitudinal study. *Social Forces* 84(2): 1131–57.

Brunsma, D.L. and Rockquemore, K.A. (2001) The new color complex: appearance and biracial identity. *Identity: An International Journal of Theory and research* 1(3): 225–46.

Burke, R. and Kao, G. (2010) Stability and change in racial identities of multiracial adolescents. In: K. Korgen (ed) *Multiracial Americans and social class: the influence of social class on racial identity.* New York, NY, and London: Routledge, pp 39–50.

Campbell, M.E. (2007) Thinking outside the (black) box: measuring black and multiracial identification on surveys. *Social Science Research* 36(3): 921–44.

Campbell, M.E. and Eggerling-Boeck, J. (2006) "What about the children?" The psychological and social well-being of multiracial adolescents. *The Sociological Quarterly* 47: 147–73.

Dalmage, H. (2000) *Tripping on the color line: black–white multiracial families in a racially divided world.* New Brunswick, NJ: Rutgers University Press.

Daniel, G.R. (2002) *More than black? Multiracial identity and the new racial order.* Philadelphia, PA: Temple University Press.

Daniel, G.R. (2006) *Race and multiraciality in Brazil and the United States.* University Park, PA: The Pennsylvania State University Press.

Davis, F.J. (1991) *Who is black? One nation's definition.* University Park, PA: Pennsylvania State University Press.

Eschbach, K. (1995) The enduring and vanishing American Indian: American Indian population growth and intermarriage in 1990. *Ethnic and Racial Studies* 18: 89–108.

Fhagen-Smith, P. (2010) Social class, racial/ethnic identity, and the psychology of choice. In: K. Korgen (ed) *Multiracial Americans and social class: the influence of social class on racial identity.* New York, NY: Routledge, pp 30–8.

Hall, C.C.I. (1980) The ethnic identity of racial mixed people: a study of black–Japanese. Unpublished doctoral dissertation, University of California, Los Angeles.

Hall, C.C.I. (1992) Please choose one: ethnic identity choices for biracial individuals. In: M.P.P. Root (ed) *Racially mixed people in America.* Newbury Park, CA: Sage Publications, pp 250–64.

Harris, C.A. and Khanna, N. (2010) Black is, black ain't: biracials, black middle-classers, and the social construction of clackness. *Sociological Spectrum* 30: 639–70.

Harris, D.R. (2002) Does it matter how we measure? Racial classification and the characteristics of multiracial youth. In: J. Perlmann and M. Waters (eds) *The new race question: how the Census counts multiracial individuals*. New York, NY: Russell Sage Foundation, pp 62–101.Harris, D.R. and Sim, J.J. (2002) Who is multiracial? Assessing the complexity of lived race. *American Sociological Review* 67: 614–27.

Herman, M.R. (2004) Forced to choose: some determinants of racial identification in multiracial adolescents. *Child Development* 27(3): 730–48.

Herman, M.R. (2010) Do you see what I am? How observers' backgrounds affect their perceptions of multiracial faces. *Social Psychology Quarterly* 73(1): 58–78.

Hitlin, S., Brown, J.S., and Elder, G.H. Jr (2006) Racial self-categorization in adolescence: multiracial development and social pathways. *Child Development* 77(5): 1298–308.

Holmes, S.A. (1997) Gingrich outlines plan on race relations. *New York Times*, 19 June. Available at: http://www.nytimes.com/1997/06/19/us/gingrich-outlines-plan-on-race-relations.html?src=pm

Humes, K.R., Jones, N.A. and Ramirez, R.R. (2011) Overview of race and Hispanic origin: 2010. US Census Bureau. Available at: http://www.census.gov/prod/cen2010/briefs/c2010br-02.pdf

Johnson, D.J. (1992) Developmental pathways: Toward an ecological theoretical formulation of race identity in Black–White biracial children. In: M.P.P. Root (ed.) *Racially mixed people in America*. Newbury Park, CA: Sage, pp 37-49.

Jones, N.A. and Bullock, J. (2012) The two or more races population: 2010. US Census Bureau, US Department of Commerce. Available at: http://www.census.gov/prod/cen2010/briefs/c2010br-13.pdf

Kana'iaupuni, S.M. and Liebler, C.A. (2005) Ponderng poi dog: place and racial identification of multiracial Native Hawaiians. *Ethnic and Racial Studies* 28(4): 687–721.

Khanna, N. (2004) The role of reflected appraisals in racial identity: the case of multiracial Asians. *Social Psychology Quarterly* 67(2): 115–31.

Khanna, N. (2010a) "If you're half black, you're just black": reflected appraisals and the persistence of the one-drop rule. *Sociological Quarterly* 51(1): 96–121.

Khanna, N. (2010b) Country clubs and hip-hop thugs: examining the role of social class and culture in shaping racial identity. In: K. Korgen (ed) *Multiracial Americans and social class: the influence of social class on racial identity*. New York, NY: Routledge, pp 53–71.

Khanna, N. (2011) *Biracial in America: forming and performing racial identity*. Lanham, MD: Lexington Books.

Kilson, M. (2001) *Claiming place: biracial young adults of the post-civil rights era*. Westport, CT: Bergin & Garvey.

Korgen, K.O. (1998) *From black to biracial: transforming racial identity among Americans*. Westport, CT: Praeger.

Korgen, K.O. (ed) (2010) *Multiracial Americans and social class: the influence of social class on racial identity*. New York, NY: Routledge.

Liebler, C.A. (2001) The fringes of American Indian identity. Unpublished doctoral dissertation, University of Wisconsin, Madison, WI.

Masuoka, N. (2011) The "multiracial" option: social group identity and changing patterns of racial categorization. *American Politics Research* 39(1): 176–204.

Morning, A. (2000) Who is multiracial? Definitions and decisions. *Sociological Imagination* 37(4): 209–29.

Portes, A. (1984) The rise of ethnicity: determinants of ethnic perceptions among Cuban exiles in Miami. *American Sociological Review* 49: 383–97.

Qian, Z. (2004) Options: racial/ethnic identification of children of intermarried couples. *Social Science Quarterly* 85(3): 746–66.

Rockquemore, K.A. (1998) Between black and white: exploring the "biracial" experience. *Race & Society* 1(2): 197–212.

Rockquemore, K.A. and Brunsma, D.L. (2002) *Beyond black: biracial identity in America*. Thousand Oaks, CA: Sage Publications.

Rockquemore, K.A. and Laszloffy, T.A. (2005) *Raising biracial children*. Lanham, MD: AltaMira Press.

Rockquemore, K.A., Laszloffy, T., and Noveske, J. (2006) It all starts at home: racial socialization in multiracial families. In: D.L. Brunsma (ed) *Mixed messages: multiracial identities in the "color-blind" era*. Boulder, CO: Lynne Rienner, pp 203–16.

Root, M.P.P. (1990) Resolving "other" status: identity development of biracial individuals. In: L.S. Brown and M.P.P. Root (eds) *Diversity and complexity in feminist therapy*. New York, NY: Harrington Park Press, pp 185–205.

Roth, W.D. (2005) The end of the one-drop rule? Labeling of multiracial children in black intermarriages. *Sociological Forum* 20(1): 35–67.

Saenz, R., Sean-Shong, H., and Anderson, R. (1995) Persistence and change in Asian identity among children of intermarried couples. *Sociological Perspectives* 38: 175–94.

Squires, C.R. (2007) *Dispatches from the Color Line: The press and multiracial America.* Albany, NY: State University of New York Press.

Stephan, C.W. (1992) Mixed-heritage individuals: ethnic identity and trait characteristics. In: M.P.P. Root (ed) *Racially mixed people in America.* Newbury Park, CA: Sage Publications, pp 50–63.

Telles, E,E, and Lim, N (1998) Does it matter who answers the race question? Racial classification and income inequality in Brazil. *Demography* 35(4) 465-74.

Twine, F.W. (1996) Brown skinned white girls: class, culture, and the construction of white identity in suburban communities. *Gender, Place, and Culture* 3(2): 205–24.

Williams, K.M. (2006) *Mark one or more: civil rights in multiracial America.* Ann Arbor, MI: University of Michigan Press.

Wright, L. (1994) One drop of blood. *New Yorker,* 25 July. Available at: http://www.newyorker.com/archive/1994/07/25/1994_07_25_046_TNY_CARDS_000367864

Xie, Y. and Goyette, K. (1997) The racial identification of multiracial children with one Asian parent: evidence from the 1990 Census. *Social Forces* 76: 547–70.

Yancey, G. (2003) *Who is white? Latinos, Asians, and the new black/non-black divide.* Boulder, CO: Lynne Rienner.

FIVE

Multiracial Americans and racial discrimination

Tina Fernandes Botts

Introduction

There are currently no US laws or court decisions specifically protecting multiracial people from discrimination (Daniel, 2006; Williams, 2006). In fact, multiracial Americans have long been left out of the antidiscrimination law loop as a result of their status as belonging simultaneously to multiple legally established racial groups and to no one legally established racial group in particular. This state of affairs is a problem for multiracial Americans because in order to bring a claim of racial discrimination, a prospective antidiscrimination plaintiff must identify as belonging to at least one and to only one legally established racial group.[1]

In the early years of antidiscrimination law, a person raising a claim of unconstitutional racial discrimination had to be a member of a particular monoracial minority group with a history of having been discriminated against. In constitutional parlance, the plaintiff first had to identify as being a member of a "suspect class." "Suspect class" has many definitions in the case law. One definition is a group of people with a history of having been discriminated against in the US. Another way of defining a "suspect class" is as a "discrete and insular minority group." Yet another way is as a group that is politically powerless. Still another way is as a group in possession of an "immutable characteristic" on the basis of which discrimination would be unfair in a particular context. In practice, this meant that one had to be a member of a monoracial minority group or ethnic group with a history of having been discriminated against in the US (Asian, Latino/a, black, or Native American). If this requirement was met, the law or policy in question would be subject to a very strict level of judicial review, and the result would likely be that the law or policy in question would be struck down as unconstitutional.

Today, the barrier for multiracial plaintiffs is different. In the present day, while the barrier of belonging to multiple legally established racial groups remains a problem, the new, practical barrier for multiracial plaintiffs in antidiscrimination cases is that they belong to *no particular* racial group. This is a barrier because, over the years, the threshold requirement for initiating a legally recognizable case of racial discrimination moved from requiring the plaintiff to identify as a member of a "suspect class" to requiring that the law or policy in question involve a "suspect classification." Between the 1938 case of *United States v. Carolene Products* (in which the Supreme Court first mentions that prejudice against "discrete and insular minorities" may be a special condition requiring closer judicial scrutiny of laws affecting such groups) and the 1978 case of *Regents of the University of California v. Bakke* (in which the Supreme Court held that racial classifications per se are racially discriminatory), the Supreme Court decided a series of cases (including, e.g., the 1944 case of *Korematsu v. United States*, where the Court held, in the midst of the Japanese internment controversy, that classifications based on nationality were inherently suspect), and gradually shifted focus in antidiscrimination cases from protecting particular, historically oppressed groups to protecting everyone from racial discrimination per se.

Race and ethnicity are the prototypical suspect classifications. What this means is that, currently, if a law or policy discriminates between people on the basis of race or ethnicity, the law is subject to a much higher level of judicial scrutiny than it would otherwise be. As antidiscrimination law is presently treated by the courts, in other words, people of *any* legally established racial or ethnic group (including white people) can bring a claim of discrimination.

While the distinction between "suspect class" analysis (based on the idea that members of "suspect classes" are the intended beneficiaries of antidiscrimination law) and "suspect classification" analysis (based on the idea that racial classification per se is the intended target of antidiscrimination law) is not altogether clear in the case law, one thing that is consistent across the board is that a prospective antidiscrimination plaintiff must first identify as a member of a single racial group before bringing an antidiscrimination claim. Judicial decisions regarding the right of people who identify as multiracial to equal protection of the laws or their rights under employment discrimination laws are always muddled and internally inconsistent, with the relevant judicial decisions often switching back and forth between recognizing the multiracial person as first a member of one race and then another, but never both or all; that is, never recognizing the multiracial person as a multiracial person.

Recent scholars of the relationship between multiracial people and the law have highlighted, however, that multiracial people very likely qualify as a "suspect class." Some of the factors cited in support of this claim are that multiracial people have experienced a history of discrimination based on the "immutable characteristic" of being mixed-race, are a "discrete and insular" minority group in virtue of facing discrimination based on their status as multiracial people, and are excluded from the political process in the sense that their racial status is not acknowledged as legitimate. In other words, multiracial people, as multiracial people, have been the subject of much racial hostility in the US, as well as structural alienation from the benefits of mainstream antidiscrimination law.

Whether multiracial people are a suspect *class* or not, however, race still remains a suspect *classification* under current antidiscrimination law theory. However, since multiracial people are not understood as a legally established racial group, in order to benefit from antidiscrimination law, the multiracial plaintiff is faced with a troubling problem: either identify exclusively as a member of one minority racial group or go without redress. This problem is troubling for at least three reasons. First, since multiracial people face discrimination *as* multiracial people and not as members of a given monoracial minority group, the remedies currently offered by the law are not adequately tailored to the wrong suffered. Second, people who identify as multiracial are required to legally suppress their multiracial identity for the sake of being able to avail themselves of the equal protection of the law. As a result of these factors, many potential multiracial plaintiffs opt to suffer discrimination in silence rather than being forced to mischaracterize the discrimination they suffer in ways that suppress their racial identity.

In this chapter, I will: (1) provide an overview of the historical engagement between multiracial people and the law; (2) identify and examine factors contributing to the failure of current antidiscrimination laws to protect multiracial Americans from racial discrimination; (3) argue in favor of a distinctive group identity for multiracial Americans, with particular emphasis placed on the need for a distinctive group identity within the framework of antidiscrimination law; and (4) suggest an additional modification to antidiscrimination law (i.e, the utilization of socio-historical race) in order to better protect multiracial Americans from racial discrimination.

Historical engagement between multiracial people and the law

Anti-miscegenation laws

As described by Nagai in Chapter One of this book, antipathy toward race mixing is a fact of US history, typified in the over 300 years of anti-miscegenation laws that began in the early British colonies in North America and continued later in the US. In colonial America, criminal sanction for those marrying or cohabitating across racial lines was common, beginning in the second half of the 17th century (Wadlington, 1966). The words "miscegenation"—Latin for "to mix types" or "to mix families," from the words "miscere" (to mix) and "genus" (type, family, or descent)—and "mulatto"—from the Latin "mūlus," meaning "mule" or the hybrid offspring of a horse and a donkey—became commonly used during the colonial period (Wadlington, 1966). Virginia and Maryland were the first colonies to enact anti-miscegenation statutes, in 1662 and 1663, respectively. Over the life of anti-miscegenation laws—roughly from the mid-17th century through to the Supreme Court's decision in *Loving v. Virginia* in 1967—punishments for violating anti-miscegenation laws varied from state to state, ranging from a "sound whipping" (for a white man who was caught "lying with a Negro" in Virginia in 1630; see Wadlington, 1966) to up to five years of prison with hard labor (see *State v. Brown*, 108 S.E.2d 233, 234 (La. 1959)). Rationales offered in support of these laws often centered on society's interest in keeping the races pure. At the root of these rationales was the idea that members of minority racial groups were physically, mentally, and morally inferior to members of the majority white racial group, so the white race was thought to be corrupted, soiled, and degraded by "mixing" with the "non-white" one.

The general understanding of race in popular American culture, in other words, included the notion that races were both biologically based and pure, necessitating anti-miscegenation laws in order to stop the impurity from spreading. The myth of racial purity continued into the 20th century, and continues to exist today in the minds of most Americans, despite evidence available at least as early as Darwin that all members of the human species have a common African genesis (see Darwin, 1871; Larson, 2006), and therefore that there really were no pure human races. The eugenics movement of the late 19th and early 20th centuries supported the erroneous claim that there were such things as pure human races, with the result that the criminalization of marriage or cohabitation (and, ultimately, procreation) between members of different races seemed justified for the good of so-called "racial progress."

Jim Crow Laws and segregation

One of the most fascinating turns in the history of multiracial people and antidiscrimination law is the case of *Plessy v. Ferguson*. As described by Nagai in Chapter One of this book, this case gave constitutional blessing to racial discrimination in public accommodations and augured in the Jim Crow era. Throughout the case, the court made reference to "the two races," as if, in the first place, there are races and, in the second place, there are only two (black and white). In the court's mind, a clear line of demarcation existed between "the two races" in terms of the ability of members of the black race to freely associate with members of the white race, even though there was some argument in the states as to how one might draw the line or even as to how to distinguish one race from the other. As the court itself pointed out: "It is true that the question of the proportion of colored blood necessary to constitute a colored person, as distinguished from a white person, is one upon which there is a difference of opinion in the different states." In support of its decision in *Plessy*, the Supreme Court cited the then constitutionality of state bans on "intermarriage" and state laws requiring racial segregation in public schools, arguing that it had repeatedly (and, presumably, justifiably) made "the distinction between laws interfering with the political equality of the Negro and those requiring the separation of the two races."

The effect of *Plessy* was official federal support for the idea that there were races in the world, that these races were distinguishable, and that these races could be legally segregated. The result was approximately 65 years of official, federally sanctioned separation of members of minority monoracial groups from white people in all sorts of public accommodations. The existence of multiracial people in the US problematized this framework. Did they belong in the white section of public accommodations or the black? The emergence of what became known as the "one-drop rule" offered a solution to that problem.

The "one-drop rule"

While early US courts relied on one or more of three traditional rules to determine a person's race (physical appearance, blood fraction, or association), between 1830 and 1840 Northern American courts began to use what became known as the "one-drop rule" instead (Spickard, 1989; Davis, 1991; Daniel, 2002; Sweet, 2005; Jordan, 2014). According to this rule, anyone with any known black ancestry was categorized as black. The one-drop rule then spread slowly southward and became the unwritten law throughout the US by the turn of the 20th century.

The pervasiveness of the one-drop rule lent popular support in the US to what is known as "hypodescent," according to which people of multiracial ancestry are identified as belonging to the "non-white" racial group aspect of their ancestry (Brunsma and Rockquemore, 2002). Within a culture that accepts the one-drop rule and hypodescent as authoritative on the question of racial identity, multiracial identity is rendered nonsensical, and therefore legally unrecognizable. Therefore, the history of the engagement between multiracial people and antidiscrimination law in the US is one in which the status of multiracial people *as multiracial* has either been systematically ignored or obliterated.

Current factors contributing to the failure of antidiscrimination laws to protect multiracial people

There are several current factors contributing to the non-recognition in US law of multiracial people as a legally established group for antidiscrimination law purposes. These include the persistence of the mistaken belief that race is rooted in biology and science and the current failure of antidiscrimination law to acknowledge that the illegality, wrong, and harm of racial discrimination is that it perpetuates historically situated, institutionalized racial oppression.

Biological races

Notions about race in the US are fraught with confusion. To help clarify this confusion, it is helpful to distinguish at least three ways in which the phenomenon of human racial categories can be understood: (1) according to colloquial understanding; (2) according to scientific understanding; and (3) according to sociological understanding. The colloquial understanding defines race in one or more of the following ways: as being based in biology; as having a genetic basis; as involving common ancestry or descent; as based on shared external physical characteristics (sometimes called phenotype); or as involving the presumption of a correlation between shared external physical characteristics and more internal traits, such as intellectual or moral features. The scientific understanding rejects all aspects of the colloquial understanding. For some time, there has been widespread, although not undisputed, acceptance in the scientific community of the fact that the phenomenon of human racial categories has no biological or genetic basis (Montagu, 1942; UNESCO, 1951; Livingstone, 1962, Lewontin, 1972; Hubbard, 1999; Graves, 2001) and, therefore, no link between any biological, physical, or genetic trait and any internal features. The sociological understanding accepts the scientific understanding but adds the fact that American culture still operates as if race exists (in the biological sense). In this sociological understanding, race is sometimes referred to as having a sociocultural or socio-historical existence. The upshot of American confusion over race is that although science has clearly shown that there are no biological or genetically based human races, American culture still operates as if there were.

Even more troubling is the inclusion of beliefs in racial purity and racial essentialism in the biological concept of race that prevails in American culture. According to this perspective, there are biological races in the world that are identifiable in terms of biological traits. These biological races are "pure" and can easily be differentiated from one another in terms of objective, observable phenomena. There are certain non-physical traits associated with these pure races as well, such as intellectual capacity, moral sensibility, and aesthetic tastes (in music, in art, etc). Multiracial people throw this picture of race into havoc. It does not make sense if they exist. In order to have rights (including rights against racial discrimination) as multiracial people, multiracial people must first be real. If biological race adequately describes race, then multiracial people are not real and do not exist.

Racial discrimination perpetuates historically situated oppression

Antidiscrimination law (including both equal protection law and employment discrimination law) was designed for the purpose of remedying racial discrimination against historically marginalized and oppressed groups rather than to remedy racial discrimination *per se* (Botts, 2013). Equal protection law originated with the ratification of the 14th Amendment to the US Constitution in 1868. The 14th Amendment included what is known as the Equal Protection Clause, which says: "No state shall ... deny to any person within its jurisdiction the equal protection of the laws" (US Const. amend. XIV § 1). A look at the historical context in which the Equal Protection Clause was created provides insight as to its meaning, purpose, and goals. The 14th Amendment is one of a set of constitutional amendments enacted shortly after the Civil War ended in April of 1865 (Rawley, 1989). In December of that year, the 13th Amendment, which banned slavery everywhere in the US, was ratified. Two and a half years later, in July 1868, the 14th Amendment (containing the Equal Protection Clause) was ratified, and then about two years after that, in March of 1870, the 15th Amendment, prohibiting discrimination in voting "on account of race, color, or previous condition of servitude," was ratified. Taken together, these Civil War amendments suggest that the Equal Protection Clause was included in the 14th Amendment to make clear that equal protection under the law for black Americans could and would be federally enforced. Therefore, Justice Miller's famous statement in the 1873 Slaughterhouse Cases to the effect that the 14th Amendment had "one pervading purpose," that is, "the protection of the newly made freeman and citizen from the oppressions of those who had formerly exercised unlimited dominion over him" seems very well justified.

The legislative history of the 14th Amendment, much of which is found in the debates that took place in 1866 during the 39th Congress, supports Miller's interpretation. This history shows that the Equal Protection Clause was meant to operate as a remedial measure to correct the widespread subjugation of black people as a group in America. When Congressman Stevens introduced the Amendment in the House, he characterized its purpose as "the amelioration of the condition of the freedmen" (Cong. Globe, 39th Cong., 1st Sess. 2459 (1866)). Additionally, proponents of the 14th Amendment repeatedly emphasized in the congressional debates of the time that one of the Amendment's primary purposes was to place in the Constitution itself the principles of section 1 of the Civil Rights Act of 1866, an Act whose entire purpose was to give citizens:

> without regard to race and color, without regard to any previous condition of slavery or involuntary servitude ... full and equal benefit of all laws and proceedings for the security of person and property, as is enjoyed by white citizens.

In other words, proponents of the 14th Amendment in the early congressional debates repeatedly stated that the 14th Amendment's primary purpose was to address the manifest unequal status of black people as a group. Therefore, the historical evidence shows that rather than being designed to address racial discrimination per se, "the [congressional] debates reveal overriding concern with the status of one racial group [i.e, black people]" (Baer, 1983: 183).

Similarly, employment discrimination law was enacted to overturn the reality that for the first 350 years of US history, the best of everything was reserved for men with white skin (Gold, 2001). It was enacted to increase the likelihood that people other than white males would benefit from meritorious hiring decisions. Employment discrimination law is rooted in the Unemployment Relief Act of 1933, which stated: "In employing citizens for the purpose of this Act no discrimination shall be made on account of race, color, or creed" (US Equal Employment Opportunity Commission, 2015). Title VII of the Civil Rights Act of 1964 ("Title VII") evolved out of the Unemployment Relief Act and serves as the basis for employment discrimination cases today. Title VII prohibits discrimination on the basis of race, color, religion, sex, or national origin and was passed primarily to protect women and "people of color" from discrimination (Jasper, 2008). Title VII was designed as a guide to the litigation of employment discrimination cases and therefore goes into great detail about the kinds of behaviors that constitute illegal discrimination (e.g., harassment), the kinds of behaviors that are protected (e.g., opposition or reporting discrimination to the employer), the kinds of employers covered, and the kinds of bases for discrimination covered by the Act (e.g., race and sex).

There is no evidence in the Act itself or in the legislative history surrounding the Act that its purpose was to promote racial understanding, eliminate racism, or eliminate racial discrimination. Nor is there evidence that by "race" or "protected class," the Act meant biological race. Instead, history reveals that Title VII was enacted during the height of the civil rights movement and was designed to allow plaintiffs facing employment discrimination on the basis of being members of historically oppressed groups a legal remedy for that discrimination.

Despite all of the preceding, antidiscrimination law operates as if the wrong to be remedied by this area of law is treating the race of a person as significant in situations in which it should not be so treated. In other words, the historical context of antidiscrimination law has been forgotten in favor of treating racial discrimination as if it occurs in a vacuum, as if it, in itself, is the problem to be addressed by antidiscrimination law rather than continued American discrimination against members of historically oppressed groups. If the goal of antidiscrimination law is not to remedy historically situated oppression, but merely to prevent or stop the utilization of race in laws or policies as a criterion for applicability, the ramifications for multiracial people seeking to bring cases of racial discrimination are clear. Those who racially identify as multiracial—having no legally established race—therefore have no basis upon which to argue that any law discriminates against them. However, if the goal of antidiscrimination law is to remedy historically situated oppression, and evidence shows a history of antipathy directed at multiracial people *as* multiracial people, then multiracial people qualify as a suspect class and may use antidiscrimination law to protect themselves.

Toward a distinctive multiracial group identity

Scholarship in multiracial studies began establishing the features of a group identity for multiracial Americans at least as early as the first half of the 20th century. For example, during this period, Robert Park (1928) and Everett Verner Stonequist (1937) produced work on what they called the "marginal man," a person (typically mixed-race, but who could also be a Jewish American or any sort of American immigrant) who, by virtue of being a member of at least two cultures, was perpetually outside of the mainstream. Characteristic features of the marginal man were living in two worlds at once and living in a state of conflict. The marginal man was a "cultural hybrid," a person:

> living and sharing intimately in the cultural life and traditions of two distinct peoples, never quite willing to break, even if he were permitted to do so, with his past and his traditions, and not quite accepted in the new society in which he now sought to find a place. The marginal man was a person on the margin of two cultures and two societies, which never completely interpenetrated and fused. (Park, 1928: 892)

What emerged was a distinctive personality type, a microcosm of cultural conflict, inherently ambiguous, and operating as a source of confusion and change for the surrounding, established cultures. Later theorists speculated on both the negative features of this personality type (e.g., a tendency to delinquency, maladjustment, insecurity, and emotional instability) and the positive features (e.g., high potential for originality and creativity, and cosmopolitanism) (Goldberg, 1941; Antonovsky, 1956; Johnson, 1960; Weisberger, 1992; Grant and Breese, 1997; Rockquemore and Brunsma, 2002). Finally, the marginal man often brings a vantage point that is removed from both or all particularized vantage points, resulting in the honing of certain skills in mediation and translation.

In the mid-20th century, much scholarship was produced on the question of whether there were certain professional pursuits particularly suited for the "marginal man." Examples included the foreman (Gardiner and Whyte, 1945; Wray, 1949), the chiropractor (Wardwell, 1952), the druggist (McCormack, 1956), the merchant-marine radio operator (Record, 1957), the university dean of student personnel (Nudd, 1961), the engineering technician (Evan, 1964), the integrative manager (Ziller et al, 1969), the university labor educator (Nash, 1978), and the academic general practitioner (Reid, 1982). The consistent theme in these occupations was a person "either unable to attain acceptance in the roles to which they aspired" or "trapped between two occupations or statuses in which they were considered outsiders" (Goldberg, 2012: 207).

Recent scholarship in multiracial studies has provided evidence of a long history of racially motivated antipathy toward multiracial people in the US that continues to the present day (Campbell and Herman, 2010; Leong, 2010). A group identity can arguably be generated based on these shared experiences of multiracial antipathy. As noted earlier, the antipathy toward multiracial people originated in the taboo against interracial relationships and interracial mixing between white people and "people of color." Incidents described in recent court cases provide proof that antipathy toward multiracial people continues to exist today. In one incident, described by the US District Court for the Eastern District of Tennessee in passing, Oreo cookies were thrown onto a high school basketball court when a biracial student entered the game (*DeFoe v. Spiva*, 2010). In another federal court case, a white supervisor of an African-American employee who had multiracial children is reported as having made a series of derisive remarks about the children directed at their status as multiracial (*Green v. Franklin National Bank*, 2006). In yet another incident of multiracial animus described in a federal court case, not only were an employee's multiracial children subjected to multiracial slurs (e.g., "half-breed"), but the employee herself was subjected to disparaging comments about her interracial relationship from her co-workers, who at one point left a magazine article condemning interracial relationships in her desk drawer (*Wheaton v. North Oakland Medical Center*, 2005). In still another incident, an employee in an interracial marriage was subjected to "pervasive harassment—a co-worker remarking at one point that the employee had "ruined herself by marrying a black man and having biracial children" (*Madison v. IBP*, 2003)—including having her children referred to as "monkeys" and "zebras."

Many theorists of group rights argue that certain experiences of individual group members may be so related that a kind of solidarity is generated by these experiences that forms the basis of legally recognizable group rights (see, e.g., May, 1987). This subjectivity-based argument in favor of group rights grants group rights to members when the people in the group understand themselves as bound together as members of a group. The key is a strong sense of intra-group solidarity (Segesvary, 1995; Galenkamp, 1998). While the fact of understanding themselves as a group is subjective, in this view, the shared understanding is nonetheless based on objective factors, such as a common history or social condition, or shared interests (May, 1987). The shared history of antipathy toward multiracialism, or the shared intersubjective experience of having been discriminated against by virtue of their multiracial status, or the shared interest that multiracial people have in protecting themselves from discrimination based on their multiracial status are all factors that can be understood as the kind of intersubjective experience that can form the basis for a legally recognizable racial group composed of those with multiracial ancestry.

An additional modification to antidiscrimination law

There is a branch of late 20th- and early 21st-century philosophy of race that has spent a significant amount of time debating whether race is "real." One strand of this branch of philosophy—often called the "eliminativist" position—has involved bringing into the philosophical mainstream evidence (available since at least the 1950s) to the effect that race as it is commonly understood to exist (i.e., as having a basis in biology) is not supported by scientific evidence (Piper, 1992, 1992–93; Appiah, 1993; Zack, 1993, 2002, 2010). For the eliminativists, belief in the existence of biological race is thought to be the core misconception driving racial oppression. This is because, for the eliminativists, a belief in biological race carries with it at least two related beliefs: (1) the belief that there is a correlation between somatic traits (like hair texture, eye shape, or skin color) and character or personality traits (like intelligence or trustworthiness); and (2) the belief in a kind of natural racial hierarchy according to which some races are superior to other races. The assumption behind the eliminativist position is that once racial hierarchy is exposed as lacking in scientific support, those holding racist views and engaging in racially oppressive practices will suddenly stop the offending practices. The eliminativists maintain, then, that in order to end racial oppression, we should eliminate "race talk" or "race thinking" because continuing to speak of race or think about race at all perpetuates the misconception that race has a biological basis, to the detriment of efforts to curb racism. Many advocates for the rights of multiracial people advocate the eliminativist position. In their view, any talk of race at all invokes the biological conception of race, and invocation of the biological concept of race undermines the interests of multiracial people.

There are ways of thinking about race other than in terms of biology, however. Another strand of contemporary philosophy of race emphasizes the social—as opposed to the biological—existence of race, building upon the evidence that biological race is unsupported by scientific evidence but acknowledging nonetheless that race operates very powerfully in our lives. From this "social constructionism" viewpoint, concepts of race "are the products of the socio-historical practices, behaviors, conventions and institutions that give rise to them" (Atkin, 2012: 47), providing race with an ontological status that is significant, if not fixed or unchangeable (Taylor, 2003; Shelby, 2005).

An interesting twist on social constructionism—sometimes called "reconstructionism"—incorporates what is known as "racial realism" or a concession to the permanence of racism (Bell, 1995) as a key aspect of the philosophical examination of the phenomenon of race. For the racial realist, it is of no importance whether race exists biologically, socially, or any other way since regardless of the outcome of that inquiry, racism is alive and well. The racial realist disentangles the problem of racial oppression from the question of whether or not race is "real" to focus instead on improving conditions for racialized minority groups (Bell, 1995). The racial reconstructionist adds to the (weak) social constructionist position a recommendation that the concept of race should be used to actually improve conditions for members of racialized minority groups rather than used in the service of oppressing them.

As long as there is a need for racial antidiscrimination law, there is a need for the utilization of the concept of race. As this chapter points out, there is much evidence to show that such a need exists today. Such utilization will not lead, as eliminitavists and some multiracial people fear, to the reification of the concept of pure, biological races so long as the socio-historical concept of race is identified as the concept of race that should be at work in antidiscrimination law. In this socio-historical concept of race, the reality of race is rooted not in biology, but in historically situated social practices, behaviors, conventions, and institutions. In other words, what makes race real is the fact that a given society or culture acts and behaves as if it is real, resulting in very tangible consequences in the lives those who have been racialized

Within the realm of antidiscrimination law, then, in order to identify a group that should be granted the status of a "suspect class" (or a group deserving of special protection under antidiscrimination laws), the relevant test is not what biology might tell us, but history. Has the group in question been the subject of widespread, institutionalized, systematized and legalized oppression or subjugation based on the identifying group characteristic or not? If so, such a group qualifies as a "suspect class." This would include multiracial Americans given the history outlined earlier. Note that within this framework, whether race is biologically real or not is completely irrelevant. The question is whether race has been treated as if it were real historically, and, if so, whether that treatment has resulted in the oppression of the members of the group in question, in this case, multiracial people.

Concluding remarks

Multiracial people currently have no protection under US laws from racial discrimination directed at them by virtue of their multiracial status, despite a long history of such discrimination in the US legal system and in US society at large. The surface reason for this lack of protection is that antidiscrimination law requires a prospective plaintiff to first identify as a member of one and only one of five legally established racial groups: Asian, black, Latino/a, Native American, or white. In the eyes of US courts, in other words, multiracial people do not constitute what the law calls a "suspect class" (i.e., a group having a history of discrimination), nor can a law that discriminates against multiracial persons constitute what the law calls a "suspect classification" (or a constitutionally impermissible basis for distinguishing one person from another, vis-a-vis access to employment opportunities or other social goods of various sorts). The deeper reason, however, is that US courts no longer acknowledge that the purpose of antidiscrimination law—with regard to cases of racial discrimination—is to provide redress for historically situated, systematized racial oppression. If US courts were to acknowledge this, then a good case could be made for multiracial people being legally established as what the law calls a "suspect class" for the same reasons that minority monoracial groups have been acknowledged as "suspect classes." However, since the courts have moved from discussing antidiscrimination cases in terms of "suspect classes" to discussing them in terms of "suspect classifications," an alternative option to protect multiracial persons from racial discrimination would be for the courts to acknowledge multiracialism as a legally established racial identity.

The argument for the recognition of multiracial people as a "suspect class" is rooted in a shared history of systemic and legalized oppression directed at multiracial people by virtue of their multiraciality. Examples of this oppression include the long history of anti-miscegenation laws in the US (which go as far back as the 17th century), the widespread enactment of Jim Crow (segregation) laws enacted after *Plessy v. Ferguson*, and the rise of the "one-drop rule" and the phenomenon of hypodescent in US society and in US laws, according to which people with any known minority group ancestry were categorized as members of the minority racial group in question. The oppression continues to this day through the persistence in US society and US courts of a belief in biological race, together with its concomitant features of racial purity and racial essentialism. This belief maintains that human races exist, are pure, are biologically based, and are associated with specific physical and non-physical traits that cannot be escaped. Within this framework, not only do multiracial people not have rights, but *they do not exist* as a first order of business. More importantly, for their ability to avail themselves of antidiscrimination law, multiracial people *have no legally established racial identity*.

Scholarship in multiracial studies, however, suggests that multiracial people do, indeed, have a group identity rooted in their multiracialism. This identity is forged in the crucible of belonging to at least two cultures or races at once, of feeling pulled between these two cultures or races, of being a "cultural hybrid," and of never quite being accepted in either or any specific race or culture. The multiracial person's identity is marginal, peripheral, a microcosm of cultural conflict, inherently ambiguous, and operating as a source of confusion and change for the surrounding, established cultures.

Most importantly for antidiscrimination law, however, the long history of shared experiences of having been oppressed or discriminated against by virtue of their multiracial status (a set of experiences that continues today) provides the basis upon which multiracial people might successfully argue that they have rights as a group and therefore qualify as a "suspect class." These experiences include name-calling ("half-breed"), disparaging remarks about oneself or one's children, and a lack of support from one or all monoracial groups to which one might belong. Systematic alienation from the body of laws designed to protect all people from racial discrimination (in virtue of a failure on the part of the law to legally recognize multiracial identity), however, may be the greatest basis upon which to argue in favor of legal protection for multiracial people as multiracial people. If multiracial people are to get their foot in the proverbial door of antidiscrimination law, their existence must first be legally established and acknowledged. At a minimum, then, US antidiscrimination law must begin to acknowledge multiracial identity as a legally established racial status. As antidiscrimination law currently operates without this step, US law is in the awkward position of allowing white people to bring cases of racial discrimination but not multiracial people.

Arguably, all educated people are waiting for the day when legally established racial categories are no longer necessary to protect Americans from racial discrimination; however, until that day comes, there is no reason why multiracial Americans should not be able to avail themselves of antidiscrimination law when discrimination happens to them in the same way that Americans who identify as members of monoracial groups are currently able to do. To accomplish this goal, and given the history of racial discrimination that multiracial people have historically faced and continue to face to this day, US antidiscrimination law should be revised so that either multiracial Americans should be granted the status of a "suspect class" or multiracialism should be added to the list of legally established racial identities.

Note

[1] Mention of "racial groups," "races," "black people," "white people," "the black race," or "the white race" and similar terms in this chapter should not be construed as an endorsement of the popularly held belief in American society in the existence of biologically based, pure, human races characterized by biological essentialism. Instead, the bare terms have been used as a convenient shorthand for "so-called racial groups," "so-called races," "so-called black people," "so-called white people," the "so-called black race," the "so-called white race," and so on.

References

Antonovsky, A. (1956) Toward a refinement of the "marginal man" concept. *Social Forces* 35(1): 57–62.

Appiah, K.A. (1993) *In my father's house*. Oxford: Oxford University Press.

Atkin, A. (2012) *The philosophy of race*. Durham: Acumen Publishing.

Baer, J.A. (1983) *Equality under the constitution: reclaiming the Fourteenth Amendment*. Ithaca, NY: Cornell University Press.

Bell, D. (1995) Racial realism. In: K. Crenshaw, N. Gotanda, G. Petter, and K. Thomas (eds) *Critical race theory: the key writings that formed the movement*. New York, NY: The New Press.

Botts, T.F. (2013) Antidiscrimination law and the multiracial experience: a reply to Nancy Leong. 10 *Hastings Race and Poverty L.J.* 191.

Brunsma, D.L. and Rockquemore, K.A. (2002) What does "black" mean? Exploring the epistemological stranglehold of racial categorization. 28 *Critical Soc.* 101.

Campbell, M. and Herman, M. (2010) Politics and policies: attitudes toward multiracial Americans. *Ethnic and Racial Studies* 33(9): 1511–36.

Daniel, G.R. (2002) *More than black? Multiracial identity and the new racial order.* Philadelphia, PA: Temple University Press.

Daniel, G.R. (2006) *Race and multiraciality in Brazil and the United States: converging paths?* University Park, PA: Pennsylvania State University Press.

Darwin, C. (1871) *The descent of man.* New York: D. Appleton and Company

Davis, F.J. (1991) *Who is black? One nation's definition.* University Park, PA: The Pennsylvania State University Press.

Evan, W.M. (1964) On the margin: the engineering technician. In: P.L. Berger (ed) *The human shape of work: studies in the sociology of occupations.* New York, NY: Macmillan, pp 83–112.

Galenkamp, M. (1998) *Individualism versus collectivism: the concept of collective rights.* Rotterdam: Sanders Instituut: Gouda-Quint.

Gardiner, B. and Whyte, W.F. (1945) The man in the middle: position and problems of the foreman. *Applied Anthropology* 4(2): 1–28.

Gold, M.E. (2001) *An introduction to the law of employment discrimination* (2nd edn). Ithaca, NY: Cornell University Press.

Goldberg, C.A. (2012) Robert Park's marginal man: the career of a concept in American sociology. *Laboratorium* 4(2): 199–217.

Goldberg, M.M. (1941) A qualification of the marginal man theory. *American Sociological Review* 6(1): 52–8.

Grant, G.K. and Breese, J.R. (1997) Marginality theory and the African American student. *Sociology of Education* 70(3): 192–205.

Graves, J.L., Jr (2001) *The emperor's new clothes: biological theories of race at the millennium.* New Brunswick, NJ: Rutgers University Press.

Hubbard, R. (1999) *Exploding the gene myth: how genetic information is produced and manipulated by scientists, physicians, employers, insurance companies, educators, and law enforcers* (3rd edn). Boston, MA: Beacon Press.

Jasper, M.C. (2008) *Employment discrimination law under title VII (Oceana's legal almanacs: law for the layperson)* (2nd edn). Oxford: Oxford University Press.

Johnson, P.A. (1960) The marginal man revisited. *Pacific Sociological Review* 3(2): 71–4.

Jordan, W.D. (2014) Historical origins of the one-drop rule in the United States. *Journal of Critical Mixed Studies* 1(1): 98–132.

Leong, N. (2010) Judicial erasure of mixed-race discrimination. 59 *Am. U.L. Rev.* 469, pp 483-504.

Lewontin, R.C. (1972) The apportionment of human diversity. *Evolutionary Biology* 6: 381–98.

Livingstone, F. (1962) On the nonexistence of human races. *Current Anthropology* 3: 279–81.

May, L. (1987) *The morality of groups: collective responsibility, group-based harm, and corporate rights.* Notre Dame: University of Notre Dame Press.

McCormack, T.H. (1956) The druggist's dilemma: problems of a marginal occupation. *American Journal of Sociology* 61(1): 308–15.

Montagu, M.F.A. (1942) *Man's most dangerous myth: the fallacy of race.* New York, NY: Columbia University Press.

Nash, A. (1978) The university labor educator: a marginal occupation. *Industrial and Labor Relations Review* 32(1): 40–55.

Nudd, T.R. (1961) The dean is a marginal man. *Journal of Educational Sociology* 35(4): 145–51.

Park, R.E. (1928) Human migration and the marginal man. *The American Journal of Sociology* 33(6): 881–93.

Piper, A. (1992) Passing for white, passing for black. *Transition* 58: 5–32.

Piper, A. (1992–93) Xenophobia and Kantian rationalism. *Philosophical Forum* 24(1–3): 188–232.

Rawley, J.A. (1989) *Turning points in the civil war* (2nd edn). Lincoln, NE: University of Nebraska Press.

Record, J.C. (1957) The marine radioman's struggle for status. *American Journal of Sociology* 62(4): 353–9.

Reid, M. (1982) Marginal man: the identity dilemma of the academic general practitioner. *Symbolic Interaction* 5(2): 325–42.

Rockquemore, K.A. and Brunsma, D. (2002) Socially embedded identities: theories, typologies, and processes of racial identity among black/white biracials. *Sociological Quarterly* 43(3): 335–56.

Segesvary, V. (1995) Group rights: the definition of group rights in the contemporary legal debate based on socio-cultural analysis. *International Journal on Group Rights* 3(2): 89–107.

Shelby, T. (2005) *We who are dark.* Cambridge, MA: Belknap Press of Harvard University Press.

Spickard, P.R. (1989) *Mixed blood: intermarriage and ethnic identity in twentieth-century America.* Madison, WI: University of Wisconsin Press.

Stonequist, E.V. (1937) *The marginal man; a study in personality and culture conflict.* New York, NY: Russell & Russell.

Sweet, F.W. (2005) *Legal history of the color line: the rise and triumph of the one-drop rule.* Palm Coast, FL: Backintyme.

Taylor, P.C. (2003) *Race: a philosophical introduction.* Cambridge: Polity Press.

UNESCO (United Nations Educational, Scientific, and Cultural Organization) (1951) *Race and science: the race question in modern science.* New York, NY: Columbia University Press.

U.S. Equal Employment Opportunity Commission. Celebrating the 40th Anniversary of Title VII Retrieved August 11, 2015 from http://www.eeoc.gov/eeoc/history/40th/panel/firstprinciples.html

Wadlington, W. (1966) The loving case: Virginia's antimiscegenation statute in historical perspective, 52 *Virginia Law Review*: 1189–1223.

Wardwell WI. (1952) A marginal professional role: the chiropractor. *Soc Forces*, 30: 339-45.

Weisberger, A. (1992) Marginality and its directions. *Sociological Forum* 7(3): 425–46.

Williams, K.M. (2006) *Mark one or more: civil rights in multiracial America.* Ann Arbor, MI: University of Michigan Press.

Wray, D.E. (1949) Marginal men of industry: the foremen. *American Journal of Sociology* 54(4): 298–301.

Zack, N. (1993) *Race and mixed race.* Philadelphia, PA: Temple University Press.

Zack, N. (2002) *Philosophy of science and race.* New York, NY: Routledge.

Zack, N. (2010) The fluid symbol of mixed race. *Hypatia* 25(4): 875–90.

Ziller, R., Stark, B.J. and Pruden, H.O. (1969) Marginality and integrative management positions. *The Academy of Management Journal* 12(4): 487–95.

Cases

Defoe v. Spiva, 625 F.3d. 324 (6th Cir. 2010).

Green v. Franklin National Bank, 459 F.3d 903 (8th Cir. 2006).

Korematsu v. United States, 323 U.S. 214 (1944).

Loving v. Virginia, 388 U.S. 1 (1967).

Madison v. IBP, Inc., 330 F.3d 1051 (8th Cir. 2003).

Plessy v. Ferguson, 163 U.S. 537 (1896).

Regents of University of California v. Bakke, 438 U.S. 265 (1978) (The) Slaughterhouse Cases, 83 U.S. 36 (1873).

State v. Brown, 108 S.E.2d 233, 234 (La. 1959).

Wheaton v. North Oakland Medical Center, 130 F.App'x 773 (6th Cir. 2005).

United States v. Carolene Products, 304 U.S. 144 (1938).

Statutes

US Const. amend. XIV § 1.
Civil Rights Act of 1866.

Other

Cong. Globe, 39th Cong., 1st Sess. 2459 (1866).

SIX

Should all (or some) multiracial Americans benefit from affirmative action programs?

Daniel N. Lipson

Introduction

When Americans discuss and debate the government's role in promoting racial equality and justice, the conversation on race commonly spirals into a debate over affirmative action. The debates continue to rage on and continue to center on the black–white divide, even as the racial paradigms and demographics have become more complicated in the face of multicultural and multiracial movements. Until recently, multiracial identity has been largely overlooked by practitioners, political entrepreneurs, and scholars of affirmative action (Leong, 2006: 1). To the extent that scholars have turned their focus to multiracial identity and race policy, it has tended to center on the Census.

When affirmative action is scrutinized not only on the basis of whether its methods are narrowly tailored and whether its rationales are compelling, but also on the basis of whether the choice of beneficiaries accords with these rationales and whether the policy methods are capable of selecting among the appropriate beneficiaries, the project of affirmative action becomes even more vulnerable to criticism. Adding multiracial Americans to the discussion raises just these sorts of questions and concerns. Critiques come from sympathetic audiences as well as staunch opponents of race-based programs. Some progressives are critical of affirmative action law and policy for preserving rigid racial categories that "often fail to comport with the complexities of race and the racial mixture in the modern United States" (Johnson, 2003: 2). On the other hand, many African-American civil rights activists and leaders feel threatened by the rise of multiracial identities because they fear the legal acknowledgment of the fluidity of racial boundaries will endanger the civil rights project of affirmative action, school integration, and other racial inclusion policies (Daniel, 2002).

What is surprising is not that critics of affirmative action have in recent years begun to capitalize on problematizing the social and legal construction of racial categories, but rather that they took so long to do so. The recent rise of high-profile, multiracial color-blind entrepreneurs (such as Ward Connerly), in addition to those whom Dillard (2001) refers to as "multicultural conservatives" (e.g., Linda Chavez, Elaine Chao, Thomas Sowell, Shelby Steele, John McWhorter, etc), has shifted the "color-blind" agenda from a cause that predominantly invoked the civil rights movement's emphasis on color-blindness as a means to combat white supremacy to an effort that strategically appropriates the technique of deconstructing racial categories (Lucas, 2014).

At the same time that some "color-blind" legal activists have begun to deploy "social construction of race" rhetoric in their effort to dismantle racial justice policies, pro-affirmative action entrepreneurs have also positioned themselves to connect their policy agenda with the rhetoric of diversity, multiculturalism, and multiracialism. They have done so primarily by rooting affirmative action's constitutional status firmly in the "diversity rationale" (Edelman et al, 2001; Schuck, 2003; Michaels, 2006; Lipson, 2007; Kennedy, 2010). The combined result of these competing "color-blind" and pro-affirmative action developments has been to collectively acknowledge the impact of contemporary affirmative action on Latinos, Native Americans, and Asian-Americans rather than continuing to focus so exclusively on the competition between African-Americans and white people. This shift from affirmative action as a racial justice policy primarily for African-Americans to affirmative action as an instrumental diversity policy to help improve organizations' performance has taken a toll on the "truly disadvantaged" African-Americans (Wilson, 1990) for whom the program was ostensibly created and for whom the program may still be quite important (Skrentny, 2002: 113; Frymer and Skrentny, 2004; Kennedy, 2010).

In this chapter, I give an overview of the origins of affirmative action, the arguments for and against affirmative action programs, and the evolution of the rationales for affirmative action programs (including a discussion of how well or poorly multiracial Americans fit with each rationale). I then focus on affirmative action programs in higher education. I conclude with some policy suggestions for how colleges and universities can most equitably include multiracial Americans in affirmative action programs.

The roots of affirmative action and the rise of diversity-based affirmative action

Since the Supreme Court's *Regents of the University of California, Davis Medical School v. Bakke* ruling in 1978, the trend has been for universities that practice affirmative action voluntarily to recast their affirmative admissions policies by rooting them in the diversity rationale. This section of the chapter will compare and contrast the diversity justification with the compensatory (or remedial) and other supplementary justifications for affirmative action. The following section will assess the assets and liabilities of the evolution of affirmative action from a civil rights policy to a diversity policy.

The origins of affirmative action

Most experts of affirmative action trace its origins to the 1960s, a tumultuous time in US history marked by the growing strength of the civil rights movement, the anti-war movement, and the environmental movement, among other forms of social unrest (Graham, 1989; Skrentny, 1996; Anderson, 2004; Stulberg and Chen, 2008). The understandable priority for civil rights leaders in the early stages of the civil rights movement was to ban Jim Crow segregation and other forms of invidious classification of individuals on the basis of their race or color. The signature victories of the movement included *Brown v. Board of Education* (1954), the Civil Rights Act 1964, the Voting Rights Act 1965, and the Fair Housing Act 1968, all of which banned discrimination against individuals on the basis of their race. Despite these historic legal and political victories, many civil rights advocates began to conclude by the late 1960s that mere color-blindness would be insufficient; securing civil rights for African-Americans would require that government and private organizations take affirmative measures to proactively include African-Americans as a way of making up for centuries of racial exclusion.

While a few scholars trace affirmative action's inception back to the 1930s, with policies in the Public Works Administration and the War Department (see, e.g., Katznelson, 2005: 168), most experts consider these to be precursors to explicit race-based affirmative action. Instead, most accounts portray affirmative action's origins as emerging out of pressure from the civil rights movement. To its proponents, the spirit of affirmative action is exemplified by the following statement by President Lyndon Johnson in his now-famous commencement address of 4 June 1965 at Howard University, titled "To fulfill these rights":

> You do not take a person who, for years, has been hobbled by chains and liberate him, bring him up to the starting line of a race and then say, "you are free to compete with all the others," and still justly believe that you have been completely fair. (Johnson, 1966: 366)

Indeed, President Johnson made civil rights progress his mission after President John F. Kennedy was assassinated. Four years prior, President Kennedy had issued Executive Order 10925, which included a provision requiring that government contractors "take affirmative action to ensure that applicants are employed, and employees are treated during employment, without regard to their race, creed, color, or national origin" (Kennedy, 1963). Republican President Richard Nixon's Revised Philadelphia Plan in 1969—which was put into place by the Department of Labor under the authority of Democratic President Johnson's Executive Order 11246 in 1965—is often attributed as the genesis of explicit race-based affirmative action in the US.

Conventional accounts typically characterize affirmative action as a civil rights policy adopted by political elites resulting from pressure from Left protest movements. Such portrayals point to quotes from Martin Luther King Jr and other civil rights leaders. However, this conventional account of affirmative action's origin has been challenged by experts who have instead found that affirmative action's inception was driven by political and organizational elites despite the lack of grassroots pressure. While King did support proportional representation of black employees shortly before he was assassinated, he prioritized race-neutral, class-based reforms that would build coalitions among working-class Americans across the racial divide. The Urban League's Executive Director Whitney Young was the sole civil rights leader who openly and stridently advocated explicit race-based affirmative action during the 1960s (Skrentny, 1996).

The support for direct, race-based affirmative action did not come primarily from organized interests. Instead, it came from presidents and administrators in federal agencies, who were responding to the crises of urban race riots and the concern that domestic racism would hamper the war on communism (Skrentny, 1996). The civil rights groups looked to the enforcement of color-blindness as an ideal in the short term. There is little evidence that they would have opposed direct, race-based affirmative action down the road, but the problems of discrimination were so severe that they were more focused on ending the discrimination rather than worrying about affirmative acts.

At the political elite level, Skrentny has traced affirmative action's origins in the late 1960s to the following three factors: crisis management, anticommunism, and Republican electoral incentives. First, crisis management refers in particular to Republican President Nixon's fear of the urban unrest occurring in the late 1960s in the form of urban race riots/rebellions. Enacting affirmative action policies served the purpose of showing commitment to racial justice, and the Nixon administration hoped that it would help to appease the urban unrest. Second, President Nixon's advisors warned him that domestic racism would hamper the war on communism. The Soviet Union and its allies engaged in propaganda efforts to paint the US as hypocritical in claiming that it was fighting the Cold War in order to further freedom and equality. By pointing to racial subordination in the US, they were able to question the US's purported motives (Skrentny, 1996; Dudziak, 2000).

In addition to the anti-communism and crisis management concerns, Nixon had an additional incentive to develop affirmative action policies. The Democratic voting base was rooted in a fragile coalition between African-Americans and working-class white people. In addition, the Democratic success in Congress and the presidency was based on another tenuous coalition of liberal Northern Democrats and conservative Southern Democrats. The success of the Republican Party in the electorate and in government was tied to the ability to break these coalitions, luring working-class white voters and conservative Southern Democratic legislators to join the Republican Party (Skrentny, 1996; Parikh, 1997). Civil rights leaders and Democratic Party leaders saw the electoral risk of pushing quickly for strong civil rights policies, whether in color-blind or affirmative action form. Nixon and his fellow Republican Party leaders, on the other hand, were well aware of the electoral benefits for their party of strong civil rights legislation. When combined with the aforementioned legitimacy concerns of anti-communism and crisis management, Nixon began to calculate that a civil rights agenda was a win–win situation and signed an executive order creating hard, race-based affirmative action in contracting (commonly known as the Philadelphia Plan).

When Nixon revived the Philadelphia Plan—which had been proposed and later dropped under the Johnson administration when the US comptroller ruled it in violation of Title VII (Anderson, 2004: 115)—he modified it by mandating that certain explicit percentages of minority groups be hired. Nixon later reversed course and opposed racial quotas but not until the Democratic Party and civil rights groups unified in favor of this hard affirmative action. Nixon's Plan required contractors and unions to show that they would make a "good faith effort" to achieve proportional representation of African-Americans in order to be eligible for federal funds (Skrentny, 1996; Anderson, 2004: 117). Republicans in the House supported the Plan by a margin of 124 to 41. The majority of Democrats opposed it—115 House Democrats voted no, while only 84 voted yes (Graham, 1989). It was an essential part of Nixon's strategy to divide the Democratic base, splitting working-class white Democrats against African-American Democrats (Kahlenberg, 1996; Skrentny, 1996; Parikh, 1997). The strategy worked—as Democrats became more supportive of racial preferences, many white Democrats felt alienated from their party and began moving toward the Republican Party. Nixon, meanwhile, disowned his own Plan, speaking out against quotas in his re-election campaign (Kahlenberg, 1996).

In short, civil rights leaders opted not to push for affirmative action for strategic reasons (despite their moral support for the policy), while a Republican president ultimately ended up creating affirmative action at the federal level also for strategic reasons (despite his moral ambivalence toward the policy). This runs contrary to the conventional account of affirmative action as a policy pushed by organized liberal civil rights interests over the opposition of conservative critics. Aside from the strategic motives responsible for the enactment of the policy, it is important to understand the explicit justifications for affirmative action where it has been enacted. Here, too, the conventional wisdom is that early affirmative action policies were rooted in civil rights justifications. This is partially correct, but many affirmative action policies had multiple justifications. By turning to the first major Supreme Court decision on affirmative action in university admissions—*Regents v. Bakke* (1978)—I will provide one example of the multiple rationales of affirmative action. The University of California, Davis Medical School articulated four justifications for its affirmative action policy:

i   "reducing the historic deficit of traditionally disfavored minorities in medical schools and in the medical profession," Brief for Petitioner 32;
ii countering the effects of societal discrimination;
iii increasing the number of physicians who will practice in communities currently underserved; and
iv obtaining the educational benefits that flow from an ethnically diverse student body. (*Regents v. Bakke*, 1978: 306)

Note that compensating for societal discrimination was one, but only one, of the justifications. Universities and other organizations created affirmative action policies with numerous rationales in mind, and only some of these rationales were rooted in civil rights notions of racial justice. Indeed, Jerome Karabel's scholarship on Harvard, Princeton, and Yale during the late 1960s concluded that "the dominant theme in the texts of the period was neither diversity nor compensation for past injustices, but rather the need for 'Negro leadership'" to help African-American communities move beyond the urban racial unrest crises (Karabel, 2005: 408).

The rise of the diversity rationale

For a variety of reasons—including somewhat conservative Supreme Court directives in cases such as *Regents v. Bakke* (1978)—colleges and universities felt pressured to recast the objectives underlying affirmative action as "diversity" instead of "compensation." In the deeply fractured *Bakke* decision, Justice Lewis Powell's sole opinion cast the tie-breaking vote in defense of the diversity rationale and against the method of quotas being used by the University of California, Davis Medical School in its voluntary affirmative action program. The four liberal justices sought to uphold both the method of quotas and the ends of diversity (and compensation, among other rationales). They wished to sustain the medical school's policy of reserving 16 out of 100 seats for socio-economically or racially disadvantaged students. The four conservative justices sought to strike down the quota method and the diversity rationale (as well as all of the other three rationales) for the University of California, Davis Medical School affirmative action policy. Ultimately, universities learned from *Bakke* that employing racial preferences that consider race as a "plus factor" (i.e., one of many factors, but not the determining factor) was constitutional for voluntary affirmative action policies if rooted in the educational value of diversity. Thus began the switch from justifying voluntary affirmative action policies as a means of addressing societal discrimination to justifying it as a means of promoting the educational value of diversity (Lipson, 2008).

Justice Powell's *Bakke* opinion was a very important contributor to the rise of the diversity rationale, but it coincided with other factors. A second factor was the professional socialization of equal employment opportunity (EEO) and other diversity professionals in organizations (such as corporations, government agencies, colleges and universities, and non-governmental organizations). The civil rights movement had been a formative, defining experience for many of these professionals when they were in high school and/or college, and they were able to spread the embrace of diversity within their organizations by convincing superiors that it would serve the interest of their organizations. Repackaging EEO and affirmative action programs via diversity management rhetoric also gave these diversity specialists leverage to "prevent, or at least forestall, the deinstitutionalization of their programs and departments" (Kelly and Dobbin, 2001: 111).

The recasting of affirmative action from a civil rights policy to an instrumental diversity policy led to a sea change in the nature of political battles surrounding this linchpin racial policy. It has gained the support of leaders and middle managers in major corporations, as well as top leaders in the military (Lipson, 2008). The corporate case for diversity-based affirmative action has several angles. First, the logic is that a diverse workforce is better able to market and sell goods and services to a diverse and growing global customer base. Second, corporations perceive that top employees increasingly wish to work in diverse workplaces; hence, having a diverse workforce today is an asset when it comes to recruiting the top talent tomorrow. Third, having a diverse company with institutionalized rules and procedures that promote and protect diversity within the company can help to insulate the company from lawsuits by disgruntled employees alleging racial or other bias. Rooting affirmative action in the diversity rationale has also created an opening for multiracial students and employees to be included as affirmative action recipients.

Not surprisingly, the military case for diversity-based affirmative action is rooted in national security imperatives. The military is already exceedingly diverse but stratified. The officer corps is disproportionately white, while the enlisted personnel are disproportionately African-American and Latino (Lipson, 2008). In such a hierarchical institution, these racial disparities contribute to racial tension, which can impede the healthy functioning of the military.

As institutions increasingly settled on the diversity rationale in the 1980s, they gained conservative supporters within the leadership of the Republican Party, the military, and the corporate world. Selective universities became more aggressive in pursuing race-based affirmative action to showcase their racial and ethnic diversity. Campuses with strong African-American enrollments touted these as their core diversity numbers. Campuses with large Latino populations but lagging African-American enrollments tended to highlight aggregate enrollments of "underrepresented students of color" in order to showcase overall diversity while obscuring their low African-American enrollments. It appears likely that campuses will tout and profile their multiracial enrollments over the coming years, as reporting requirements and media coverage lead to greater calls for multiracial Americans to be identified and celebrated rather than recoded back into monoracial identities.

Assets and liabilities of diversity-based affirmative action

The rise of diversity-based affirmative action has as many defenders as detractors. For some supporters of a civil-rights conception of affirmative action, diversity-based affirmative action can feel like a watered-down, packaged, and superficial alternative (Frymer and Skrentny, 2004; Michaels, 2006; Anderson, 2010). To others, the embrace of the diversity rationale is a success story—recasting affirmative action as diversity-focused enabled the policy to endure at a time when many were predicting its impending demise (Bok and Bowen, 1998; Kennedy, 2010). Critics of race-based affirmative action tend to see the rise of diversity-based affirmative action as an organizational and judicial subterfuge (Lynch, 1997).

On the Left, one concern with the diversity rationale tends to be that it severs the civil rights roots of affirmative action and replaces them with instrumental bases focused on helping organizations manage diversity in order to achieve their goals. One of the central controversies surrounding the rise of diversity-based affirmative action is whether the switch from civil rights to instrumental diversity results in the exclusion of underprivileged African-Americans. As the Latino population grows rapidly, universities are able to showcase their increasingly diverse student body while deflecting attention away from their lagging enrollments of disadvantaged African-Americans. Elite universities have been criticized for producing diverse classes disproportionately from elite and wealthy international students from Africa, Asia, and Latin America while not doing enough to maximize enrollments of truly disadvantaged African-American students (Brown and Bell, 2008; Massey et al, 2007).

On the Right, one objection to the diversity rationale is that it creates a permanent rationale for a policy that, at least in the eyes of many conservatives, ought to be temporary. Another is that the diversity rationale gives organizations free reign to pick and choose whom to prefer and how to prefer them in ways that are incoherent and incur little risk of being punished for discriminating. It gives organizations cover to continue race-conscious policymaking with little oversight. Across the ideological spectrum, one criticism of the diversity rationale is that it (allegedly) encourages universities and employers to prefer privileged candidates of color while neglecting low socio-economic status (SES) candidates of all races (Kahlenberg, 1996, 2014; Carnevale and Rose, 2003; Cashin, 2014).

Another criticism gaining increasing traction among conservative critics of affirmative action is that affirmative action promotes the very kind of arbitrary and dangerous racial classifications that the civil rights movement sought to prohibit (Lucas, 2014). Even worse, the allegation goes, the "box-checking" nature of affirmative action rewards applicants who fraudulently check boxes claiming "non-white" heritage on the gamble that it might increase such applicants' chances of admission. The controversy surrounding US Senator Elizabeth Warren's (Democrat from Massachusetts) claiming of Native American heritage (Rich, 2013) has focused attention on such allegations of fraudulent self-identification. Instead of explicitly harping on about white men as the new racial victims, conservative critics of affirmative action have increasingly deployed the frame of race as a social and legal construction in their effort to dismantle affirmative action. This quote by conservative commentator David Frum (2014) provides but one of many examples of this technique:

> As intermarriage between ethnic groups accelerates—one in six Americans now marries a person outside his or her own race or ethnicity—the task of adjudicating these preferences becomes ever more baroque and absurd. I once worked alongside a woman whose mother was a Cuban of partly African descent and whose father was Irish via Australia. Her first name was Latino, her last name was purest Hibernian. Preference? No preference? What about the children of an Anglo-Canadian multimillionaire and an African-American Rhodes Scholar, to mention another prominent example? Preference? No preference? Both Puerto Rico and the Philippines were conquered and colonized by the United States. Yet migrants from the one commonwealth and their descendants receive legal preferences; migrants from the other do not.

Since it is now increasingly difficult to determine clear racial boundaries, so this argument goes, we should no longer have race-based policies, such as affirmative action.

On the other hand, one of the distinctive features of the diversity rationale is that it provides more leverage for expanding and reassessing the appropriate targets of race-based affirmative action. For example, the diversity rationale opens the door for universities affirmatively seeking Latino, Native American, Asian,[1] African–American, and multiracial students. Doing so, they can argue, is good for both their institution and society at large. Students who live in a diverse society should be educated in a diverse setting.

Affirmative action in higher education

Universities have great discretion in choosing which groups, and which subgroups, deserve affirmative action. They can decide what form the affirmative action shall take, including how aggressive the preference is, whether it comes in a low-discretion formula-based system (e.g., a point system) or a high-discretion individualized review, whether it will extend to financial aid and in what form, and so on. That said, colleges and universities do not have complete autonomy. Many operate in states that have banned explicit race-based (and gender-based) affirmative action via ballot measure or even via legislation (in the case of New Hampshire) or executive action (in the case of Florida). Universities in Texas were banned from using affirmative action policies by the *Hopwood v. Texas* (1996) Fifth Circuit Court of Appeals decision from 1998 until this decision was nullified by *Grutter v. Bollinger* in 2003.

Many colleges and universities operating in states where affirmative action programs are against the law have nonetheless found ways to effectively pursue their diversity commitments while still complying with these bans on affirmative action by pursuing what Daniel Sabbagh calls "indirect affirmative action" (Lipson, 2001; Frymer and Skrentny, 2004; Leonhardt, 2007; Sabbagh, 2011). The then-Democratic-controlled Texas legislature pioneered the Top Ten Percent Plan following the aforementioned *Hopwood* ban on direct race-based affirmative action. Percentage plans offer guarantees of admission to graduates of in-state public high schools who are at the top of their senior class, regardless of how well or poorly they perform on standardized tests. Their grade point average relative to their classmates is all that matters. While percentage plans are entirely race-neutral and hence comply with bans on race-based affirmative action, the motivation behind putting them into place was to restore the diversity levels that existed before race-based affirmative action was prohibited. In effect, percentage plans succeed in highly diverse and highly segregated states. Percentage plans are bittersweet in the eyes of affirmative action supporters in that they capitalize on racial segregation in Kindergarten through 12th grade (K-12) public education in order to integrate public higher education.

The individualized review of applicants has served as a second method of indirect affirmative action in states with bans on direct race-based affirmative action. The logic of individualized review—as an indirect way of working around legal bans on race-based affirmative action—is that admissions officials evaluate the applicant holistically, especially preferring applicants who demonstrate a record of overcoming adversity. Often, the applicants reveal to the admissions officials that they are underrepresented applicants of color in their application files, even though the admissions officers (in states with bans on affirmative action) are not given access to which racial/ethnic boxes the applicants have checked (Carbado and Harris, 2008; Kirkland and Hansen, 2011). Their racial/ethnic identity can often also be easily discerned from their name, their home address, their high school, or other information in their application.

Some colleges and universities engage in geographic preferences that also serve as indirect affirmative action. For instance, Wayne State University responded to the 2006 Proposal 2 ban on affirmative action in Michigan by instituting preferences for applicants from Detroit. This geographic preference was race-neutral and hence complied with Proposal 2. Wayne State University is located in Detroit, and it is plausible that the administration would genuinely wish to increase the enrollment of residents from the blighted city in which it operates. That said, Detroit is 85% African-American, and providing preferences to applicants from Detroit hence operates as an "indirect affirmative action" workaround.

While universities (in states that allow race-based affirmative action) have great leeway in designing their affirmative action and admissions procedures, they do nonetheless face some pressures to follow certain guidelines. Beyond the legal guidelines imposed by federal courts and state ballot measures, universities also face pressure to adhere to standards required by accreditation agencies (Welch and Gruhl, 1998), the US Department of Education (especially via its reporting standards via the Integrated Postsecondary Education Data System [IPEDS]), and the Common Application (for the more than 500 universities now relying on this unified college application). They also face informal pressures in the competitive higher education marketplace to recruit the best students, which entails winning over the parents. Maintaining a successful institution in an era of declining state and federal assistance requires funding the institutions increasingly through tuition dollars and donations, the latter of which requires courting alumni and wealthy patrons. To the extent that having a diverse student body and faculty assist in any of the aforementioned dimensions, most universities (though not all; e.g., Texas A&M chooses not to have an Affirmative Action (AA) program) will pursue racial and ethnic diversity.

The Department of Education—via the IPEDS system—has also influenced how colleges and universities report racial and ethnic student enrollment data and, hence, how they practice direct and indirect affirmative action. All colleges and universities that participate in, or apply to participate in, any federal financial assistance program as authorized by Title IV of the Higher Education Act 1965 must submit educational data to the Institute for Education Sciences within the US Department of Education. The following section will address the recent changes in IPEDS reporting requirements regarding racial and ethnic enrollment data, focusing in particular on the guidelines for deciding how to code students with multiple racial or ethnic identifications.

Where do multiracial Americans fit into the debate over affirmative action?

In order to understand what role multiracial identity currently plays in the domain of university admissions, it is necessary to pay attention to racial identification at two levels: first, how multiracial applicants self-identify on admissions applications; and, second, how the admissions officials evaluate the applicants' multiracial identification (Leong, 2006: 2). Prior to the 2010/11 academic year, universities tended to rely on the common list of five official minority groups in the US: African American/black; Native American/Alaska Native; Asian American; Hispanic/Latino; and white (Leong, 2006: 6). Colleges and universities differed in what they did with these categories, however. Prior to the widespread adoption of the Common Application in 2006, some higher education institutions asked students to check one box that best captured their racial or ethnic heritage. Others allowed applicants to "check all that apply" (Leong, 2006: 6). Some schools allowed applicants to select a "multiracial" option; others required students to select "other" and provide further information. Other schools provided a large laundry list of specific categories.

The Common Application currently begins by asking students: "Are you Hispanic/Latino?" If the students respond "Yes, Hispanic or Latino (including Spain)," then they are asked to "please describe your background." Question two asks them: "Regardless of your answer to the prior question, please indicate how you identify yourself. (Check one or more and describe your background.)." If they choose "American Indian or Alaska Native (including all Original Peoples of the Americas)," then they are asked "Are you Enrolled?" If they answer yes, then they are asked to "please enter Tribal Enrollment Number." The other options are Asian (including Indian subcontinent and Philippines), black or African American (including Africa and Caribbean), Native Hawaiian or Other Pacific Islander (Original Peoples), and/or white (including Middle Eastern).

Since 2011, the Department of Education has required that colleges and universities comply with a broad federal order to report ethnic and racial data more precisely and thoroughly. This change has made it easier for students to claim a multiracial identity. According to the new rules:

> Institutions MUST give students and staff the opportunity to self-report their race and ethnicity. Students and staff do NOT have to respond. Institutions MUST use a 2-part question to collect these data. The first part of the question collects ethnicity, and the second part of the question collects race. (Source: nces.ed.gov/ipeds/reic/ collecting_re.asp)

The first question asks: "Are you Hispanic or Latino?" The second question asks the respondent to select one or more of the following races: American Indian or Alaska Native; Asian; black or African American; Native Hawaiian or Other Pacific Islander; and/or white. Institutions must ensure that students and staff are always shown both parts of the question. The wording for the second part must read: "one or more" instead of alternatives such as "all that apply." Institutions are not allowed to offer the following response options: unknown; refuse or decline to respond; none of the above; other; or nonresident alien. Institutions are permitted to collect subcategories of the six race and ethnic categories listed earlier. If the individual self-identifies as Hispanic only, or Hispanic and any race category, then the institution is required to report this individual to IPEDS as Hispanic. If the individual self-identifies as not being Hispanic but identifies with more than one race category, then the institution is required to report the individual as "two or more races." In fall 2013, 1.7% of all undergraduates at Title IV institutions were counted as "two or more races," and 3.4% were reported as "Race/ethnicity unknown" (source: nces.ed.gov/ pubs2015/2015012.pdf).

Of the top 10 public institutions, as measured by the *U.S. & World Report* rankings, five (the University of Virginia, the University of Michigan, the University of North Carolina at Charlotte, the College of William and Mary, and the Georgia Institute of Technology) rely on the Common Application. Among the other five, four (The University of California, Berkeley; The University of California, Los Angeles; The University of California, Davis; and The University of California, San Diego) are part of the same University of California system, which relies on its own application. The Pennsylvania State University is the only top-ranked public institution that uses its own application. Of the 10 top-ranked private institutions, the Massachusetts Institute of Technology stands out as the only one declining to use the Common Application. The rest (Princeton University, Harvard University, Yale University, Columbia University, Stanford University, the University of Chicago, and Duke University) all use the Common Application

Of the few aforementioned institutions declining to use the Common Application, the design of the questions soliciting applicants' racial/ethnic identifications are nonetheless rather similar. The University of California institutions ask applicants to check one or more boxes (41 questions in total!) under a category titled "Ethnicity, National Origin or Religion." The other top public school not relying on the Common Application—Pennsylvania State University—follows the more conventional box-checking set of questions. Pennsylvania State University first asks whether the applicant's ethnicity is Hispanic/Latino (Cuban, Mexican, Puerto Rican, South or Central American, or other Spanish culture of origin). Then the applicants are asked to select all racial categories that apply: white; black or African American; Asian; American Indian or Alaska Native; and/or Native Hawaiian or other Pacific Islander.

Overall, as seen earlier, the leading universities have largely settled on asking applicants to choose among one or more of the five "official minority" groups. Note that none of these university applications has a dedicated "multiracial" category to check on their applications. When reporting data to the Department of Education, these institutions have to follow the IPEDS requirements about multiracial reporting. However, they can still rely on other counting methods to provide themselves and the public with a more complete picture of their student body. Some institutions—including Bryn Mawr College—double-count multiracial students and note this in the data. That is, Bryn Mawr reports students in every category they check. Other institutions disaggregate the "two or more races," listing the various combinations of multiracial students (e.g., African American and American Indian or Alaska Native; Asian and white; etc).

One of the big objections to the "two or more races" category is that it is so nebulous. When the Department of Education required that the Pacific Islander category be split off from the Asian category in 2006 in draft guidelines (Jaschik, 2006), students with one parent of Asian ancestry and another of Pacific Islander ancestry would now appear in the "two or more" category. Previously that student would have appeared as Asian.

Preliminary research suggests that many multiracial applicants are most likely to claim the most disadvantaged identity only and thereby pass on the opportunity to check multiple racial categories (Schemo, 2000). Doing so is seen as a strategic move, based on the calculus that picking the most disadvantaged group will increase the chances of admission via affirmative action preferences. As Leong (2006: 22) points out, several admissions consultants coach their applicants to do exactly that. However, this strategic act is at least in part counteracted by an opposing strategic calculus: applicants declining to answer the race question at all (Moreno et al, 2005; Rich, 2009; "Students who decline to identify their race in college applications," News and Views,1996).

In 2008, 6.3% of all college students earning bachelor's degrees were of unknown race/ethnicity. This is more than double the percentage (3.0%) 10 years prior (source: acenet.edu/news-room/Documents/ Minorities-in-Higher-Education-Twenty-Fourth-Status-Report-2011-Supplement.pdf). The percentages are even higher at selective institutions (Leong, 2006: 19). For example, at the University of Michigan, 8.4% of enrolled new first-year students declined to report their race or ethnicity on their applications (source: ro.umich.edu/ enrollment/ethnicity.php). At the University of Texas at Austin in 1998, 29% of admitted first-year students declined to state their race. More than one in seven admitted students at the University of California system did not check any racial categories. Some anecdotal evidence suggests that much of this population is made up of white students who thought that their chance of being admitted would increase if they avoided checking white. An exploratory analysis of three California college campuses has found that "a sizeable portion of students in the unknown category are white, in addition to multiracial students who may have selected white as one of their categories" (Moreno et al, 2005).

As noted in other chapters in this text, the trend of allowing applicants to self-identify has been in place since the Census first administered a system of self-reporting in 1960. This switched the focus from how others identify citizens to how citizens identify themselves. Since applicants are identifying their racial and ethnic background without any authorities responsible for verifying this self-identification, some scholars and laypersons alike have raised concerns about applicants' fraudulent self-reporting (Rich, 2013). The rise of multiracial consciousness is seen by such skeptics as opening the door even more to fraud. It is easy for an applicant to claim to have some Hispanic or Native American or even African ancestry. Whether or not this is true can be difficult to determine.

Conclusion and policy suggestions

To conservative critics of affirmative action, the rise of multiracial identification is further evidence that the enterprise of classifying individuals on the basis of race and ethnicity and providing benign race-based preferences is fundamentally flawed. To staunch defenders of a civil-rights conception of affirmative action, the rise of multiracial identity poses complications to a policy they would prefer to defend on simple, compensatory grounds. Ultimately, the battle between the critics and defenders will continue to play out in statewide ballot measures, litigation, and even proposed legislation and executive action. Lurking beneath the heated battle over affirmative action's legality, however, are numerous controversies over specific affirmative action policies. Barring a major liberal shift in Supreme Court precedent, the shift in rationales from compensation to diversity appears likely to endure. There is always the possibility that the Supreme Court will overturn the ruling in *Grutter* that diversity is a compelling governmental objective justifying the use of race-based preferences. However, the justices passed on opportunities to rule that diversity is not a compelling governmental interest in *Parents Involved v. Seattle* (2007), *Fisher v. University of Texas* (2013), and *Schuette v. Coalition to Defend Affirmative Action* (2014).

The role of multiracial identity in the practice of affirmative action needs to be examined from the vantage points of both the applicants and the institutions' admissions officials. It is important that the applicants be able to express their identity in a way that is as true as possible to their experience. Therefore, the trend of allowing individuals to identify with multiple racial and ethnic identifications is a positive one, despite the unavoidable concerns about fraudulent box-checking. There is no perfect system for allowing individuals to identify with multiple racial/ethnic identities. However, the move to allow applicants to select multiple races is surely an improvement.

Similarly, the move to allow institutions to report the multiracial identification of applicants—from the Common Application, to accreditation agencies, to the Department of Education—is a step in the right direction. Having standardized procedures for guiding institutions on how to report this data can only help in gaining a more accurate measure of multiracial identification in the US. That said, the "two or more races" category required by the IPEDS system is a poor category as it is a catch-all that fails to provide accurate information on the "details of the groups that constitute biracial and multiracial identities" (Moreno et al, 2005: 11).

Colleges and universities exercise significant leeway in how they design their admissions procedures. Institutions operating in places where voluntary, race-based affirmative action remains legal can use any number of options in designing their procedures. How they treat various combinations of multiracial identity is largely their prerogative. To the extent that campus leaders are committed to actively reaching out to less privileged applicants of color, as they should be, it is important that they continue to reach out to the least privileged monoracial and multiracial applicants. As Campbell and Barron point out in Chapter Two, "the most educated multiracial groups on average are white–Asian and Asian–Some Other Race adults." The groups that are least likely to attend college are Latina/o–white–Some Other Race and Latina/o–black–Some Other Race. Campbell and Barron also document that "of the five multiracial groups with incomes below $45,000, four are part-black, and the fifth is part-Native American." Colleges and universities ought to prioritize enrolling low SES monoracial and multiracial applicants, and doing so requires accurately compiling the racial identification of the applicants.

In the end, much of the fate of (multi)racial policy rests in the hands of the professionals who enact such policies in their organizations. Regardless of what lawmakers decide, these organizational professionals still hold substantial power over the fate of diversity and racial inclusion. For better or worse, such organizational professionals are influenced by the same societal forces as are ordinary citizens; hence, the stakes are high when it comes to which side wins the legal/political battles to shape public opinion regarding multiracial identity and racial equality.

Note

[1] Over the past few years, critics of affirmative action have stepped up their efforts to turn Asian-American citizens against race-based affirmative action, alleging that Asian-Americans are the new victims of affirmative action as universities seek to increase African-American and Latino enrollments at the expense of white and Asian applicants (see Park, 2015). A large majority (70%) of Asian-American registered voters support affirmative action in higher education (see: aapidata.com/wp-content/uploads/2014/11/APV-AAJC-issues-nov7.pdf).

References

Anderson, E. (2010) *The imperative of integration.* Princeton, NJ: Princeton University Press.

Anderson, T.H. (2004) *The pursuit of fairness: a history of affirmative action.* New York, NY: Oxford University Press.

Bok, D. and Bowen, W.G. (1998) *The shape of the river: long-term consequences of considering race in college and university admissions.* Princeton, NJ: Princeton University Press.

Brown, K. and Bell, J. (2008) *Demise of the talented tenth: affirmative action and the increasing underrepresentation of ascendant blacks at selective higher educational institutions.* Ohio State Law 69: 1229.

Carbado, D.W. and Harris, C.I. (2008) *The new racial preferences. California Law Review* 96(5), 1139-214.

Carnevale, A.P. and Rose, S.J. (2003) Socioeconomic status, race/ethnicity, and selective college admissions. The Century Foundation. Available at: http://www.tcf.org/assets/downloads/tcf-carnevale_rose.pdf

Cashin, S. (2014) *Place, not race: a new vision of opportunity in America.* Boston, MA: Beacon Press.

Daniel, G.R. (2002) *More than black? Multiracial identity and the new racial order.* Philadelphia, PA: Temple University Press.

Dillard, A.D. (2001) *Guess who's coming to dinner now? Multicultural conservatism in America, American history and culture.* New York, NY: New York University Press.

Dudziak, M.L. (2000) *Cold War civil rights: race and the image of American democracy.* Princeton, NJ: Princeton University Press.

Edelman, L.B., Fuller, S.R., and Mara-Drita, I. (2001) Diversity rhetoric and the managerialization of law. *American Journal of Sociology* 106: 1589–641.

Frum, D. (2014) Why affirmative action no longer works. *The Atlantic.* Available at: http://www.theatlantic.com/politics/archive/2014/04/why-affirmative-action-no-longer-works/361113/ (accessed 16 June 2014).

Frymer, P. and Skrentny, J.D. (2004) SYMPOSIUM: the rise of instrumental affirmative action: law and the new significance of race in America. *Connecticut Law Review* 36: 677–723.

Graham, H.D. (1989) *The civil rights era: origins and development of national policy, 1960–1972.* New York, NY: Oxford University Press.

Jaschik, S. (2006) An end to picking one box. *Inside Higher Education,* August 8. Available at: https://www.insidehighered.com/news/2006/08/08/race

Johnson, K.R. (2003) *Mixed race America and the law: a reader, Critical America*. New York, NY: New York University Press.

Johnson, L.B. (1966) To fulfill these rights: commencement address at Howard University. In *Public papers of the presidents of the United States*. Washington, DC: Government Printing Office, pp 635–40.

Justia. US Supreme Court. *Regents of Univ. of California v. Bakke 438 U.S. 265* (1978) Retrieved August 11, 2015 from https://supreme.justia.com/cases/federal/us/438/265/case.html

Kahlenberg, R.D. (1996) *The remedy: class, race, and affirmative action*. New York, NY: BasicBooks.

Kahlenberg, R.D. (ed) (2014) *The future of affirmative action: new paths to higher education diversity after Fisher v. University of Texas*. New York: The Century Foundation Press.

Karabel, J. (2005) *The chosen: the hidden history of admission and exclusion at Harvard, Yale, and Princeton*. Boston, MA: Houghton Mifflin.

Katznelson, I. (2005) *When affirmative action was white: an untold history of racial inequality in twentieth-century America* (1st edn). New York, NY: W.W. Norton.

Kelly, E. and Dobbin, F. (2001) How affirmative action became diversity management: employer response to antidiscrimination law, 1961–1996. In: J.D. Skrentny (ed) *Color lines: affirmative action, immigration, and civil rights options for America*. Chicago, IL: University of Chicago Press, pp 87–117.

Kennedy, J.F. (1963) *The American promise to African Americans*. Washington, DC: Congressional Record.

Kennedy, R. (2010) The enduring relevance of affirmative action. *The American Prospect*, July 29. Available at: http://prospect.org/article/enduring-relevance-affirmative-action-0

Kirkland, A. and Hansen, B.B. (2011) "How do I bring diversity?" Race and class in the college admissions essay. *Law & Society Review* 45: 103–138.

Leong, N. (2006) Multiracial identity and affirmative action. UCLA *Asian Pacific American Law Journal* 12: 1–34.

Leonhardt, D. (2007) *The new affirmative action. New York Times* September 30. Available at: http://www.nytimes.com/2007/09/30/magazine/30affirmative-t.html?pagewanted=all&_r=0

Lipson, D.N. (2001) Affirmative action as we don't know it: the rise of individual assessment in undergraduate admissions at UC-Berkeley and UT-Austin. In: A. Sarat and P. Ewick (eds) *Studies in law, politics, and society*. New York, NY: Elsevier Science Ltd, pp 137–84.

Lipson, D.N. (2007) Embracing diversity: the institutionalization of affirmative action as diversity management at UC-Berkeley, UT-Austin, and UW-Madison. *Law & Social Inquiry* 32: 985–1026.

Lipson, D.N. (2008) Where's the justice? Affirmative action's severed civil rights roots in the age of diversity. *Perspectives on Politics* 6: 691–706.

Lucas, L.S. (2014) Undoing race? Reconciling multiracial identity with equal protection. *California Law Review*, 102: 1243–302.

Lynch, F.R. (1997) *The diversity machine: the drive to change the "white male workplace."* New York, NY: Free Press.

Massey, D.S., Mooney, M., Torres, K.C., and Charles, C.Z. (2007) black immigrants and black natives attending selective colleges and universities in the United States. *American Journal of Education* 113: 243.

Michaels, W.B. (2006) *The trouble with diversity: how we learned to love identity and ignore inequality* (1st edn). New York, NY: Metropolitan Books.

Moreno, J., Clayton-Pedersen, A., Smith, D.G., Teraguchi, D., and Parker, S. (2005) *"Unknown" students on college campuses: an exploratory analysis.* Available at: http://www.cgu.edu/PDFFiles/UnknownStudentsCDI.pdf: James Irvine Foundation.

News and views: Students who decline to identify their race in college applications (1996) *The Journal of Blacks in Higher Education*, p 51.

Parikh, S. (1997) *The politics of preference: democratic institutions and affirmative action in the United States and India.* Ann Arbor, MI: University of Michigan Press.

Park, J.J. (2015) The misleading lawsuit accusing Harvard of bias against Asian Americans. *Washington Post*, Retrieved August 11, 2015 from https://www.washingtonpost.com/opinions/the-misleading-lawsuit-accusing-harvard-of-bias-against-asian-americans/2015/01/02/cc7a7c52-91e5-11e4-ba53-a477d66580ed_story.html

Rich, C.G. (2009) Decline to state: diversity talk and the American law student. *Southern California Review of Law and Social Justice* 18: 539–85.

Rich, C.G. (2013) Affirmative action in the era of elective race: racial commodification and the promise of the new functionalism. *Georgetown Law Journal* 102: 179–218.

Sabbagh, D. (2011) The rise of indirect affirmative action: converging strategies for promoting "diversity" in selective institutions of higher education in the United States and France. *World Politics* 63: 470–508.

Schemo, D.J. (2000) Despite options on Census, many to check "black" only. *New York Times.* Available at: http://www.nytimes.com/2000/02/12/us/despite-options-on-census-many-to-check-black-only.html

Schuck, P.H. (2003) *Diversity in America: keeping government at a safe distance*. Cambridge, MA: Harvard University Press.

Skrentny, J.D. (1996) The ironies of affirmative action: politics, culture, and justice in America, Morality and society. Chicago, IL: University of Chicago Press.

Skrentny, J.D. (2002) Inventing race. *Public Interest* 146: 97–113.

Stulberg, L.M. and Chen, A.S. (2008) Beyond disruption: the forgotten origins of affirmative action in college and university admissions, 1961–1969. Available at: http://fordschool.umich.edu/research/pdf/chen-stulberg.pdf

Welch, S. and Gruhl, J. (1998) Affirmative action and minority enrollments in medical and law schools. Ann Arbor, MI: University of Michigan Press.

Wilson, W.J. (1990) The truly disadvantaged: the inner city, the underclass, and public policy. Chicago, IL: University of Chicago Press.

SEVEN

Multiracial students and educational policy

Rhina Fernandes Williams and E. Namisi Chilungu

The role of race in schooling and the education system has been studied extensively but with minimal attention to the intricacies of the experiences of multiracial students. In this chapter, we help fill that gap through: (1) an overview of existing research on this topic; (2) a discussion of the influence of national trends in education on the curriculum and the experiences of multiracial students; and (3) providing specific suggestions for policymakers and teachers on how to create optimal learning environments in schools that are more inclusive of and welcoming toward multiracial students.

The field of multicultural education, which developed after the Civil Rights movement in the 1970s, began with a focus on changing education policies to provide fair and equal opportunities to all children in recently desegregated schools. Education researchers and advocates for equity demanded an inclusive curriculum rooted in affirming diversity within schools. Hence, a large focus in the early stages of multicultural education was on ethnic studies. Equal educational opportunities were sought largely for African-American students, with some attention offered to Latino students. Multiracial students were not on the radar as a separate group.

As the field grew and evolved, scholars and researchers extended the focus to equity issues among a broader spectrum of oppressions, including language, gender, sexual orientation, ability, and social class (Grant, 2014). Important strides were made in schools as well as in the preparation of teachers to teach diverse students. Multicultural training began to be part of teacher education programs.

Although all state certification boards in the US address diversity in their standards, the specific requirements vary and are ambiguous (Akiba et al, 2010). In a few states, Georgia for example, the Board of Regents stipulated that all teacher certification programs had to include a cultural foundations course. More recently, since 2007, as a prerequisite for admission into a teacher certification program in the university system of Georgia, students have been required to take three courses that address critical issues and social, cultural, political, and psychological perspectives on diversity, teaching, and learning in order to ensure that teachers have a clear understanding of the larger context of education.

Despite this broadening of the field of multicultural education, however, multiracial students were still not considered as a separate group for whom equal educational opportunities and policies needed to be sought. In fact, tension developed between the multicultural education movement and the multiracial movement. This tension became evident during multiracial organizations' efforts to change the 2000 US Census survey classifications to include a multiracial category (Spencer, 1999; DaCosta, 2007; Williams, 2009; Daniel, 2010). Many in the multicultural education movement were concerned that a new multiracial category would lead to lowered numbers for the African-American population, leaving fewer resources available for African-American students.

Over the last few decades, as the field of multicultural education evolved and expanded into numerous subfields with differing foci and philosophies, the experiences and specific needs of multiracial students remained unexplored. Multiracial students, despite the growing multiracial movement, remained, for the most part, off the radar of multicultural education researchers and educators. While the intersections of multiple identities such as race, gender, social class, and religion were explored widely, nuances of racial identity, specifically multiracial identity, remained unnamed and unattended to in discussions about schooling and identity.

Critical and culturally responsive pedagogy

Having a deeper understanding of issues related to multiracial students is one way for teachers to become critical and culturally responsive educators. Critical and culturally responsive pedagogy developed out of the work of multicultural education, with the intention of developing teachers who critically examine their own biases and assumptions in order to best understand the systems that work against equal opportunities for all students (Ladson-Billings, 1994; Freire, 2000; Nieto, 2004; Gay, 2010). When teachers are critically conscious, they are able to teach their students to think critically and work to dismantle systems that support racism, sexism, classism, and other inequities. Although this type of education has been highly effective in raising the achievement of marginalized students (Freire, 2000; Nieto, 2004), it is often met with resistance and has, in some cases, been forbidden (e.g., the banning of Ethnic Studies in Tucson, Arizona) (Martinez, 2011).

Although teacher education programs typically require at least one cultural foundations course, the content and goals of such courses vary from a "heroes and holidays" and contributions approach to a social justice approach. Similarly, standards and assessments that guide teacher preparation programs—for example, the Interstate Teacher Assessment and Consortium (InTASC) standards or edTPA (formerly the Teacher Performance Assessment)—often contain broad standards regarding diversity or multiculturalism. A quality teacher education program includes the exploration of biases as well as historical, social, economic, and political understandings of race and culture and in-depth knowledge of critical pedagogy in practice. Even high-quality teaching programs, however, rarely incorporate training related to multiracial students. Educators remain largely unaware of the unique circumstances and experiences of multiracial students and, thus, can be oblivious to the need to alter their pedagogy for them (Williams, 2013).

Research on the experiences of multiracial students in schools

Critical education researchers agree that successful teachers should be aware of their students' cultures and identity and explore and incorporate their knowledge about these into their teaching approaches (Ladson-Billings, 1994). A critical and multicultural education, meaning an education that is anti-racist, important for *all* students, social justice-oriented, pervasive, and involving critical pedagogy, is recommended for all teachers (Ladson-Billings, 1994; Freire, 2000; Sleeter, 2007; Gay, 2010). However, as we have noted, attention to the educational experiences of multiracial students is scarce (Williams, 2009).

In recent years, researchers have begun developing newer models and ways of understanding the experiences and context of multiracial youth, with the assumption that there are challenges and problem issues connected to being multiracial. Udry and colleagues (2003) found that multiracial students are more likely than monoracial students to experience educational difficulties, such as truancy and suspension. Reid (2003) argued that these findings were an indication that the specific needs of multiracial students are less likely to be met than the needs of their single-race classmates, and that, in many school districts, they may be "invisible" given the lack of data collected on multiracial students (Reid, 2003). However, this type of research is scant and dated and further research on the experience of multiracial students is needed.

Much of the recent research on multiracial youth has revolved around multiracial identity development (Root, 1996; Rockquemore and Brunsma, 2002a, 2002b; Miville et al, 2005; Renn, 2008; Jackson, 2009; Daniel, 2010). Some studies have focused on the academic achievement of multiracial students, revealing that multiracial students tend not to do as well academically as monoracial students or fall in between their White and minority peers (e.g., Kao, 1999; Herman, 2002, 2009; Burke and Kao, 2013; Burton, 2014). Recent changes to federal guidelines requiring multiple-race options in national survey data have begun to offer researchers more options for researching multiracial individuals (Meyer and Setzer, 2009).

Researchers have already investigated trends in college expectations and enrollment among various monoracial racial groups (Hurtado et al, 1997; Carter, 1999; Perna, 2000) and the relationship between African-Americans' racial identity and academics (Nasir et al, 2009; Chavous et al, 2003). These studies inform the education community about ways to support students from these groups. However, a need persists for developing similar empirical evidence on multiracial students' school experiences. Until fairly recently, multiracial students were often considered to be part of only one racial group, and were represented as monoracial in terms of relevant school and college enrollment data (as Johnston-Guerrero and Renn note in Chapter Eight of this book).

We now turn to findings from our own research studies that provide important insights for educators concerned about multiracial students. In our two studies, one mixed-methods and one qualitative, we explored the schooling experiences of multiracial youth. One study (Chilungu, 2006, 2009) examined the relationship between Black–White biracial college students' identity and the factors that influence their pursuit of higher education. The biracial cohort was part of a larger study that included monoracial participants. All biracial participants completed two surveys: a modified version of the Survey of Biracial Experiences (Rockquemore and Brunsma, 2002a) and Factors Influencing the Pursuit of Higher Education (FIPHE) (Harris and Halpin, 2002). Additionally, seven biracial students completed follow-up interviews.

Quantitative analyses revealed that biracial students who reported feeling close to middle-class White people were more likely to agree that they received support from their high school to enroll in college. This may reflect the type of support and access to college resources provided in middle-class, White communities and social networks.

Also, among the participants, Black and biracial students were more likely to report financial aid concerns—again suggesting that systemic socio-economic issues affect minority groups more consistently than their middle-class White peers.

Several themes emerged from the interview data related to racial identity development and school environments. All of the participants identified overt and subtle experiences of inclusion and exclusion because of their racial background, and discussed a sense of "duality" or having multiple racial perspectives. Also, the data made clear that the participants' racial identity development was inextricably linked to their experiences with family, friends, or others in their social network.

The second study (Williams, 2013) used a phenomenological qualitative study to explore the schooling experiences of 10 Black–White biracial youth between the ages of 16 and 24 in various regions of the US. Each participant was interviewed a minimum of two times, with each interview lasting 45 minutes to 1.5 hours. Interviews were also conducted with at least one of each student's parents to gain their insights and obtain additional information that would contextualize the experiences of the participants.

Collectively, these two studies offered key insights into some unique schooling experiences of multiracial individuals. Our findings indicated that there were common experiences related to region and school diversity, peers, the curriculum, teachers, and socio-economic status. We outline some of these findings that could potentially contribute to developing policy and schooling that is inclusive of multiracial students below in the following.

Common to the participants was the evocation of discomfort and/or self-consciousness over the "What are you?" question. For example, one participant, Mary, relayed an anecdote from her high school experience in which she was approached by another student and questioned about her background (Chilungu, 2006):

> [H]e was like, "What are you?" And I looked at him and I was like, "What?"… And he's like, "What are you?" And I just didn't know what to say, I didn't know what he meant…. And my friend looks at me and she kind of rolled her eyes … and she's like, "She's mixed. Her mom's White and her dad's Black." And he's like, "Oh" and then just like walked away. It made me feel kind of, I don't know, dumb and I just stood there and was like, okay, and kept walking. And I've had that happen a lot.

Mary's description of being asked "What are you?" is not an isolated or unusual phenomenon for those with multiracial heritage. It is an interaction to which many multiracial individuals can relate and simply one example of the type of racial discourse happening in schools. School personnel should be prepared to notice and support students who have these experiences and to knowledgeably address issues raised during these types of significant interactions. Mary was left "feeling dumb," wondering what to make of this question about her identity that she found herself facing repeatedly.

Williams (2013) found the same experience to be common for the participants in her study, with one teacher even telling her Black–White biracial student that "in this country, honey, if you have a parent who is Black, then you are Black." The teacher directed this statement to a biracial teen who was being raised by two White parents in a small, predominantly White town. The teacher who made the statement had grown up prior to the desegregation of schools at a time when the one-drop rule was the unquestioned norm in terms of racial identification. An interview with the mother of this participant stated that she was unaware of her daughter's experience of being labeled by the teacher as Black, nor was she aware of many of the other experiences her daughter had surrounding her racial identity.

Our research also highlights the impact of racism on multiracial students. Racist ideology negatively affects racial identity development (for further discussion on this topic, see Chapters Four and Five in this book). This can be exacerbated for multiracial students when they face rejection by both majority and minority racial groups.

Multiracial students' physical appearance may be a source of curiosity for others and can impact multiracial individuals' identity development (Korgen, 1998; Rockquemore and Brunsma, 2002a). For example, in Williams' (2013) study, a biracial participant shared that her female friends in the predominantly White middle school were White and they often expressed attraction to various boys who were also White. However, she was puzzled as to why the White boys never seemed to be interested in her. She assumed that she was not attractive. Later, when she entered high school, which was far more diverse, she was surprised that the Black boys were immediately interested in her, assuming that she was Black like them. She eventually came to the realization that the White middle-school boys had not been interested in her due to her skin color and racial identification. The participant had to grapple with her racial identity and chose to shift her friendships from mostly White to almost exclusively Black in order to be able to fit in and eventually date boys who were Black. In essence, although she was raised by White parents and saw herself as having a shared identity with her family, her experiences forced her to identify in the way that she was seen in society. Her experience of developing a racial identity that was different from that of her family demonstrates the powerful effects of a racialized society and the social construction of race on one's personal experience.

Many US Americans are still uncomfortable with Black–White romantic relationships and the multiracial offspring of such unions (Herman and Campbell, 2012). For example, a 2013 Cheerios commercial featuring a young biracial child and her Black father and White mother generated so much negative backlash that General Mills deactivated the comments section for the YouTube video (Elliott, 2013). While there was considerable positive response to the commercial, the negative responses and the ensuing media storm highlight a pervasive attitude that Black people and White people should not couple.

In addition to anti-miscegenation attitudes, multiracial individuals may also confront colorism. Colorism generally benefits lighter-skinned individuals and presents obstacles for darker-skinned people of various racial and ethnic groups. Research on the impact of colorism on African-Americans reveals that lighter-skinned Black people tend to attain jobs and promotions more readily and have higher incomes than darker-skinned Black people. In general, darker-skinned Black people experience more negative treatment (Hochschild and Weaver, 2007; Monroe, 2013). Recent research has demonstrated the real consequences of colorism in schools, showing a connection between darker skin and a significantly increased chance of being suspended (Hannon et al, 2013).

However, while advantages exist for light-skinned Black people, they may face skepticism regarding their Black identity and others' resentment of their preferential treatment (Monroe, 2013), experiences that many multiracial individuals have described. One Black–White biracial student described his experience during high school in which other students taunted him for being "light-skinned" (Chilungu, 2006):

> You know, they always telling me, you not Black, dadada, you not this, you not that, being mad, rude, disrespectful, you know, call me names and stuff ... people call me light-skinned nigger and stuff like that. You know, that kind of stuff. Like, half-Black, half-White kid. Nigger, wigger and stuff. You know—all types of rude [names].

His experience highlights the type of negative racial interactions that can occur within schools and which school personnel may not be adequately prepared to address.

Williams (2013) described her own experiences with a first-grade teacher who repeatedly and openly discussed her problems with a particular student in the teachers' lounge and then announced one day that she had figured out the source of the student's problems—the fact that the student was biracial. Apparently, the teacher attributed all the challenges faced by the first grader to the fact that her parents were in an interracial marriage.

Most of the participants in our studies were left to deal with these negative interactions on their own. Williams (2013) found that none were able to discuss them with adults in school and few talked about them with their parents. When schools and teachers do not explicitly acknowledge or address the multiracial experience, multiracial students are overlooked, with families and students left to navigate their unique experiences on their own (Wardle, 2000b). In reality, this means that these students are largely left to deal with issues related to their multiracial background by themselves. Through interviews with parents of biracial youth, Williams found that the parents rarely discussed issues of race with their children and were generally unaware of their children's personal experiences with racial issues in school.

Because the parents of the children had not been raised as multiracial, they were unaware of the kinds of experiences that their children could and did encounter. Findings suggested that parents were generally aware of race issues and had, themselves, faced racial challenges in their interracial unions. However, an understanding of the development of multiracial identity might have proved useful to them in raising their children.

Formal and hidden curriculum issues

It is necessary to understand the roles of both the formal and hidden curriculum in relation to multiracial students' schooling experiences in order to understand their school environment. The formal curriculum refers to lessons and activities planned and implemented within schools. It is what we typically think of when using the word "curriculum" and includes the noted content area standards, goals, and objectives. The hidden curriculum refers to knowledge or ideas that students learn from school that are not overtly planned as part of the formal curriculum. Both the formal and informal curriculum can work to perpetuate social inequality (Jackson, 1968; Gatto, 1992).

In the formal curriculum, schools may select a social studies textbook that casts Christopher Columbus as an explorer "discovering" America. This not only diminishes the historical experience of Native Americans, but also suggests to students that some people's narratives are more important than others. When it comes to the formal school curriculum and teacher preparation, Wardle (2000a, 2000b) argues that multiracial students are often excluded or overlooked. Few resources in the classroom, such as textbooks and children's literature or stories, include multiracial children and even fewer identify them in that way. Wardle (2000a, 2000b, 2007) has written about these concerns, describing how formal curriculums often exclude the multiracial experience. For example, schools often highlight certain racial and ethnic groups by studying historical or well-known members during their respective heritage awareness months (e.g., studying Martin Luther King Jr during Black History Month, or César Chávez during Hispanic Heritage Month). Multiracial students may feel pressure to focus on only one part of their whole identity at a time.

When history is taught, little is included about multiracial people—at least, not explicitly. Many students may learn that some US slave-owners, for example, fathered children with one or more of their Black female slaves. Are teachers prepared to have classroom discussions about the consequences of this time period and the evolution of these couplings through US history (e.g., from "tragic mulatto" figures in literature, to anti-miscegenation laws, to current conversations of interracial relationships)? Understanding the history of multiracial people would promote a deeper understanding of the context of US history.

One Black–White biracial participant expressed her experience of feeling extremely self-conscious and ashamed during a history lesson on slavery in which all the other students identified as Black (Williams, 2013). Her feeling of shame stemmed from her love of and identification with her White mother and the depiction of White people as the perpetrators of horrific acts during times of slavery and segregation. The teacher seemed to be unaware of her biracial identity and of her discomfort, and generally used "us" and "them" language throughout the lesson. This scenario makes clear the need for teachers to be knowledgeable and prepared to use a critical culturally responsive pedagogy that includes the multiracial experience.

Several multicultural education researchers have written about implementing a multicultural curriculum that addresses both the formal and the hidden curriculum (Banks, 1993; Gorski, 1995–2014; Freire, 2000, McIntosh, 2000). Gorski (1995–2014) summarized five stages of a multicultural curriculum often found in schools and classrooms, ranging from the first, maintaining the status quo, which excludes non-dominant groups' perspectives ("curriculum of the mainstream"), to the last, which highlights students' varied experiences to create a student-centered, student-empowered multicultural classroom. What is typical in most classrooms is the first stage, maintaining the status-quo mainstream curriculum.

A critical multicultural education curriculum should go beyond a celebration of "Heroes and Holidays" found in most first-stage multicultural curriculums (e.g., studying African-American leaders in Social Studies during February) and involve a "deliberate questioning of power relations in society, the interrogations of the persistence of racist, classist, and sexists [sic] systems of oppression, and the fervent quest for social justice" (Jay, 2003, p 6). For example, a teacher might engage students in critical conversations about representations of "people of color" in social studies textbooks or ask students to complete a class project that draws upon resources from their community (e.g., interviewing elders) and integrates multiple content areas (where the traditional multicultural curriculum has been incorporated only in Social Studies).

Naming and critiquing bias and racist ideology is part of such a critical multicultural approach, for example, exploring the idea of President Obama as the first Black president of the US could be explored more critically to understand how and why his identity was limited to Black rather than biracial. This type of complex understanding would be inclusive of multiracial students and would aid in dismantling the widely accepted belief that race is biological rather than socially constructed. Teachers and school personnel who effectively implement the last stage of this multicultural education framework acknowledge and work to combat a hidden curriculum that often ignores the experiences of students of color.

Given the response to the previously mentioned Cheerios commercial or even well-known figures like President Obama and Tiger Woods (e.g., initially evoking a collective "What is he?"), many US Americans still seem uneasy with conversations about multiracial individuals. Truly understanding multiracial experiences in a country with deeply embedded monoracial structures and also a varying regional racial makeup is a complex task. How, then, do we prepare teachers to have these conversations with students, and acknowledge their own understanding (and possible biases) around the multiracial experience?

With standardized testing heavily influencing the climate of schools, the impact of the Common Core Curriculum is far-reaching. The

Common Core is not explicitly inclusive of the experiences of multiracial US Americans, but it gives school districts latitude in how they design their curriculum. In the cases where Common Core guidelines do suggest specific content as an example, it is usually along the lines of studying Shakespeare, Ovid, or the Bible. There is certainly room for teachers and schools to intentionally incorporate content addressing the multiracial experience within the Common Core Curriculum. However, as previously discussed, the danger is that the multiracial experience is often not on many educators' radar and is, thus, unlikely to be incorporated.

Implications for policymakers, researchers, and educators

In light of our review of the research relevant to the schooling of multiracial children, we now offer some suggestions for policymakers and educators. Policymakers must consider the use of the data collected on multiracial students on official school forms. Official school forms requesting racial identification are now federally mandated to offer *multiracial* as an option. This mandate recognizes multiracial students as an official racial group. However, as other chapters in this book describe, it is an umbrella term that includes people from a wide variety of racial heritages with wide-ranging experiences. Teachers must be aware of the differences within the multiracial group experience, as well as between multiracial and monoracial students.

Given the findings from our and other studies on the teasing and bullying of multiracial students, teachers must be alert and prepared to intervene when necessary. Teachers who are conscious of the experiences of their students are better able to help their students develop a critical and deeper understanding of race issues in society. Teacher preparation standards and assessments (e.g., InTASC, edTPA) should explicitly call upon schools and teachers to develop a critical consciousness by reflecting upon the history and experiences of their multiracial students.

When implementing Common Core Curriculum, teachers should make explicit connections to the experiences of multiracial people and select content that reflects those experiences. Classroom resources should include a variety of images, stories, authors, and books representative of multiple identities and multiracial experiences. Teachers should teach their students to read and interpret media representations of multiracial individuals with a critical eye and an understanding of the impact of past and present race relations on these images. Creating opportunities for children to have critical dialogues centered on race, gender, and social inequalities (e.g., the intersection of gender, socio-economic, and multiracial identities) will also enable students to question and change societal beliefs and attitudes and, ultimately, systems of oppression. This approach to education, of developing culturally responsive pedagogy in all classrooms, is essential to promoting social, economic, and political equality.

Multiracial students and families offer an important perspective and set of lived experiences that should be meaningfully incorporated into culturally responsive pedagogy and multicultural education frameworks. As communities change and reflect the growing multiracial population, people's awareness of multiracial identity will continue to grow. With a deep understanding of the history and context of multiracial students, teachers will be better able to serve all their students.

References

Akiba, M., Cockrell, K.S., Simmons, J.C., Han, S., and Agarwal, G. (2010) Preparing teachers for diversity: examination of teacher certification and program accreditation standards in the 50 states and Washington, DC. *Equity & Excellence in Education* 43(4): 446–62.

Banks, J. (1993) Approaches to multicultural curriculum reform. In: J. Banks and C. Banks (eds) *Multicultural education: issues and perspectives*. Boston, MA: Allyn & Bacon.

Burke, R. and Kao, G. (2013) Bearing the burden of whiteness: the implications of racial self-identification for multiracial adolescents' school belonging and academic achievement. *Ethnic and Racial Studies* 36(5): 747–73.

Burton, B.A. (2014) A quantitative analysis of resiliency and academic achievement among multiracial students in urban high schools. Unpublished doctoral dissertation, Northern Illinois University.

Carter, D.F. (1999) The impact of institutional choice and environments on African-American and White students' degree expectations. *Research in Higher Education* 40(1): 17–41.

Chavous, T.M., Bernat, D.H., Schmeelk-Cone, K., Caldwell, C.H., Kohn-Wood, L., and Zimmerman, M.A. (2003) Racial identity and attainment among African American adolescents. *Child Development* 74(4): 1076–90.

Chilungu, E.N. (2006) Black/White biracial identity and the pursuit of higher education. Unpublished doctoral dissertation, State University of New York at Buffalo.

Chilungu, E.N. (2009) Black/White biracial identity and college enrollment factors. Paper presented at American Educational Research Association (AERA) Annual Conference, San Diego, CA, 13–17 April.

DaCosta, K.M. (2007) *Making multiracials: state, family, and market in the redrawing of the color line.* Stanford, CA: Stanford University Press.

Daniel, G.R. (2010) *More than Black: multiracial identity & new racial order.* Philadelphia, PA: Temple University Press.

Elliott, S. (2013) Vitriol online for Cheerios ad with interracial family. *The New York Times*, 31 May. Available at: http://www.nytimes.com/2013/06/01/business/media/cheerios-ad-with-interracial-family-brings-out-internet-hate.html

Freire, P. (2000) *Pedagogy of the oppressed.* New York, NY: Continuum.

Gatto, J.T. (1992) *Dumbing us down: the hidden curriculum of compulsory schooling.* Philadelphia, PA: New Society Publishers.

Gay, G. (2010) *Culturally responsive teaching: theory, research, and practice.* Teachers College Press.

Gorski, P. (1995–2014) Critical multicultural pavillion: multicultural curriculum reform. EdChange project. Available at: http://www.edchange.org/multicultural/curriculum/steps.html

Grant, C.A. (2014) Systems of oppression, the globalization of neoliberalism and NAME's calls to action. *Multicultural Perspectives* 16(2): 99–109.

Hannon, L., DeFina, R., and Bruch, S. (2013) The relationship between skin tone and school suspension for African Americans. *Race and Social Problems* 5(4): 281–95.

Harris, S.M. and Halpin, G. (2002) Development and validation of the factors influencing pursuit of Higher Education Questionnaire. *Educational and Psychological Measurement*, 62(79): 79-96.

Herman, M.R. (2002) The Black–White–other test score gap: academic achievement among mixed-race adolescents. Working paper, Institute for Policy Research, Northwestern University.

Herman, M.R. (2009) The Black–White–other achievement gap: testing theories of academic performance among multiracial and monoracial adolescents. *Sociology of Education* 82(1): 20–46.

Herman, M.R. and Campbell, M.E. (2012) I wouldn't, but you can: attitudes toward interracial relationships. *Social Science Research* 41(2): 343–58.

Hochschild, J.L. and Weaver, V. (2007) The skin color paradox and the American racial order. *Social Forces* 86(2): 643–70.

Hurtado, S., Inkelas, K.K., Briggs, C., and Rhee, B.-S. (1997) Differences in college access and choice among racial/ethnic groups: identifying continuing barriers. *Research in Higher Education* 38(1): 43–75.

Jackson, K.F. (2009) Beyond race: examining facets of multiracial identity through a life-span developmental lens. *Journal of Ethnic and Cultural Diversity in Social Work* 18(4): 293–310.

Jackson, P.W. (1968) Life in classrooms. New York, NY: Holt, Rinehart and Winston.

Jay, M. (2003) Critical race theory, multicultural education, and the hidden curriculum of hegemony. *Multicultural Perspectives: An Official Journal of the National Association for Multicultural Education* 5(4): 3–9.

Jones, N.A. and J. Bullock. (2012, September). *The Two Or More Races Population: 2010. 2010 Census Briefs*. Retrieved August 12, 2015 from https://www.census.gov/prod/cen2010/briefs/c2010br-13.pdf

Kao, G. (1999) Racial identity and academic performance: an examination of biracial Asian and African American youth. *Journal of Asian American Studies* 2(3): 223–49.

Korgen, K.O. (1998) *From Black to biracial: transforming racial identity among Americans*. Westport, CT: Praeger Publishers.

Ladson-Billings, G. (1994) *The dreamkeepers: successful teachers of African American students*. San Francisco, CA: Jossey-Bass.

Martinez, M. (2011) Arizona education chief moves to ban ethnic studies in Tucson schools. CNN, 5 January. Available at: http://www.cnn.com/2011/US/01/04/arizona.ethnic.studies.ban/

McIntosh, P. (2000) Interactive phases of personal and curricular revision with regard to race. In: G. Shin and P. Gorski (eds) *Multicultural resource series: professional development for educators*. Washington, DC: National Education Association.

Meyer, J.P. and Setzer, J.C. (2009) A comparison of bridging methods in the analysis of NAEP trends with the new race subgroup definitions. *Journal of Educational Measurement* 46(1): 104–28.

Miville, M.L., Constantine, M.G., Baysden, M.F., and So-Loyd, G. (2005) Chameleon changes: an exploration of racial identity themes of multiracial people. *Journal of Counseling Psychology* 42(4): 507–16.

Monroe, C.R. (2013) Colorizing educational research: African American life and schooling as an exemplar. *Educational Researcher* 42(1): 9–19.

Nasir, N.S., McLaughlin, M.W., and Jones, A. (2009) What does it mean to be African American? Constructions of race and academic identity in an urban public high school. *American Educational Research Journal* 46(1): 73–114.

Nieto, S. (2004) Black, White, and us: the meaning of *Brown v. Board of Education* for Latinos. *Multicultural Perspectives* 6(4): 22–5.

Perna, L.W. (2000) Differences in the decision to attend college among African-Americans, Hispanics, and whites. *The Journal of Higher Education* 71(2): 117–41.

Reid, K. (2003) Mixed-race youths found more prone to school troubles. *Education Week* 23(11): 1–3.

Renn, K.A. (2008) Research on biracial and multiracial identity development: overview and synthesis. In: K.A. Renn and P. Shang (eds) *Biracial and multiracial students*. San Francisco, CA: Jossey-Bass/ Wiley Periodicals, pp 13–32.

Rockquemore, K.A. and Brunsma, D.L. (2002a) *Beyond Black: biracial identity in America*. Thousand Oaks, CA: Sage Publications.

Rockquemore, K.A. and Brunsma, D.L. (2002b) Socially embedded identities: theories, typologies, and processes of racial identity among Black/White biracial. *The Sociological Quarterly* 43: 335–56.

Root, M.P.P. (ed) (1996) *The multiracial experience: racial borders as the new frontier*. Thousand Oaks, CA: Sage Publications.

Sleeter, C.E. (2007) Preparing teachers for multiracial and historically underserved schools. In: G. Orfield and E. Frankenburg (eds) *Lessons in integration: realizing the promise of racial diversity in America's schools*. Charlottesville, VA: University of Virginia Press, pp 171–98.

Spencer, R. (1999) *Spurious issues: race and multiracial identity politics in the United States*. Boulder, CO: Westview Press.

Udry, J.R., Li, R.M., and Hendrickson-Smith, J. (2003) Health and behavior risks of adolescents with mixed-race identity. *American Journal of Public Health* 93(11): 1865–70.

Wardle, F. (2000a) Children of mixed race—no longer invisible. *Educational Leadership* 57(4): 68–71.

Wardle, F. (2000b) Multiracial and multiethnic students: how they must belong. *Multicultural Perspectives* 2(4): 11–16.

Wardle, F. (2007) Multiracial children in child development textbooks. *Early Childhood Education Journal* 35(3): 253–9.

Williams, R.M.F. (2009) Black–White students in American schools: a review of the literature. *Review of Educational Research* 79(2): 776–804.

Williams, R.M.F. (2013) When gray matters more than Black or White: the schooling experiences of Black–White biracial students. *Education and Urban Society* 45: 175–207.

EIGHT

Multiracial Americans in college

Marc P. Johnston-Guerrero and Kristen A. Renn

In fall 2012, US institutions of higher education enrolled over 21 million students, with 2.3% of these students (over 486,000) identified as "Two or More Races" (National Center for Education Statistics, 2013). The 2010 Census reported nearly 50% more multiracial children than the 2000 Census, making the "Two or More Races" youth demographic the fastest-growing of all reported racial groups (Saulny, 2011). As these children grow up and enter higher education, the percentage of multiracial college students will increase. This increase lies at the foundation for this chapter, which will focus on the complications attached to the enumeration of this population within US higher education and related policy concerns.

As others have pointed out (see Chapter Four), there is a positive relationship between higher levels of education and multiracial identification. What is it about higher education that might relate to such differences in identification? How are policies and practices on college campuses supportive (or not) of multiracial identity development? In this chapter, we answer these questions and explore how to improve higher education policies that impact multiracial college students

Although most of the attention of policy issues regarding increasing numbers of multiracial college students has focused on admissions and affirmative action programs (see Chapter Six), there are also policy issues related to the growing presence of multiracial college students after they matriculate. We discuss the importance of the campus racial climate for multiracial students and how they navigate potentially hostile structures and interactions on college campuses. For example, many multiracial college students must deal with micro-aggressions during interpersonal interactions on campus. These subtle, yet everyday, experiences with discrimination stem from a larger system of discrimination against multiracial individuals called monoracism (Johnston and Nadal, 2010). A pervasive and persistent belief that an individual is monoracial (of one race only), and that being monoracial is superior to being multiracial, is rooted in inaccurate, racist, and pseudo-scientific notions of so-called racial purity that undergirded the US's foundation as slave-holding colonies (Daniel, 1996; see also Chapter One). These beliefs persist today in social and organizational systems that assume and prefer that individuals are one race only, an assumption and preference we term *monoracialism*. To be clear, we argue that monoracialism is the social force shaping a monoracial paradigm while monoracism is the system of oppression that results from such a paradigm. Although distinct, they are interrelated. Individuals who do not fit such monoracial norms stemming from monoracialism experience subtle, covert, and overt unintended micro-aggressions targeting their multiracial heritage or identity, which is how monoracism manifests on the interpersonal level. For instance, the common experience of being asked "What are you?" can be perceived as a multiracial micro-aggression as it implies that the individual is not normal and can be objectified in order for someone to place them into the schemes that fit monoracialism (Johnston and Nadal, 2010).

Campus policies and practices should be designed to address monoracism, starting with reducing monoracialism and unintended micro-aggressions against multiracial students. For example, traditional structures and services targeting students of color (e.g., Multicultural Affairs offices, Cultural Centers) have been identified as important spaces for students to escape hostile climates (Ozaki and Johnston, 2008). However, these services and programs tend to be designed with only monoraciality in mind, leading to questions about where multiracial students fit, and whether they are informing changes in these structures and services provided to support student diversity efforts (e.g., Literte, 2010; Ozaki and Renn, 2014). Additionally, pedagogical innovations designed to improve campus climates for diversity include intergroup dialogue programs. However, these also tend to be monoracially designed and can lead to multiracial students feeling ostracized or forced to choose (Ortiz, 2013).

Outside of faculty- and staff-administered services and programs, multiracial students have created their own spaces through student organizing. However, many of these groups dissolve shortly after founding members graduate, likely due to a lack of institutionalization (e.g., not having a corresponding academic program) (Ozaki and Johnston, 2008; Ozaki and Renn, 2014). The lack of multiracial representation in the curriculum can also be a source of micro-aggressions that college students face. The biannual Critical Mixed Race Studies conference held at DePaul University since 2010 set the stage to develop and institutionalize mixed race studies as its own field of study, including the launching of the *Journal of Critical Mixed Race*

Studies in 2011 (Daniel et al, 2014). Before multiraciality can become fully integrated into the higher education landscape, however, higher education policies must come to terms with some of the complexities associated with the diversity of students and institutions.

Complicating policies: the diversity of students and institutions

It is critical in the 21st century to be able to disaggregate and observe trends in college student data by race, sex, and family income, among other key factors, in relation to student outcomes, including learning, persistence, and graduation rates. While many progressive educators look forward to a time when such monitoring will no longer be necessary, that time has not yet arrived. As of the 2010/11 academic year, postsecondary institutions must collect data on student race and ethnicity in a format that allows individuals to indicate more than one race and enables institutions to report the following to the Department of Education's Integrated Postsecondary Education Data System (IPEDS):

1. Number of students who are "Hispanic or Latino" and "Not Hispanic or Latino" (the federal government considers "Hispanic or Latino" to be an ethnic rather than a racial category; see Renn, 2009).
2. Unduplicated numbers of students in each of six categories based on single or multiple responses regarding race: American Indian or Alaska Native; Black or African American; Asian; Native Hawaiian or Other Pacific Islander; White; Two or More Races, in any number or combination (see Renn, 2009).

Scholars and educators differ in their opinions about these categories and the separation of ethnicity and race, though there is an emerging consensus that adolescents and young adults consider "Hispanic or Latino" identity a racial construct and that the contexts under which they self-identify as Hispanic or Latino vary (Brown et al, 2006). Current postsecondary data policy centers on the key principle of self-identification (i.e., no one else determines into which categories an individual falls).

For the purposes of reporting to IPEDS, the vast majority of institutions ask students to self-identify their sex, ethnicity, and race only at the time of admissions. Renn and Lunceford's (2004) empirical study found that 98% of institutions collected these data only on admissions applications. There has been no change in this practice since then, though in the immediate aftermath of the change to the new reporting categories, some institutions attempted to re-survey students after admission. Institutions have since dropped this practice due to practical considerations (cost, low response rates). Outside of IPEDS mandates, institutions may report this demographic data internally (i.e., for institutional assessment purposes) in any way they choose, and many institutions elect to report in ways that meet local interests in understanding the student population. For example, an institution may report locally represented groups of Hispanic or Latino students (e.g., Mexican-American, Dominican-American, Puerto Rican).

Before the 2010/11 school year, IPEDS required postsecondary institutions to report in the "old" one-race-only categories. The result is that there is a break in trend data on student race at any given institution, with an apparent one-year decrease in some racial categories from the fall 2009 entering class to the fall 2010 entering class. A Black and Asian student who entered in fall 2009 would have been reported in one category at admission, but her sister who entered the following fall could have been reported in the "Two or More Races" category. If the older sister was reported as "Black," and the younger sister as "Two or More Races"—and this phenomenon was repeated at institutional scale—it would appear that the number of Black students had decreased.

Additional complications arise when considering that any student may change identities over time, and, as pointed out in Chapter Two, multiracial individuals may change their racial identity over their lifetime, from one setting to another, and depending on how racial demographic questions are asked (Harris and Sim, 2002; Doyle and Kao, 2007; Harper, 2014; Johnston et al, 2014). Moreover, just as there is more than one way to be "Black," "Latino," "Asian American," or "American Indian," there is more than one way to be "Two or More Races" on campus.

Multiracial students represent a variety of heritage groups, and identify themselves in varied ways, including situationally. Renn's extensive work on mixed-race college student identity revealed five patterns of racial identification among her research participants (similar to patterns found by other scholars; see Wallace, 2001; Daniel, 2002; Rockquemore and Brunsma, 2002): (1) a student in the *monoracial* pattern claims only one racial group; (2) a student in the *multiple monoracial* pattern claims two or more monoracial groups; (3) a student in the *multiracial pattern* may claim identities such as biracial, mixed, blended, or other terms that signify a singular, yet mixed, identity; (4) a student who identifies outside of race altogether, attempting to deconstruct race by opting out of racial identification or outside of the common racial landscape, fits the *extraracial* pattern; and (5) a student who identifies across the patterns, depending upon the context, fits the *situational* pattern of racial identification.

Not only can the diversity of how students identify complicate counting and tracking, but how scholars and educators operationalize race in the first place can influence campus policies and practices. Given the diversity inherent in the population considered "multiracial college students," and given the various patterns of racial identification outlined earlier, locating this population in the data is complicated even further when considering different ways of operationalizing race. For instance, is "race" about ancestry or identity? This question needs to be clarified by practitioners before moving forward in designing practices to meet the needs of multiracial students since some students might fit the multiracial ancestry category but not claim a multiracial identity (e.g., a student who has some Native American ancestry but lives her life as a White person), while others claim a multiracial identity but might not get counted as "Two or More Races" based on what boxes they may have checked at the time of admissions (e.g., a biracial Black–Asian-American student who worries about higher standards for Asian-American applicants and so checks only "Black" on the admissions form) (Saulny and Steinberg, 2011).

Rockquemore, Brunsma, and Delgado (2009) argued that "race" can be distinguished in three different ways, depending on whether it is based on ancestry, self-labeling, or how others view the person racially. Johnston and colleagues (2014) expanded and clarified this typology of racial meanings by outlining five distinct, yet related, meanings: *racial ancestry* refers to an individual's racial heritage (which could be perceived to be something biological/genetic and/or cultural); *racial identity* is defined as an individual's understanding of her or his racialized self; *racial identification* is defined as the available and chosen racial category that an individual selects in a certain situation; *racial ascription* refers to how others racially understand and categorize an individual; and *racial conceptualization* refers to an individual's fundamental understanding of what race is and how she fits within that conception.

Although these constructs are interrelated (e.g., how others racially classify an individual may influence the individual's racial identity), they are not the same. When students are asked about their "race," they may utilize one or many of these meanings in formulating their answers. For researchers and institutions that attempt to measure racial demographics through data collection methods, it is important to consider how students may enact these varied understandings of race in any given situation. Such common situations where students enact such understandings include within the high-stakes context of filling out a college admissions application or completing a standardized test, or something that may seem as having lower stakes, such as participating in a research study or joining a student organization's social media group. These nuanced meanings of race may be helpful for explaining some of the variability in racial identification found in the literature. Underlying this fluidity may be a disconnect between how individuals prefer to identify and the racial and ethnic categories and options available to them (Rockquemore et al, 2009), as well as the various ways in which students understand and enact the multiple meanings of race.

Institutional diversity

Not only are students diverse themselves, but campuses also differ—especially in terms of the percentage of their students who are of color, the fluidity of racial boundaries, and the historical legacies of inclusion and exclusion of individuals of different heritage groups (Renn, 2004; Renn and Reason, 2013). Campuses differ by institutional type and control (e.g., public, private, religiously affiliated, for-profit, community college, liberal arts, comprehensive university, research university), the size and number of campuses, the residential nature of the student population, the history of racial inclusion (exclusively White at founding by practice or by law, predominantly White but enrolling all races, Historically Black Colleges and Universities [HBCUs], Hispanic-Serving Institutions [HSIs], Tribal Colleges and Universities [TCUs], and Asian American, Native American, Pacific Islander-Serving Institutions [AANAPISIs]), curriculum, location (rural, suburban, urban), and so forth. All of these factors and more influence the ways in which contemporary students experience and express racial identities.

The extent to which multiracial students are comfortable expressing identities situationally is also, in part, a function of how open the peer culture is to students moving among groups (Renn, 2004). A campus with a strong culture of monoracialism will resist such situational expressions through multiracial micro-aggressions and overt discrimination. Myriad factors of individual, peer, and campus-by-campus specificities go into students' experiences with racial identity.

A hypothetical example of multiracial college students helps to illustrate the importance of identity and identification for policy considerations. Imagine two cousins, Jovan Garcia and Bella Garcia.

144

Their Mexican-American fathers are brothers but Jovan's mother is Black and Bella's mother is White. They arrive as first-year students on the same campus, a public research university located in the Southern US. Upon arrival, they have very different experiences navigating campus policies and politics, which seemed to start at their applications. Asked to indicate ethnicity, both marked "Hispanic or Latino," and asked to "check all that apply" for race, Jovan indicated Black and White, whereas Bella indicated only White because she had no other option for a racial category that included her Mexican-American father. When their university reported them to the IPEDS, it included both as Hispanic or Latino, Jovan as "Two or More Races," and Bella as White (Hispanic/Latino). When the university drew up lists for the multicultural office to use for outreach, Jovan ended up in a singular "African-American" category and Bella ended up in a singular "Hispanic" category; this approach mirrors the historic concept of "hypodescent," which assigns the individuals to the "lower-status" category (see Daniel, 2002).

During orientation, Jovan and Bella received different types of messages from school groups. For example, Bella received emails from the Latinos Unidos (LU) organization while Jovan received emails from the Black Student Union (BSU), but not LU. When the cousins got together for lunch after a few weeks on campus, they compared experiences and realized that they were being set up to have very different cultural experiences of the same institution. Furthermore, neither could find a comfortable space to bring their "whole selves"— Mexican-American, White, Black, mixed-race. Fortunately for Jovan and Bella, they had each other. They could debrief one another and know that they had someone to talk to who understood what they were experiencing. Other multiracial students on their campus may not have known where to turn to discuss racial dynamics. Many multiracial students in real life are left on their own to figure out their identities, identity expression, and campus racial climate.

Strategies

Considering the diversity of the population of multiracial Americans in college and the complications discussed earlier, we present some recommendations for supporting this population. These recommendations focus on service delivery programming for students, institution-level policies, and system-wide policies that impact multiracial students.

A typical model of serving racially and ethnically diverse students on campus is through multicultural student services, often in the form of an office or center (Stewart, 2011; Shek, 2013). Shek (2013) identified a taxonomy of cultural resource centers in US higher education: (1) institutions that have one centralized cultural resource center to serve students of color (e.g., Multicultural Center, Intercultural Center); (2) institutions with separate centers that focus on specific racial and ethnic populations (e.g., Black Cultural Center, Asian-American Student Center); and (3) institutions that have both multicultural and race-specific centers. Within each type, there are subtypes related to staffing. For instance, the majority of multicultural-only centers in Shek's sample had multiple staff members with generalist positions, as opposed to staff members whose titles reflected a focal group (e.g., Coordinator of Latina/o Student Affairs).

Within cultural centers, or other race-oriented student services (ROSS), clarity about whether and where multiracial students fit remains elusive (Literte, 2010). Through case studies of ROSS at two California campuses, Literte (2010) found that many biracial students did not participate in ROSS because peers questioned whether they belonged. Although Literte (2010) noted that the ROSS administrators did not intentionally leave out multiracial students, there were few examples of explicit inclusion, often an artifact of the historical legacy of the ROSS establishment and focal groups. Questions still remain as to how best to make sure that multiracial students feel included in ROSS. Should a separate center or office be established solely for this diverse population? Or at campuses with a multicultural center, should a staff member be hired for specific outreach to multiracial students? The answers to these questions do not come easily, as institutional contexts—both contemporary and historical—must be considered.

A campus with a long history of race-specific cultural centers, for example, might see resistance to creating another center, especially when other communities might fear that it will mean reduced resources for them. A campus with a newly established multicultural center might have more flexibility to rearrange their services to promote more explicit inclusion of multiracial students. In any case, changes of this nature tend to be dependent on student advocacy and institutional politics. Given the diversity of multiracial students and the prevalence of a monoracial paradigm that diffuses such efforts to organize, building community and organizing for such changes can be difficult (Hamako, 2014).

Wong and Buckner's (2008) review of student services for multiracial college students used three cases to illustrate how different institutions provide support specifically for multiracial students, if at all. Two main factors influenced the types of services: the existence of professional staff dedicated to serving multiracial students; and the strength of multiracial student leadership. Institutions deemed to have stronger student services had both staff and student leaders dedicated to increasing multiracial awareness. Wong and Buckner posited that institutions with student groups but without staff support/infrastructure might face higher turnover rates for such student groups. Additionally, institutions with staff and programs but not much push from the student community might struggle with attendance and not deem the continuation of multiracial-specific services and programs necessary.

Brown University's office supporting students of color provides a successful model of inclusion for multiracial students since it specifically puts multiracial students on an equal footing with other racial populations. Its mission statement declares its intent "to provide an environment in which Arab, Asian, Black, Latino, Multiracial, and Native American students can feel comfortable celebrating their cultural heritages" (Brown University, 2014). In addition to explicitly mentioning multiracial students in the office's mission statement, multiracial students are integrated into Brown's programs and services, including having a multiracial student welcome event and multiracial heritage series, alongside similar programs for other groups.

The imperative of language

The inclusion of multiracial students by name is integral to their feeling included and supported, but what should such a diverse group of students be called? The language of multiraciality spans from using specific heritage combinations (e.g., Black–White biracials, Mexipinos) to broader terms (e.g., mixed-heritage students) and it is clear that scholars and policymakers do not all agree on the best naming. Even the "Two or More Races" category presents conceptual challenges for understanding what unites such a diverse group of students. Hamako (2014) recently argued that what unites these students are the contexts and social experiences that signify one as multiracial, for example, monoracism and micro-aggressions. A term for this group that might capture this common experience better is "multiracialized" students, which signifies that "one is treated as Multiracial" (Hamako, 2014: 244). Moreover, scholars and practitioners might use the term "multiracial-identifying" students, signaling that these students actually identify as multiracial, which may be distinct from those who check "Two or More Races" on their admissions form. Although potentially clunky to speak, utilizing different terms—such as biracial/multiracial/multiracialized—serves three key functions: clarifying who is included within the multiracial category (i.e, those who are treated as multiracial); highlighting the common experiences of multiracial students (rather than just their identification); and disrupting assumptions that everyone agrees on the best language to use to design policies in support of multiracial students.

Such specifications and clarifications in language usage are important for designing policies and practices to meet the needs of multiracial students, particularly since students may not see themselves as any one chosen term. For instance, differences exist in preferences for using "multiracial" and "mixed race" given various histories and interpretations (e.g., "mixed" perpetuating being "mixed up" or confused) (Daniel et al, 2014). Yet, the usage of "mixed" is becoming increasingly popular among undergraduate students, as seen in "Mixed Student Unions" across the West Coast and even the creation of the National Association of Mixed Student Organizations (NAMSO). No matter what one calls this diverse group of students, it is important that they be named and clearly included in outreach efforts by institutions of higher education. It is important to counter monoracialism and multiracial micro-aggressions through the use of explicit and inclusive language.

The language and policy implications of underrepresentation

Often used as a codeword for students of color, and particularly African-American, Latina/o, and Native American (and, in some cases, Pacific Islander and certain Asian ethnic groups), the term "underrepresented" permeates higher education policy. For example, the recently announced federal fund for innovation in higher education, or the First in the World Program (FITW), names "underrepresented" students in four of its five "absolute priorities" (e.g., increasing the enrollment and retention of underrepresented or low-income students in science and technology programs) (Lederman, 2014). However, it is unclear whether and when multiracial students fit into this umbrella term of "underrepresented," and especially those multiracial students who may partially or fully identify as White (but check the "Two or More Races" box). How institutions of higher education count multiracial students will determine if multiracial students (or what type of multiracial students) get tracked in such measurements of achievement, persistence, and completion.

Part of FITW funding is set aside for Minority-Serving Institutions (MSIs). As noted earlier, MSIs fit traditional monoracial categories: HBCUs, HSIs, TCUs, and AANAPISIs. There are different criteria for eligibility for each of these institutions to obtain MSI status and compete for MSI-specific grants. The Higher Education Act 1965 defined a fixed group of HBCUs, which has persisted regardless of changes to the student population. TCUs are approved for inclusion in federal programs by the American Indian Higher Education Consortium. AANAPISIs must have a student body of at least 10% Asian-American or Native Hawaiian or other Pacific Islander students along with a majority of the student body meeting income eligibility requirements. HSIs must have at least 25% Hispanic students. How are multiracial students counted in the demographics of campuses seeking eligibility for AANAPISI or HSI status? If they are being counted, how are grant-seekers including multiracial minority students in their grants and services (if at all)?

Future issues of policy and practice to consider

Four ongoing and future policy issues bear attention from postsecondary educators. First, since 2010/11, when postsecondary education began to align its data collection with the 1997 Office of Management and Budget determination that individuals should be allowed to self-identify in more than one racial category, postsecondary educators, leaders, and policymakers have adjusted to the change and begun to cope with the complexity of policy implementation during the transition. Earlier in the chapter, we discussed the break in trend data across the implementation of the change to multiple-race reporting. The actual number of students who are, for example, of Black and White heritage might be the same, but in fall 2009, their institution would have asked them to choose one racial category only, while in fall 2010, the instructions would have been to choose all that apply. All other things being equal, depending on how the fall 2009 cohort chose their one category, there would appear to be a decrease in Black students and White students—matching the appearance of the new "Two or More Races" category—in fall 2010.

How does the institution report multiracial students in their six-year graduation rate? What does it mean for meeting the goals of the "completion agenda" to close differences among racial groups if the data on which those outcomes are being measured is in transition? Similarly, how does the institution understand its trend data in student diversity across that transition in data? We recommend that institutions that did not collect "Two or More Race" data until fall 2010 use proportionality—the ratio of students indicating various racial combinations—in the two years following the change to estimate the proportion of racial heritage combinations in the four years prior to the change, and then make the comparisons across cohorts to track trends.

Second, students have multiple identities in addition to their race and ethnicity. The ways in which gender, class, sexuality, ability, nationality, and citizenship status—among others—interact with multiracial identity is a rich area for research and an additional consideration for practice. This phenomenon is not unique to multiracial students, and they may, in fact, have a developmental advantage in their ability to consider identity categories as social constructions (Shih et al, 2007) that influence one another. When assessing multiracial students' needs, educators should take the opportunity to take into account other salient identities. For example, offices providing programs and services to students of specific identity groups (e.g., based on gender or sexual orientation) should be required when doing assessments and conducting research to include the option for students to report race and ethnicity in more than one category; similarly, offices providing programs and services based on students' racial and ethnic identities should inquire about students' other identities and attempt to avoid repeating the "choose one only" effect of making students choose between race and ethnicity and their other identities. Collaborating and communicating in order to avoid simultaneous counter-programming is one example of how to achieve this goal.

Third, the increasing globalization and internationalization of higher education will provide additional opportunities to consider multiracial identities on campus. International students who come to the US will have varying experiences with the concept of "race" and thus the concept of "multiracial." Multiracial students who engage in international study, work, internships, or tours may encounter historical and contemporary components of their heritages in ways that are enlightening and overwhelming, as well as educational and personally meaningful. A student with, for example, one parent from a European colonizer and one from an indigenous, colonized heritage group may come face to face—literally—with an additional part of the complicated legacy of her ancestry when abroad. Postsecondary educators should seek to maximize opportunities to consider multiracial identities and histories in the context of globalization and campus internationalization. Discussing the history of racial categorization in the US during orientation for domestic and international students and offering a study abroad curriculum that explores post-colonial cultures are two ways to engage this material.

Finally, there may be policy and practical issues related to the influence of social media on multiracial student identity and organizing. Gasser (2008) pointed to the ways in which the Internet in general and social media in particular have become means for exploring a host of identities, including multiracial identities of countless combinations of heritage groups. Anyone, anywhere, can get online and find someone else who shares a specific heritage combination. The potential validation that comes from locating other people like oneself is a powerful tool for developing and expressing identity through text, audio, images, and video. The simultaneous emergence of multiracial voices and faces in public life and the emergence of the Internet have created a generation of multiracial young adults adept at using social media for organizing for social change (e.g., Census categories), visibility, and community-building (for examples, see www.lovingday.org and www. mavinfoundation.org). Although institutions are still trying to figure out policies and practices related to social media overall, whatever direction online communication and social media take, postsecondary educators concerned about creating optimal campus environments for multiracial students would be wise to pay attention.

Conclusion

In this chapter, we have described key factors for understanding and serving the needs of multiracial college students. Thoughtful policies and practices can work against the forces of monoracialism and seek to eliminate multiracial micro-aggressions on campus and monoracism within the larger society. Data collection and reporting and campus programs and services are two key areas for action.

We urge educators and policymakers to consider the importance of language and to implement policies and practices that will reduce monoracialism and micro-aggressions against multiracial students within the context of adapting to the new data policy guidelines. We also encourage them to recognize and address students' multiple identities, to account for globalization and internationalization, and to attend to multiracial identity construction and expression in the digital age. No matter what changes future federal policies may hold for the US Census and education data policy, students of mixed-heritage backgrounds will continue through the educational pipeline to college, and they will do so in increasing proportions of the population.

Postsecondary institutions must adapt to this present reality and make their campuses welcoming places for multiracial students.

References

Brown, J.S., Hitlin, S., and Elder Jr, G.H. (2006) The greater complexity of lived race: an extension of Harris and Sim. *Social Science Quarterly* 87(2): 411–31.

Brown University (2014) *Third-World Center mission and philosophy.* Providence, RI: Brown University. Available at: www.brown.edu/campus-life/support/third-world-center/about/mission-and-guiding-philosophy

Daniel, G.R. (1996) Beyond Black and White identity in the new millennium: unsevering the ties that bind. In: M.P.P. Root (ed) *The multiracial experience: racial boundaries as the new frontier.* Thousand Oaks, CA: Sage, pp 333–41.

Daniel, G.R. (2002) *More than Black? Multiracial identity and the new racial order.* Philadelphia, PA: Temple University Press.

Daniel, G.R., Kina, L., Dariotis, W.M., and Fojas, C. (2014) Emerging paradigms in critical mixed race studies. *Journal of Critical Mixed Race Studies* 1(1): 6–65.

Doyle, J.M. and Kao, G. (2007) Are racial identities of multiracials stable? Changing self-identification among single and multiple race individuals. *Social Psychology Quarterly* 70(4): 405–23.

Gasser, H.S. (2008) Being multiracial in a wired society: using the Internet to define identity and community on campus. In: K.A. Renn and P. Shang (eds) *Biracial and multiracial college students: new directions for student services, 123.* San Francisco, CA: Jossey–Bass, pp 63-72.

Hamako, E. (2014) Improving anti-racist education for multiracial students. Unpublished dissertation, University of Massachusetts, Amherst.

Harper, C.E. (2014) Pre-college and college predictors of longitudinal changes in multiracial college students' self-reported race. *Race, Ethnicity and Education,* online pre-print, DOI: 10.1080/13613324.2014.911161.

Harris, D.R. and Sim, J.J. (2002) Who is multiracial? Assessing the complexity of lived race. *American Sociological Review* 67: 614–27.

Johnston, M.P. and Nadal, K.L. (2010) Multiracial microaggressions: exposing monoracism in everyday life and clinical practice. In: D.W. Sue (ed) *Microaggressions and marginality: manifestation, dynamics and impact.* Hoboken, NJ: Wiley and Sons, pp 123–44.

Johnston, M.P., Ozaki, C.C., Pizzolato, J.E., and Chaudhari, P. (2014) Which box(es) do I check? Investigating college students' meanings behind racial identification. *Journal of Student Affairs Research and Practice* 51(1): 56–68.

Lederman, D. (2014) Federal fund for innovation. Inside Higher Ed, 16 May. Available at: http://www.insidehighered.com/news/2014/05/16/us-unveils-75-million-fund-spur-higher-ed-innovation#ixzz31tNlkRiu

Literte, P.E. (2010) Revising race: how biracial students are changing and challenging student services. *Journal of College Student Development* 51(2): 115–34.

National Center for Education Statistics (2013) Digest of education statistics: 2012. Available at: http://nces.ed.gov/programs/digest/d12/

Ortiz, A.J. (2013) Understanding and supporting multiracial students. In: L.M. Landreman (ed) *The art of effective facilitation: reflections from social justice educators.* Sterling, VA: Stylus, pp 117–32.

Ozaki, C.C. and Johnston, M. (2008) The space in between: issues for multiracial student organizations and advising. In: K.A. Renn and P. Shang (eds) *Biracial and multiracial college students: new directions for student services, 123.* San Francisco, CA: Jossey-Bass, pp 53–72.

Ozaki, C.C. and Renn, K.A. (2014) Creating engaging and supporting spaces for multiracial college students. In: S.R. Harper and S.J. Quaye (eds) *Student engagement in higher education: theoretical perspectives and practical approaches for diverse populations* (2nd edn). New York, NY: Routledge, pp 91–104.

Renn, K.A. (2004) Mixed race college students: the ecology of race, identity, and community. Albany, NY: State University of New York Press.

Renn, K.A. (2009) Educational policy, politics, and mixed heritage students in the United States. *Journal of Social Issues* 65: 165–83.

Renn, K.A. and Lunceford, C.J. (2004) Because the numbers matter: transforming racial and ethnic data in postsecondary education to meet the challenges of a changing nation. *Educational Policy* 18: 752–83.Renn, K.A. and Reason, R.D. (2013) *College students in the United States: characteristics, experiences, and outcomes.* San Francisco, CA: Jossey-Bass.

Rockquemore, K.A. and Brusnma, D.L. (2002) *Beyond Black: biracial identity in America.* Thousand Oaks, CA: Sage.

Rockquemore, K.A., Brunsma, D.L., and Delgado, D.J. (2009) Racing to theory or retheorizing race? Understanding the struggle to build a multiracial identity theory. *Journal of Social Issues* 65(1): 13–34.

Saulny, S. (2011) Census data presents rise in multiracial population of youths. *New York Times*, 24 March. Available at: http://www.nytimes.com/2011/03/25/us/25race.html?_r=0

Saulny, S. and Steinberg, J. (2011) On college forms, a question of race, or races, can perplex. *New York Times*, 13 June. Available at: http://www.nytimes.com/2011/06/14/us/14admissions.html

Shek, Y.L. (2013) Strategizing for the future: evolving cultural resource centers in higher education. Doctoral dissertation, University of California, Los Angeles.

Shih, M., Bonam, C., Sanchez, D., and Peck, C. (2007) The social construction of race: biracial identity and vulnerability to stereotypes. *Cultural Diversity and Ethnic Minority Psychology* 13(2): 125–33.

Stewart, D.L. (ed) (2011) *Multicultural student services on campus: building bridges, re-visioning community*. Sterling, VA: Stylus.

Wallace, K.R. (2001) *Relative/outsider: the art and politics of identity among mixed heritage students*. Westport, CT: Ablex.

Wong, M.P. and Buckner, J. (2008) Multiracial student services come of age: the state of multiracial student services in higher education in the United States. In: K.A. Renn and P. Shang (eds) *Biracial and multiracial college students, new directions for student services, 123*. San Francisco, CA: Jossey-Bass, pp 43–9.

NINE

Multiracial Americans, health patterns, and health policy: assessment and recommendations for ways forward

Jenifer L. Bratter[1] *and Christa Mason*

Health and mortality rates in the US continue to be stratified by race and ethnicity (Williams, 2012). For example, African-Americans continue to live shorter lives and have higher rates of infant mortality and death from a range of causes when compared to White people (Williams, 2012). Closing these gaps has been a long-standing goal of health officials (Geiger, 2005; Bleich et al, 2013). As the US becomes more diverse, tracking racial health disparities will require engaging a more complex set of racial identities, including multiracial Americans.

The population identifying with multiple races has expanded dramatically, providing new opportunities, as well as challenges, in measuring racial disparities in health conditions and crafting effective health policy to address those gaps. As noted in previous chapters, relative to 2000, the number of US residents selecting multiple races has grown 32%, to over 9 million people, or 2.9% of the population (Jones and Bullock, 2012). What is this group's health profile and how does it differ from monoracial groups? Do multiracial Americans face unique health challenges or are their patterns essentially reflective of their component monoracial groups? Should the health experiences of multiracial people be included among larger monoracial groups with whom they may identify most closely (Bratter and Gorman, 2011), or should they be treated as a unique stand-alone group (or multiple groups, depending on their particular racial backgrounds) (Chavez and Sanchez, 2010)?

In this chapter, we bring multiracial people into the discussion of policies concerning racial health disparities by addressing four issues. First, we provide a brief overview of the work on the health of multiracial populations, including the types of health challenges noted and the gaps in research on this topic. Second, we provide an analysis of nationally representative data on the health of multiracial adults, a subgroup usually absent in studies. Third, we turn to health policies that target the reduction of health disparities and ask how such policies, in light of what we have uncovered, can best speak to the health needs of multiracial groups. Fourth, we argue that more and broader data must be collected on multiracial people in order to effectively measure and address racial health disparities. As a point of terminology, we use the term "multiracial" to refer to persons who self-identify as multiracial, usually through selecting multiple racial groups on an official form. We acknowledge that this is a selective slice of the multiracial population as this group may be defined in a variety of ways (Woo et al, 2011), but it is standard for most work conducted on multiracial populations.

Overview of multiracial health: a focus on risk?

The existing research conducted on racial health disparities compares the relative health standing of minority groups to those of the majority to delineate race-based health needs (Williams, 2012). Similarly, the overriding question that shapes most of the scholarship on multiracial health is whether multiracial status confers a different risk on health when compared to a monoracial counterpart. This reflects a larger question driving sociological inquiry into multiracial lives, which is whether the status of being "betwixt and between" races produces some unique impact on an individual's life. To begin to estimate this population's common health challenges, we focus our attention on where multiracial people stand out among their monoracial counterparts on mental health, health behaviors, and physical health.

Mental health and health behaviors

Several studies of multiracial adolescents show that they demonstrate a greater risk profile for smoking, alcohol usage, and illicit drug abuse compared to most other racial groups (Choi et al, 2006; Whaley and Francis, 2006; Chavez and Sanchez, 2010; Chen et al, 2012), and that they may begin negative health behaviors at relatively younger ages (Clark et al, 2013). Furthermore, works on multiracial adults' mental health and health behaviors show similar results. In their review of research on multiracial people's psychological adjustment and well-being, Shih and Sanchez (2005) find that in several qualitative studies and one quantitative study, multiracial adults are more likely to report feeling sad or depressed. Additionally, utilizing the 2001 California Health Interview Study, Chavez and Sanchez (2010) conclude that multiracial adults smoke tobacco and drink alcohol at higher rates than other minority racial groups, with the exception of American Indian/ Alaska Native (AIAN) people.

More than risk: what are the challenges to a complete picture?

While the aforementioned research provides important sites of concern for health policy, we highlight two issues that distinguish research on multiracial people when compared to other work connecting race and health. First, much of the previous works aggregate all self-identified multiracial people into one group as opposed to referencing conditions of particular combinations (e.g., White–Asian, Black–AIAN), prompting the question: do these patterns extend across all multiracial people regardless of racial background? As studies do not always distinguish multiracial respondents according to racial make-up, it is often unclear if these patterns are general to anyone of a mixed-race background or only certain racial combinations.

Some research on multiracial adolescents does consider their specific multiracial backgrounds and provides some evidence of higher levels of depression across several mixed-race subgroups (Campbell and Eggerling-Boeck, 2006; Campbell and Troyer, 2007; Cheng and Lively, 2009). Additionally, Clark et al (2013) draw attention to White–AIAN and White–Asian youth due to the comparatively young ages that they begin engaging in various forms of substance use. Other research that distinguishes race and ethnic combinations shows that those of partial AIAN ancestry are more likely than certain monoracial peers to display symptoms of depression (Shih and Sanchez, 2005; Udry et al, 2003) and are at a greater risk of suicide (Udry et al, 2003; Whaley and Francis, 2006; Wong et al, 2012).

Unfortunately, teasing out specific combinations is beyond the reach of many public data sets. Data collections fielded by the Centers for Disease Control or the National Center for Health Statistics are obligated to employ federal Office of Management and Budget (OMB) guidelines, which, since the late 1990s, mandate that they ask respondents their race or *races*. However, as multiracial people are still a proportionately small segment of the population (and thus represent a small share of nationally representative samples), researchers must often combine all multiracial respondents into one category in order to have a sample large enough to yield reliable estimates. Furthermore, some data sets do not indicate the specific races that respondents selected as this information poses a risk to maintaining the confidentiality of the respondents (for more information, see NCHS, 2011). The Behavioral

Risk Factor Surveillance System does provide information on race and ethnic combinations but users are recommended to pool multiple years to get large enough estimates of multiracial people for analysis (Bratter and Gorman, 2011).

Second, the types of health outcomes and age-specific subgroups explored remain limited. Although efforts to document racial health disparities generally focus on patterns of chronic illness, morbidity, and mortality (Williams, 2012), studies of multiracial people's health focus largely on mental health issues and risky health behaviors (Shih and Sanchez, 2005; Campbell and Eggerling-Boeck, 2006; Choi et al, 2006; Whaley and Francis, 2006; Cheng and Lively, 2009; Chavez and Sanchez, 2010; Wong et al, 2012; Chen et al, 2012; Clark et al, 2013). Arguably, this reflects an underlying notion that health distinctions result from developing or forming a multiracial identity (Campbell and Eggerling-Boeck, 2006), as opposed to concerns driving race and health in general, such as segregation, discrimination, and socio-economic disadvantage (Williams, 2012). This is also evident in the focus on those who most actively contend with identity formation—adolescents (Udry et al, 2003; Campbell and Eggerling-Boeck, 2006; Choi et al, 2006; Whaley and Francis, 2006; Cheng and Lively, 2009; Chen et al, 2012; Wong et al, 2012; Clark et al, 2013; Flores and Lin, 2013)—as opposed to adults. Studies on adults and the elderly are relatively less common, particularly those that draw on nationally representative samples (see Parker, 2006; Pleis and Barnes, 2008; Bratter and Gorman, 2011).

We begin to address a few of these shortcomings by examining whether multiracial adult health is actually distinctive. In the following section, we present an analysis of adults sampled in the National Health Interview Survey (NHIS), pooled across 11 years (2001–11). Through this, we can gauge whether multiracial people have distinctive or parallel health profiles to members of the monoracial group with which they identify most closely.

Patterns of multiracial adult health

The NHIS collects health data by surveying approximately 35,000 households across the nation annually. While NHIS respondents can report multiple races, multiracial respondents are subsequently prompted to select one race that "best describes" their identity. In Table 9.1, we present the rates of several health conditions, controlling for age, among "non-Hispanic," US-born adults. These figures are generated from a series of statistical models[2] predicting each outcome that introduces age and race/ethnic identity as covariates. These are essentially baseline patterns that provide an initial assessment of health patterns prior to considering the roles of other demographic, socio-economic, or acculturative issues. We present the data divided by each racial group and further divided by whether adults solely identify with this category or whether they identify this group as the race that "best describes" them. Please note that only multiracial adults can select a race that "best describes" them. This approach, similar to those of Bratter and Gorman (2011) and Parker (2006), reveals how much multiraciality matters for the patterns of general health, even among those who identify with the same racial category.

Some other researchers have simply folded multiple-race respondents into the monoracial groups that the respondents say best describe their racial background (Mays et al, 2003; Parker, 2006). This may obscure health concerns faced by multiracial people that are not shared by their monoracial peers (see Table 9.1), perhaps related to being misclassified as members of groups with which they do not identify (see Campbell and Troyer, 2007). In addition, in cases where multiracial individuals have better health profiles, including them as members of monoracial groups may actually shift the aggregate profile of a disadvantaged group and could lead to a misattributed indication of improved health experiences of group members (see Mays et al, 2003).

These reporting strategies also leave out those who do not select a race that "best describes" them. Analyses by Bratter and Gorman (2011) do show that a small number of respondents (less than 1% of the sample) opt to not report a race that "best describes" them and these respondents are more likely than White people to report their health as poor, with comparable rates of poor (self-reported) health to the most disadvantaged multiracial groups, those of partial AIAN ancestry.

In our analysis of the NHIS data (shown on Table 9.1), we assess the degree to which all groups statistically stand apart from (monoracial) White people ("non-Hispanic"). These differences (noted with asterisks if significant) show the degree of difference for the corresponding group relative to the reference category, "non-Hispanic" White people who solely identified with this race. We have also included comparisons between each single racial group and its multiracial counterpart, with significant differences ($p < .05$) noted with the superscript "a." Multiracial people who identify "White" as the race that "best describes" them experience significantly poorer health than White people in many respects. They are more likely to suffer from many chronic health conditions, such as diabetes, heart attack, and hypertension. Multiracial respondents who selected this

Table 9.1: Expected probabilities of health measures among non-Hispanic US-born adults by race

	White		Black		AIAN		Asian	
	Single-race	Multi-racial	Single-race	Multi-racial	Single-race	Multi-racial	Single-race	Multi-racial
	N = 540,427	N = 5,873	N = 140,113	N = 3,174	N = 4,983	N = 1,000	N = 48,205	N = 1,165
Health conditions								
Diabetes	5.1	8.5*ᵃ	9.1*	9.6*	12.8*	8.9**	6.0*	7.7
Heart attack	3.2	5.8*ᵃ	3.0	4.3	4.7**	10.8*ᵃ	1.7*	1.4
Hypertension	24.4	29.6*ᵃ	35.3*	34.6*	33.2*	35.0*	21.0*	24.9
Heart disease	4.1	5.5*ᵃ	3.9	4.9	5.0	9.1**	2.9*	2.0
Angina pectoris	2.3	4.1*ᵃ	1.9*	5.3*ᵃ	2.2	6.9*ᵃ	1.3*	1.3
Heart condition/ disease	7.6	11.2*ᵃ	6.2*	8.9ᵃ	8.8	12.0*	3.7*	4.9
Stroke	2.2	4.5*ᵃ	3.7*	4.2**	4.1*	4.4*	1.9	3.7
Emphysema	1.8	3.4*ᵃ	1.1*	1.6	2.8*	8.8*ᵃ	0.6*	0.3
Cancer	8.0	9.1	4.1*	4.9*	6.6	9.8	2.9*	5.4
Other heart condition	9.0	13.5*ᵃ	8.1*	11.0ᵃ	11.0*	14.1**	5.0*	4.7
Self-rated health								
Poor/fair	8.5	14.9*ᵃ	15.8**	14.9*	17.0*	19.6*	7.6**	8.2
Health behaviors								
Obesity	24.0	30.9*ᵃ	35.6*	36.1*	37.9*	36.9*	8.0*	19.9a
Current smoking	23.7	31.0*ᵃ	21.3*	23.1	33.1*	42.8*	11.2*	19.1a
Binge drinking	39.4	42.9*ᵃ	26.7*	28.9*	45.6**	51.8**	23.8*	31.8
Vigorous exercising	48.2	49.8	36.3*	43.9a	33.2*	43.4ᵃ	39.7*	55.6ᵃ
Health care								
Health insurance	89.3	85.1*ᵃ	83.2*	86.3*	68.1*	72.7*	85.6*	90.2ᵃ
Dental visit	68.1	60.6*ᵃ	58.4*	63.9*ᵃ	58.3*	55.2*	65.1*	71.5ᵃ
Eye care visit	37.0	30.8*ᵃ	27.9*	28.3*	33.8*	34.4	30.3*	28.0*

Notes: With the exception of health-care variables, age is controlled for. * Significant difference from single-race White adults at the $p \leq .05$ significance level. ᵃ Significant difference from corresponding single-race category at the $p \leq .05$ significance level.

category are also more likely to report their general health as poor, exhibit negative health behaviors, be obese, and have inadequate health care. Only multiracial people who report "Asian" as the race that "best describes" then resemble monoracial White people across the majority of health measures. Notably, multiracial people whose race that "best describes" them is AIAN stand out among all racial groups as having the highest likelihoods of experiencing the most chronic conditions and negative health behaviors.

Does a declaration of a race that "best describes" respondents unify health experiences among specific racial groups? By and large, no. As previously mentioned, multiracial people who select "White" as the race that best describes them are unfavorably distinct from their White monoracial counterparts. Additionally, multiracial people whose reported "best describes" races are "Black" or "AIAN" are *more* likely than their monoracial counterparts to experience several negative health conditions, while multiracial people whose race that best describes them is "Asian" have increased probabilities for obesity and smoking statistically different from monoracial Asians' (and statistically similar to White people). Nevertheless, the data do reveal one positive health disparity: multiracial people who report "Black," "AIAN," or "Asian" as the race that best describes them are more likely to engage in vigorous exercise than their monoracial counterparts. Ultimately, these significant—and generally negative—differences across a variety of health measures demonstrate that collapsing multiracial people into best single-race categories obscures their unique health statuses and challenges, as Parker (2006) also supports.

Overall, we find that multiracial adults do face disproportionate chronic health challenges, some of which occur to a greater extent than in the monoracial group with which they identify most closely. While the mechanisms producing this pattern are not clear, it is likely not due to enhanced structural disadvantage as multiracial groups tend to have socio-economic status patterns that are in-between their component groups (Campbell, 2010), and our table shows that these multiracial groups tend to be more likely to have health insurance. These relatively high rates of health challenges may be due, in part, to the adoption of more risky behaviors that enhance the risk of chronic conditions as we find that several multiracial groups are more likely to be current smokers (see Table 9.1). They may also reflect the role of racially specific stressors such as perceived discrimination in the lives of multiracial Americans, issues of health-care access, or other behavioral concerns, such as diet or the prevalence of exercise. Regardless of their sources, to what degree can policy address these issues? We now turn to health policy and place our discussion within a larger context of how health policy addresses race in general.

Health policy issues in multiracial America

Although racial disparities are persistent features of health in the US, policy initiatives aimed at reducing health inequalities emerged only in recent decades (McDonough et al, 2004; Geiger, 2005; Koh et al, 2011; Bleich et al, 2013). The government agency dedicated to eliminating racial gaps in health, the Department of Health and Human Services (Office of Disease Prevention and Health Promotion, 2015: 28), defines this form of disparity as "a particular type of health difference that is closely linked with social, economic, and/or environmental disadvantage [due to membership in a specific racial or ethnic group]." Examining existing research on both racial disparities and relevant health policies, we review the transition from goal-setting to strategizing and describe recommendations and community interventions that characterize the governmental response to health inequities in the US. We conclude with a discussion of how multiracial health might benefit from these policy foci if these recommendations were pursued.

Plans and policies addressing racial disparities during earlier decades largely focused on establishing general health objectives, rather than providing explicit strategies for closing racial gaps in health. For example, the HHS uses Healthy People, the national health promotion and disease prevention initiative, to outline its targets for health. Since the 1990s, Healthy People has included either reducing or eliminating racial disparities as one of its major objectives. While generating goals is a progressive initial step, health inequality cannot be eliminated without more extensive planning and guidance at the federal level. Two major obstacles have hindered the development of more productive health policies: the lack of adequate data on minority groups' health statuses; and the inability to identify the leading causes of and practical solutions to racial health disparities (Geiger, 2005; Zambrana and Dill, 2006; Ulmer et al, 2009; Bleich et al, 2013).

Despite these challenges, in 2011, the HHS developed recommendations in the form of an "Action plan to reduce racial and ethnic disparities" (HHS, 2011), authored by the HHS and supplemented by provisions from the Affordable Care Act. Described as the "first federal strategic disparities plan and the most comprehensive federal commitment in this area to date" (Koh et al, 2011: 1822), it joined other HHS health initiatives with more universal target populations, such as Healthy People 2020. Broadly, the HHS Disparities Action Plan aims to: (1) transform and increase access to health care; (2) further develop and diversify the health infrastructure and workforce; (3) advance the health of all Americans through awareness, prevention, and improved health programs; (4) gather and report uniform data on racial groups' health; and (5) restructure and better monitor HHS programs. By and large, existing programs generally focus on establishing health objectives that serve as frameworks for progress, but their effectiveness in closing racial gaps is unclear.

The existence of socially conscious communities is critical to the success of health policies, as demonstrated by the National Partnership for Action to End Health Disparities (NPA). The Office of Minority Health (OMH) established the NPA to "mobilize a nationwide, comprehensive, community-driven, and sustained approach to combating health disparities and to move the nation toward achieving health equity" (Arizona Department of Public, 2013). With goals complementary to the government's Disparities Action Plan, the NPA represents a community-based response to reducing health disparities that encourages individuals, beginning at the local level, to mobilize for health equality (Koh et al, 2011). The purposes of existing community health programs range from addressing issues deemed specific to certain communities to advocating for a health-care workforce that more ably speaks to the needs of community members. A case study on one of these community projects, the Racial and Ethnic Approaches to Community Health (REACH) in South Carolina, emphasizes the need for health programs to develop an articulate definition of "community" that speaks to the intersection between individuals' memberships in racial groups and geographic locations (Jenkins et al, 2010).

To create a more holistic discussion of racial and mixed-racial health disparities, communities should be placed at the center of health policies aimed at reducing racial disparities in health. Employing racial and ethnic communities, as opposed to racial and ethnic categories, provides a richer and more localized understanding of group identity. While the notion of a US-based "multiracial community" is still young and according to some not fully formed (Nobles, 2000; Farley, 2004), it is useful to know how multiracial people affiliate themselves among monoracial communities. Identifying the group that "best describes" them is a critical first step; however, the notion of community carries a somewhat distinctive meaning that highlights participation. Notably, REACH's primary goal is to recognize the "unique social, historical, economic, and cultural circumstance[s]" (Center for Disease Control, 2009) of communities in an effort to mobilize residents and improve their health knowledge and health-care access. Exposing the role of social and historical forces arguably provides the best opportunity for addressing the most powerful drivers of racial health disparities.

As Williams (2012) has argued persistently, what fundamentally underlines racial disparities in health is racial residential segregation, a historical and current process of lived separation and isolation of racial groups. However, policies have yet to place the issues that emerge from living in historically segregated circumstances (e.g., concentrated disadvantage), or even segregation itself, at the forefront of policy intervention. These and other forms of racial disadvantage that are found in specific places and characterize the experience of community members drive the more proximate concerns (e.g., poor diet, lack of exercise) that impact health status.

Focusing on communities rather than racial and ethnic categories addresses the health needs of both multiracial and monoracial individuals by incorporating context into health initiatives. This is a critical consideration, particularly for multiracial people, as the identities of mixed-race people can often be a moving target, expressed in multiple ways and varying across time and context (Tashiro, 2005; Woo et al, 2011; see also Chapters Two, Three, Four, Eight, and Eleven). For example, multiracial people of Black and White descent are more likely to identify as Black if most of their neighbors are Black (see Chapter Four).

Community-based health initiatives recognize that neighborhood quality strongly impacts the health of the residents, and has emerged as a critical mechanism factoring into racially different health profiles (LaVeist et al, 2011). The characteristics of neighborhoods related to health, such as levels of home-ownership, the availability of amenities such as parks and grocery stores, areas of concentrated poverty, and other characteristics, vary considerably by racial composition. Neighborhoods dominated by African-Americans and Latinos experiencing heavily concentrated poverty have higher levels of health problems and lower life expectancies than others (Robert Woods Johnson Foundation, 2013). Health studies using community-based initiatives can help us to better understand the relations among communities, race, socio-economic status, and health for both monoracial and multiracial people.

Health-care inequalities impacting multiracial people

Still unclear is to what degree multiracial Americans experience certain health-care inequalities that affect minority racial groups at large. These include physician stereotyping (for an overview, see Dovidio et al,

2008), perceived discrimination (Chen et al, 2005; Malat and Hamilton, 2006), and access to a limited number of minority health-care providers (Betancourt et al, 2003; Meghani et al, 2009), among other issues (Smedley et al, 2002; Geiger, 2005). What this means for multiracial people is complicated by the fact that few established stereotypes of multiracial people exist that would pattern the assumptions of health-care providers. Some multiracial people may be perceived as members of multiple groups (Herman, 2010) and, oftentimes, a group with which they do not identify (Campbell and Troyer, 2007). Their health experience and vulnerabilities to health risks, like those of all persons of color, are framed by the ways in which they are understood by outsiders (Saperstein and Penner, 2012). This also raises the question of whether any additional health challenges arise if that understanding conflicts with an "internal" or personal sense of identity (Campbell and Troyer, 2007; Khanna, 2010).

Other health-care concerns related to multiracial people include multiracial adults' lower health literacy relative to White people and Asians/Pacific Islanders (Kutner et al, 2006). Also, when compared to White youth, multiracial children are less likely to have a personal doctor, obtain all required dental care, receive specialty care, and feel that they spend adequate time with their physicians (Flores and Lin, 2013). Similarly, as shown in Table 9.1, we find that multiracial adults are less likely than White people to have health insurance and to report receiving eye and dental exams in the previous year. What this tells us is that meaningful gaps in health care do exist that policies may address. However, better data must be marshaled to address to what degree these challenges match those experienced by monoracial people of color or whether these are unique moments of marginalization for those of mixed heritage.

Conclusions

Although the focus of this volume is on policies, we would like to close on a note of calling for better data as a key foundation for quality research and effective policies. Multiracial adults do face unique health concerns that are not conveyed when folded into OMB categories. For example, we find that multiracial people who choose "White" as the race that "best describes them" do not have health experiences that parallel White people. Instead, they have more risky health behaviors and social-psychological health and chronic illness. Policies aimed at resolving gaps in health levels among racial groups could be enhanced with more information about the complexities of identification that may drive the health experiences of multiracial populations.

We advance three recommendations for expanding the data collected to enhance our ability to observe and track multiracial health:

1. As multiracial people are often not perceived to be multiracial, tracking how health-care providers racially identify them would be helpful. It is important to note that multiracial is being deployed as an identity here, not a descriptor of genetic or even parental ancestry. Therefore, the question is not whether a doctor can "read" an individual's identity correctly, but rather acknowledging that reading is occurring that may create unique concerns for individuals whose identity is rarely recognized as a viable option. Also, given the role of perceived discrimination on health, physicians should report *their* race or ethnicity and their sense of the race of their patients on medical records. When combined with a self-report of race by patients, researchers can isolate cases when these reports conflict and explore the impact on quality of care.

2. We need more complex information about racial identity to better gauge both the number of multiracial individuals and how they are perceived by others. Following the recommendation by Woo et al (2011), we advocate for gathering data on parents' races and self-identified race. Doing so can give precision in terms of enumerating multiracial populations. Those who self-report as multiracial will not include all persons directly descending from interracial heritage. Also, not all those who identify as multiracial have parents of different races; some have multiracial heritage that precedes their parents (see Campbell and Eggerling-Boeck, 2006). Without knowing both a person's racial ancestry and how they identify racially, we have no way of teasing out how each operates on health experiences (ancestry or racial identity). While these recommendations may seem cumbersome, they are necessary steps to gauge to what degree multiracial health is informed by processes related largely to issues of race, or to issues related to being *multiracial* and in-between monoracial racial and ethnic groups.

3. Finally, we need an analytical commitment among researchers and health-care practitioners to reporting *more* racial complexity not less. Efforts to place multiracial and other complex group identities into the current racial classification system serve to maintain consistency in reporting, a core issue for conveying trends over time (Liebler and Halpern-Manners, 2008), but they leave out the ways in which race is operating and could ultimately harm the cause of capturing

the ways in which race shapes health. The three-year gap in life expectancy between White people and Black people, while succinct, may be masking narrower or wider disparities among those who identify as "partial members" of these groups, and those who may be perceived in ways differently than they identify.

As multiracial groups continue to grow, the mechanisms that drive their health will challenge conventional assumptions of how race identity is organized—such as fitting into a narrow range of mutually exclusive categories or a perfect alignment between self-identity and perceived identity. Crafting effective policies that serve everyone will require us to meet these data collection challenges.

Notes

[1] Please direct all correspondence to the first author, Jenifer L. Bratter, Department of Sociology, Rice University, Mail Stop 28, 6100 Main Street, Houston, TX 77005, USA. Email: jbratter@rice.edu

[2] Using logistic regression.

References

Arizona Department of Public (2013) Campaigns & initiatives. Available at: http://www.azdhs.gov/hsd/health-disparities/campaign-initiatives/npa.htm

Betancourt, J.R., Green, A.R., Carrillo, J.E., and Ananeh-Firempong, O., II (2003) Defining cultural competence: a practical framework for addressing racial/ethnic disparities in health and health care. *Public Health Reports* 118: 293–302.

Bleich, S.N., Jarlenski, M.P., Bell, C.N., and LaViest, T.A. (2013) Addressing health inequalities in the United States: key data trends and policy action. *Frontiers in Public Health Services and Systems Research* 2(4): 1–10.

Bratter, J.L. and Gorman, B.K. (2011) Does multiracial matter? A study of racial disparities in self-rated health. *Demography* 48(1): 127–52.

Campbell, M. and Eggerling-Boeck, J. (2006) "What about the children?" The psychological and social well-being of multiracial adolescents. *Sociological Quarterly* 47(1): 147–73.

Campbell, M.E. and Troyer, L. (2007) The implications of racial misclassification by observers. *American Sociological Review*, 72, 750–765.

Center for Disease Control (2009). *Racial and ethnic approaches to community health (REACH U.S.)*. At A Glance 2009. Available at: http://www.cdc.gov/nccdphp/publications/aag/pdf/reach.pdf, p 3.

Chavez, G. and Sanchez, D. (2010) A clearer picture of multiracial substance use: rates and correlates of alcohol and tobacco use in multiracial adolescents and adults. *Race and Social Problems* 2: 1–18.

Chen, F.M., Fryer, G.E., Phillips, R.L., Wilson, E., and Pathman, D.E. (2005) Patients' beliefs about racism, preferences for physician race, and satisfaction with care. *Annals of Family Medicine* 3(2): 138–43.

Chen, H., Balan, S., and Price, R.K. (2012) Association of contextual factors with drug use and binge drinking among White, Native American, and mixed-race adolescents in the general population. *Journal of Youth and Adolescence* 41: 1426–41.

Cheng, S. and Lively, K. (2009) Multiracial self-identification and adolescent outcomes: a social psychological approach to the marginal man theory. *Social Forces* 88(1): 61–98.

Choi, Y., Harachi, T.W., Gillmore, M.R., and Catalano, R.F. (2006) Are multiracial adolescents at greater risk? Comparisons of rates, patterns, and correlates of substance use and violence between monoracial and multiracial adolescents. *American Journal of Orthopsychiatry* 76(1): 86–97.

Clark, T.T., Doyle, O., and Clincy, A. (2013) Age of first cigarette, alcohol, and marijuana use among biracial/ethnic youth: a population based study. *Addictive Behaviors* 38: 2450–4.

Dovidio, J.F., Penner, L.A., Albrecht, T.L., Norton, W.E., Gaertner, S.L., and Shelton, J.N. (2008) Disparities and distrust: the implications of psychological processes for understanding racial disparities in health and health care. *Social Science & Medicine* 67: 478–86.

Farley, R. (2004) Identifying with multiple races: A social movement that succeeded but failed? In: M. Krysan and A. Lewis (eds) *The changing terrain of race and Ethnicity*. New York: Russell Sage Foundation, pp 123-8.

Flores, G. and Lin, H. (2013) Trends in racial/ethnic disparities in medical and oral health, access to care, and use of services in US children has anything changed over the years? *International Journal for Equity in Health* 12(10): 1–16.

Geiger, J.H. (2005) Health disparities. What do we know? What do we need to know? What should we know? In: A.J. Schulz and L. Mullings (eds) *Gender, Race, Class and Health: Intersectional Approaches*. San Francisco, CA: Jossey-Bass, pp 261–88.

Herman, M.R. (2010) Do you see what I am? How observers' backgrounds affect their perceptions of multiracial faces. *Social Psychology Quarterly* 73(1): 58–78.

HHS (US Department of Health and Human Services) (2011) HHS action plan to reduce racial and ethnic health disparities. Available at: http://minorityhealth.hhs.gov/npa/files/Plans/HHS/HHS_Plan_complete.pdf

Jenkins, C., Pope, C., Magwood, G., Vandermark, L., Thomas, V., Hill, K., Linnen, F., Shelton Bock, L., and Zapka, J. (2010) Expanding the chronic care framework to improve diabetes management: the REACH case study. *Progress in Community Health Partnerships Research, Education, and Action* 4: 65–79.

Jones, N. and Bullock, J. (2012) The two or more races population 2010. *2010 Census Briefs C2010BR-13*, US Department of Commerce, Economics and Statistic Administration, US Census Bureau.

Khanna, N. (2010) Country clubs and hip-hop thugs: Examining the role of social class and culture in shaping racial identity. In K. Korgen (ed) *Multiracial Americans and social class: The influence of social class on racial identity*. New York: Routledge, pp 53-71.

Koh, K.H., Graham, G., and Glied, S.A. (2011) Reducing racial and ethnic disparities: the action plan from the Department of Health and Human Services. *Health Affairs* 30(10): 1822–9.

Kutner, M., Greenberg, E., Jin, Y., and Paulsen, C. (2006) *The health literacy of America's adults: results from the 2003 National Assessment of Adult Literacy (NCES 2006—483)*. Washington, DC: National Center for Education Statistics.

LaVeist, T., Pollack, K., Thorpe, R., Fesahazion, R., and Gaskin, D. (2011) Place, not race: Disparities dissipate in Southwest Baltimore when Blacks and Whites live under similar conditions. *Health Affairs* 30(10): 1880–7.

Liebler, C. and Halpern-Manners, A. (2008) A practical approach to using multiple-race response data: a bridging method for public-use microdata. *Demography* 45(1): 143–55.

Malat, J. and Hamilton, M.A. (2006) Preferences for same-race health care providers and perceptions of interpersonal discrimination in health care. *Journal of Health and Social Behavior* 47: 173–87.

Mays, V., Ponce, N., Washington, D.L., and Cochran, S.D. (2003) Classification of race and ethnicity: implications for public health. *Annual Review of Public Health* 24: 83–110.

McDonough, J.E., Gibbs, B.K., Scott-Harris, J.L., Kronebusch, K., Navarro, A.M., and Taylor, K. (2004) *A state policy agenda to eliminate racial and ethnic health disparities.* New York, NY: Commonwealth Fund of New York.

Meghani, S.H., Brooks, J.M., Gipson-Jones, T., Waite, R., Whitfield-Harris, L., and Deatrick, J.A. (2009) Patient–provider race-concordance: does it matter in improving minority patients' health outcomes? *Ethnicity & Health* 14(1): 107–30.

National Center for Health Statistics (2011) *Health, United States.* Retrieved August 12, 2015 from http://www.cdc.gov/nchs/data/hus/hus11.pdf

Nobles, M. (2000) *Shades of citizenship.* Stanford, CA: Stanford University Press.

Office of Disease Prevention and Health Promotion (2015). *Disparities,* August 11, para 6. Available at: http://www.healthypeople.gov/2020/about/foundation-health-measures/Disparities

Office of Minority Health and Health Disparities (2013) Multiracial populations. Available at: http://www.cdc.gov/omhd/populations/Multiracial.htm

Parker, J.D. (2006) The role of reported primary race on health measures for multiple race respondents in the National Health Interview Survey. *Public Health Reports* 121: 160–8.

Pleis, J.R. and Barnes, P.M. (2008) A comparison of respiratory conditions between multiple race adults and their single race counterparts: an analysis based on American Indian/Alaska Native and White adults. *Ethnicity & Health* 13(5): 399–415.

Robert Woods Johnson Foundation (2013) City maps. Available at: http://www.rwjf.org/en/about-rwjf/newsroom/features-and-articles/Commission/resources/city-maps.html

Saperstein, A. and Penner, A.M. (2012) Racial fluidity and inequality in the United States, *American Journal of Sociology* 118(3): 676-727.

Shih, M. and Sanchez, D. (2005) Perspectives and research on the positive and negative implications of having multiple racial identities. *Psychological Bulletin* 131(4): 569–91.

Smedley, B.D., Stith, A.Y., and Nelson, A.R. (eds) (2002) *Unequal treatment: confronting racial and ethnic disparities in health care.* Washington, DC: National Academy Press.

Tashiro, C.J. (2005) Health disparities in the context of mixed race: challenging the ideology of race. *Advances in Nursing Science* 28(3): 203–11.

Udry, J., Li, R., and Hendrickson-Smith, J. (2003) Health and behavior risks of adolescents with mixed-race identity. *American Journal of Public Health* 93(11): 1865–70.

Ulmer, C., McFadden, B. and Nerenz, D.R. (2009) *Race, ethnicity and language data: standardization for healthcare quality improvement.* Washington DC: National Academies Press.

Whaley, A. and Francis, K. (2006) Behavioral health in multiracial adolescents: the role of Hispanic/Latino ethnicity. *Public Health Reports* 121(2): 169–74.

Williams, D.R. (2012) Miles to go before we sleep: racial inequities in health. *Journal of Health and Social Behavior* 53(3): 279–95.

Wong, S., Sugimoto-Matsuda, J., Chang, J., and Hishinuma, E. (2012) Ethnic differences in risk factors for suicide among American high school students, 2009: the vulnerability of multiracial and Pacific Islander adolescents. *Archives of Suicide Research* 16: 159–73.

Woo, M., Bryan Austin, S., Williams, D.R., and Bennett, G.G. (2011) Reconceptualizing the measurement of multiracial status for health research in the United States. *Du Boise Review* 8(1): 25–36.

Zambrana, R.E. and Thornton Dill, B. (2006) Disparities in Latina health: an intersectional analysis. In A.J.Schulz and L. Mullings (eds) *Gender, race, class, and health intersectional approaches.* San Francisco, CA: Jossey-Bass.

TEN

Racial identity among multiracial prisoners in the color-blind era

Gennifer Furst and Kathleen Odell Korgen

As many race scholars have pointed out (e.g., Bonilla-Silva, 2013; Brunsma, 2006; Gallagher, 2007), growing numbers of Americans have turned against the one-drop rule and other traditional forms of racial identification. The spread of the color-blind ideology and the multiracial movement have led to vigorous debates about the necessity of racial categorizations and the move by the US Census to allow people to select more than one race. As other authors note in this volume, many people with mixed racial backgrounds demand a multiracial label and/or the abolishment of all racial labels (see also Daniel, 2002; Rockquemore and Brunsma, 2002; Spencer, 2006; Williams, 2008; Project Race, 2014).

The color-blind perspective on race goes along with the notion that we are in a post-racial society, as evidenced by the election of Barack Obama. The media often portray President Obama (who acknowledges his mixed racial background but identifies as Black), like other high-status multiracial persons, as able to make their race disappear by "transcending race" (e.g., Helman, 2007; Will, 2007). Noting that a Black President is indicative of a post-racial society, they maintain that racism is a remnant of the past and that racial categorizations—and discussions about racial inequality—only serve to needlessly divide people (Bonilla-Silva, 2013). Angie Beeman (2015: 237) describes the negative consequence of this color-blind practice as "racism evasiveness," explaining that "what people are ultimately avoiding when they say they do not see color, when they overlook differences in power, or avoid 'race words' is racism." The fact that increasing numbers of people with mixed-race heritages identify as multiracial indicates that racial identity and boundaries have become more fluid. It does not mean that racism no longer exists. The color-blind ideology and practices of racism evasiveness have, however, made the prevalence of racism, as well as people's racial identity, harder to gauge.

Researchers such as Harris and Sim (2002), Campbell (2010), and Burke and Kao (2010) show that different types of questions (open- or close-ended), answer selections (a "check all that apply" or a multiracial option), and where the survey is conducted (e.g., home or school) can influence whether or not people identify as monoracial or multiracial. Racial identity among those of mixed racial heritage is determined by multiple factors and may be fluid for many individuals these days.

The facade of a post-racial, multiracial, and/or color-blind society tends to fade and racial categorizations become more fixed farther down the social class ladder. This can be seen when looking at the influence of social class on the racial identity of Americans with both a Black and a White parent. Lower-class, less-educated Americans with one Black parent tend to be portrayed as Black—and see themselves as having no option but to identify as Black—because they fit the stereotypical image of Black people that equates blackness with poverty and low levels of education (Khanna, 2010; Saperstein and Penner, 2010; see also Chapter Four).

Male prisoners of a multiracial background with Black, Hispanic, or Native American heritage tend to find themselves fitting the worst of the stereotypes of young men of color—poor, uneducated criminals (Saperstein et al, 2014). Recent quantitative research has revealed that experiences with the criminal justice system increase the chances of people being identified by others as Black, Hispanic, or Native American, as opposed to White (Saperstein et al, 2014). It also shows that even one's racial *self*-identity can be shaped by time in prison. For example, Saperstein and Penner's (2010) research indicates that Latinos and other multiracial people with partially Black backgrounds are more likely to identify themselves as Black and less likely to identify as White after entering prison.

Moreover, prisoners of multiracial heritage find themselves in institutions where, at least officially, multiracial categories do not exist. Governmental sources of data, which are used by researchers, academics, and professionals to understand the people under the control of the criminal justice system in the US, categorize people according to monoracial categories. Historically, prison inmates have found themselves in highly racialized institutions that actively segregate them into racial "tribes." Even Goodman's (2008: 751) recent examination of racialization in California prisons, through his observation of the intake process, revealed that prisons are race-making "machines" in which inmates must racially identify themselves with "one (and only one) racial category" or be "labeled 'crazy.'"

The aforementioned findings led us to believe that we would discover that most of the inmates of multiracial descent interviewed for this study would identify, monoracially, as Hispanic, Black, or Native American and that the color-blind ideology would not have penetrated prison walls. We realized though, as Goodman (2008), Wacquant (2002), and others have pointed out, that "prisons are, to put it simply, woefully understudied locales, and the lack of attention to the construction of 'race' inside carceral facilities is a prime example of this paucity of research in prisons" (Goodman, 2008: 740). While the recent quantitative research on the relationship between prison and racial identity is helpful, it needs to be supplemented with more qualitative research.

We build upon the research described earlier by providing a qualitative analysis of the influence of prison on the racial identity of multiracial prisoners. In doing so, we provide information through semi-structured interviews of men incarcerated for having committed felonies in a north-eastern state. The information gained from these interviews allows us to begin to answer the following questions:

1. Is it possible to identify as multiracial in prison?
2. How does the prison experience impact the racial identification of prisoners from a multiracial background?
3. Has the color-blind ideology, so dominant in the larger society, permeated prison walls?

Methods

Participants were recruited at a residential risk assessment and re-entry treatment center that receives offenders from prisons run by the state Department of Corrections (DOC). The institution is operated by a corporation with facilities throughout the US. Inmates, referred to as residents while housed at the facility, receive a variety of therapeutic services focused on addiction, communication and life skills, and cognitive, behavioral, and emotional management. The facility houses up to 500 adult males. Residents must be eligible for community release, which means that inmates convicted of arson and sexual offences are excluded. Residents remain at the facility for approximately 90 days before being placed on parole and released into the community, transferred to a halfway house, or released into the community without supervision ("maxing-out"). New residents arrive at the facility three days per week and are transported out of the facility one day per week. Residents who violate the rules of the facility can be returned to prison.

As of 2 January 2014, 60% of inmates in the state where the facility is located were categorized as "Black," 23% as "White," 16% as "Hispanic," and 1% as "Asian." The state labels as "Hispanic" anyone who is of Mexican, Puerto Rican, Cuban, South American, or any other Spanish culture, regardless of skin color. The state does not specify how the determination of country of origin is made, but leaves it up to the discretion of the intake counselor to apply the labels.

Participants were recruited at the facility while attending their daily core curriculum lecture, which all the residents attend. The researcher who conducted the interviews introduced residents to the project. She identified herself as an independent researcher, unaffiliated with the state DOC or the corporation that operates the facility. She explained that the project was designed to investigate how incarceration affects racial identity. She informed the residents that they would not be compensated for their participation and that interviews would be confidential. She asked residents who were of multiracial descent, defined as having parents or grandparents of different races, to volunteer to participate. She also asked monoracial inmates interested in talking about race in prison to volunteer. She passed around a sign-up sheet and left the room so no one would feel pressured to volunteer.

Sample

A total of 71 male felony offenders were interviewed. Twenty-nine participants were monoracial, their parents and grandparents were of the same race; 42 participants were of multiracial descent, their parents and/or grandparents were of different races. Of the 29 monoracial participants, 13 identified as Black, seven identified as White, eight identified as Hispanic, and one identified as Indian (from Asia). Of the 42 participants with multiracial heritage, 18 were the first generation in their family to be multiracial (each parent was of one different racial group), while 24 were from a family of multigenerational multiracial descent. Of the 18 first-generation participants with parents of different races, six identified as Black, one identified as White, three identified as Hispanic, one identified as mixed, two identified as Hispanic and White, one identified as Hispanic and Black, two reported they have no racial identity, and two said that they identified as "other" (see Table 10.1). Of the 24 multigenerational participants, 13 identified as Black, one identified as White, two identified as Hispanic, three identified as Hispanic and Black, two reported they have no racial identity, one said that he identified as "other," one described himself as a "mutt," and one said he identifies as "multiracial" (see Table 10.2). In order to protect the identities of the participants and to make their respective racial backgrounds clear throughout the chapter, we refer to particular respondents by the numbers assigned to them in Tables 10.1 and 10.2.

According to information provided by the state's DOC webpage, the median age of inmates incarcerated in the state is 34 years; approximately one third are between each of the following age brackets: 21–30, 31–39, and 40 years or older. The median age of participants in this study was 31 years and the average age was 30 years (SD = 11 years). The median age of the 29 monoracial participants was 36 years, and the mean was 38 years (SD = 13 years). Of the 42 participants of multiracial descent, the median age was 28 years and the average age was 30 years (SD = 8 years). The median age of the 18 first-generation participants of multiracial descent was 27 and the average was 30 years (SD = 7 years). The median age of the 24 multigenerational participants with multiracial heritage was 29 years and the average age was 31 years (SD = 8 years).

Table 10.1: Racial identity of first-generation multiracial descent prisoners

ID#	Parents' race Mother	Father	Age	Racial identity	Speaks Spanish?	Total
5	BL	BL	29	BL	NO	N = 10
6	BL	H[1]	30	BL	NO	
8	NA	Haitian	37	BL	NO	
13	H[1]	WH	37	H[1]	YES	
53	WH	H[1]	24	WH	NO	
57	BL	H[2]	38	BL	NO	
64	BL	H[2]	26	BL	NO	
66	WH	H[1]	39	H[1]	YES	
70	H	BL	40	H	YES	
71	WH	BL	27	BL	NO	
11	NA	BL	36	Mixed	NO	N = 1
23	BL	WH	42	Does not identify racially	NO	N = 2
69	WH	BL	21	Does not identify racially	NO	
15	PR	WH	27	Identifies as H[1] and WH	YES	N = 2
47	WH	H[1]	24	Identifies as H[1] and WH	NO	
43	H[1]	BL	22	Identifies as H[1] and BL	NO	N = 1
63	H[1]	BL[1]	27	Identifies as "other"	YES	N = 2
68	WH	BL	21	Identifies as "other"	NO	

Notes: N = 18. H = Hispanic; BL = Black; WH = White; NA = Native American; H[1] = Puerto Rican; H[2] = Dominican; H[3] = Panamanian; BL[1] = Jamaican.

Table 10.2: Racial identity of multigenerational multiracial descent prisoners

ID#	Parents' race Mother	Father	Age	Racial identity	Speaks Spanish?	Total
4	BL	WH&BL	29	BL	NO	N = 16
7	H¹&WH	WH	32	WH	NO	
10	H¹	BL&H¹	38	H¹	YES	
17	BL	BL&WH	37	BL	NO	
24	PR&WH	H¹	21	H¹	YES	
25	H³&BL	BL	31	BL	NO	
26	BL	BL&NA	22	BL	NO	
29	BL,H,&WH	BL	22	BL	NO	
32	BL&NA	BL&BL²	44	BL	NO	
36	BL	WH&BL	33	BL	NO	
44	H¹&Haitan	BL²	42	BL	NO	
45	BL&WH	BL	43	BL	NO	
55	BL&NA	BL	43	BL	NO	
59	BL&NA	BL	26	BL	NO	
62	BL&WH	BL&NA	44	BL	NO	
65	WH&BL	BL	25	BL	NO	
9	BL&NA	BL&H¹	20	BL&H¹	YES	N = 3
14	H¹	H¹&BL	26	BL&H¹	NO	
67	H¹&BL	Haitan&BL	20	BL&H¹	NO	
19	H¹	WH&H¹	25	"Other"	NO	N = 3
21	WH&NA	WH&BL	29	"Mutt"	NO	
28	Does not know birth parents		22	Multiracial	NO	
3	NA,WH&P	BL	36	Does not racially identify	NO	N = 2
18ª	WH¹ &WH²	WH³	21	Does not racially identify	YES	

Notes: N = 24. H = Hispanic; BL = Black; WH = White; NA = Native American; P = Portuguese; H¹ = Puerto Rican; H² = Dominican; H³ = Panamanian; BL¹ = Jamaican; BL² = West Indian; WH¹ = Moroccan; WH² = Algerian; WH³ = Middle Eastern. ª He identified himself as being of multiracial ancestry when recruited for the study.

Researchers were not permitted to ask participants about their criminal charges. While participants' crimes did frequently come up in interviews, the researchers did not include questions about the nature of their crimes or the length of their sentences in the interviews. Therefore, the sample cannot be compared to the state population regarding criminal offense or length of sentence.

Findings

We now address each of the three research questions in turn.

Is it possible to identify as multiracial in prison?

Officially, people are not able to identify as multiracial in prison. As one respondent (#28, a 22-year-old who identifies as multiracial) reported: "they told me to just pick one, that I wasn't special and no one was gonna do extra work 'cause of me.'" Another respondent, #21, a 29-year-old with an Irish and Native American mother and an Irish and Black father, who described himself as a "mutt," described how he was categorized in the monoracial classification system:

> "[When I came into prison] they would check 'White.' I would check 'other.' Officer crossed it out and checked 'White' for me. I remember it quite clearly. They do that all the time. They have distinct things they go by."

As #3, a 36-year-old with a Native American, German, and Portuguese mother and an African-American father, who does not identify racially when given a choice not to, describes, in prison, "you are definitely boxed in with trying to explain who you are. Either Black, White, or Hispanic. DOC doesn't want to hear you're biracial or mixed. People don't want to hear it." He went on to describe how he would help the guards keep track of prisoners using a monoracial racial classification system: "I would run count slips at night. It had the officer's name, time, his radio number, and the number of Black, White, Hispanic in and out of the unit. They didn't have any in-betweens."

A 33-year-old with an African-American mother and an Italian and Black father, #36 explains how he and all other prisoners are given a monoracial label: "If they ask me my race, I say half-White, half-Black but they still put 'Black' on my tag. In prison you Black—that's it." The prison administration does not allow prisoners to identify as multiracial or to refuse to identify with a racial group.

On the other hand, the respondents indicated that they had more flexibility in how they identify themselves racially (or not) in conversations with fellow prisoners. As #15, a 27-year-old who identifies as both Puerto Rican and White, says:

> "some people can tell. I been going through it for so long. If they assume, let them. If they ask I tell them. It really don't make a difference to me. Most people in here call me a 'mutt'.... They say I talk like a White person, look Hispanic, and I'm in a Black gang."

As Table 10.1 indicates, eight out of 18 of the first-generation multiracial prisoners identify with more than one race or refuse to identify racially when describing themselves to others.

Relatively little research has been done on the racial identity of people of multigenerational multiracial descent (those with a multiracial background stemming from their grandparents rather than parents). Bratter's (2010) research on how multiracial parents racially identify their children indicated that nearly all of the children of parents who both identify as multiracial are also identified as multiracial by their parents. The majority (between 62% and 75%) of couples consisting of a partially Black and a monoracially Black person identify their children as Black alone. It seems likely, but not certain, that these children will identify themselves in similar ways when they are adults. The results of this study lend some support to that assumption. All eight of the prisoners of multigenerational multiracial descent who had three grandparents of the same race (Black) identified as Black.

How does the prison experience impact the racial identification of prisoners from a mixed racial background?

Nikki Khanna (2010: 55) compared public and internalized racial identities of multiracial persons when she looked at "how they label themselves to others" and the race with which they more strongly identify. Khanna found that public and internalized racial identities varied among her interviewees. Her sample consisted primarily of middle- and upper-middle-class young adults in college or recently graduated from college. The great majority (82.5%) identified themselves to others as multiracial but most tended to identify internally more strongly as either Black (60%) or White (22.5%).

Among our sample, however, almost all of the first-generation and multigenerational multiracial participants in this study indicated that how they racially identify to others (not including prison officials) and how they view themselves racially are consistent. The exception to this was #18, an interviewee with a racially ambiguous appearance, who has a mother of Moroccan and Algerian descent and a Palestinian father. He does not generally identify racially but has learned to put down "White" on employment forms:

> "I put 'White' on forms to get the job faster. I had five jobs from June 2011 to May 2012. Before that I'd say 'Asian' or 'African-American' or 'Other.' Never heard from them.

After they call me in, now I can present myself. 'White' works for me."

He is aware, through personal experience, of the discrimination that persons of color face on the job market (Pager et al, 2009).

As noted earlier, in prisons, a third type of identity, the monoracial race by which the institution racially classifies multiracial people, also comes into play. The prisoners interviewed in this study indicated that they did not care how they were officially racially classified in prison. These labels were just part of a system that labels them as bad—a label that they reject along with the racial identity assigned to them by administrators of the system.

A strong majority (80%) of the multiracial interviewees indicated that they did not face pressure to identify with one racial group or another by other inmates. A multigenerational multiracial of Black, Puerto Rican and Native American descent, #9 describes his experience this way: "I'm Black and Puerto Rican. Spanish people, Black people, I chill with everybody. It don't matter. I'm a fly person. I'm with everybody." Likewise, #11, who has a Native American mother and an African-American father, says that he is free to identify as multiracial and to interact with whomever he pleases:

> "I always tell people I'm mixed. When I first came to prison 20 years ago, 'Blacks' hung with 'Blacks,' and Hispanics with Hispanics. Now they hang out by gang. Then, I was expected to hang out with Spanish guys but not as much now. People asked, 'Why you always with them [Black guys]? If you Spanish, [why you] with Black guys?' People aren't as racist as they were back then."

Sharing #11's perspective is #15, who has a Puerto Rican mother and a White father:

> "Prison didn't influence me racially. I'll come out like I came in: I'm mixed.... You can be biracial in prison. You'll see all types of mixes in here. It's what you choose. 'Blacks' and PRs [Puerto Ricans] are Bloods. Some be Crips. Maybe I can relate to you a little better if you're a Crip [like me]. Most people are cool with whoever."

The vast majority of interviewees indicated that they felt free to share with other inmates their racial background.

The notable exception to this sense of freedom to racially identify as they please with fellow prisoners came from multiracial respondents who have Hispanic ancestry but do not speak Spanish. Hispanic respondents reported that, to be considered truly Hispanic or, as most of the interviewees described someone of Hispanic ethnicity, "Spanish," you must speak Spanish. The following representative quotes illustrate that trend:

> "A lot of Hispanics stick together. As long as you speak Spanish, it doesn't make a difference to them. A little more tighter-knit. They got music, language the same." (#15, 23-year-old, Puerto Rican mother and Italian father)

> "Puerto Ricans think I'm fake because I don't speak Spanish. I hit them with, 'Well, if you're African, do you speak African? And if you're White do you speak Polish?'" (#19, 25-year-old, Puerto Rican mother and three quarters Polish and one quarter Puerto Rican father)

> "If a guy is Spanish and Black and looks more Black, they'll say he's Black and he'll hang with 'Blacks.' But if he talks both [Spanish and English], he can be with both." (#24, 21-year-old, Puerto Rican and White mother and Puerto Rican father)

Among the first-generation multiracials with one Hispanic parent, all of the three who identified solely as Spanish speak Spanish. One of the two who identified as Puerto Rican and White speaks Spanish, and the one participant who identified as Puerto Rican and Black does not speak Spanish.

The other pattern of note was that none of the participants identified as Native American. Participants with Native American heritage mentioned their Native American ancestry but did not indicate any racial identification with it. Three first-generation multiracial participants reported having a Native American mother or father and eight second-generation multiracial participants indicated that they have a mother or father with some Native American ancestry. However, none of the participants racially identified as Native American.

Has the color-blind ideology, so dominant in the larger society, permeated prison walls?

The findings from the interviews provide ample evidence of the color-blind ideology permeating prison walls, especially among multiracial inmates. For example, #21 (a 29-year-old of multigenerational multiracial descent), a self-described "mutt," reported: "I like the idea that it shouldn't matter what [race] you are." Four of the 18 (22%) first-generation interviewees of multiracial heritage refuse to identify themselves in racial terms. Sixteen (89%) first-generation participants made some sort of statement that could be categorized as "color-blind." Seventeen (71%) of the multigenerational participants made a color-blind statement during the interview. Twenty (69%) monoracial participants also made color-blind statements.

Many interviewees of multiracial descent, however, proclaimed that race no longer matters in one sentence but shortly thereafter made a statement indicating the persistence of racial discrimination. For example, #6, who has a Black mother and a Puerto Rican father, said: "I don't think people get picked on for ethnicity [race] anymore." He went on to relate that his children (with White women) like being multiracial: "They say to me, 'Dad, I get a lot of girls cause of my looks, my hair.'… They got nice hair and skin." He described his children as having "the best of both worlds." A little later in the same interview, however, #6 shared that, when he first moved to his predominantly White suburb, "the cops used to stop me all the time" and noted that "it was probably racial profiling." Likewise, in the same interview, #11 said, "I don't look at people racially. If you're a nice person and I get along with you, we can talk" and "I try to stick to my own people in prison. Your own will have your back."

These statements exemplify how while they have been influenced by, and adopt the language and racial evasiveness tactics of, the color-blind perspective, many of the experiences of the participants of multiracial decent tend to contradict the message of the color-blind ideology that race no longer matters.

Fathering children across color lines

The percentage of respondents who have fathered children across racial lines, however, provides a very tangible indication of the diminishing impact of race on social interactions among this sample, particularly those with a multiracial background. Of the interviewees, 52 out of 71 (73%) had fathered children. Many had fathered multiple children with women of a variety of races. Of the 26 who had fathered children with more than one partner, half (13) had done so with women of different races. More than twice as many respondents of multiracial (9/13; 69%) as monoracial (4/13; 31%) heritage had fathered children with multiple women of different races.

The color-blind perspective was also less evident in the interviews with the monoracial participants. In general, monoracial respondents appeared to pay more attention to what they perceived as race-based differences among people. Unlike the respondents with multiracial backgrounds, the monoracial respondents did not have as many close interracial experiences. The following quotes are representative of the monoracial respondents' opinions of different racial groups and the influence of race in prison:

> [Regarding Black people.] "Everybody owe them something. The way they talk to they own family. They demand. Are dominant. Demanding." (#1, 49-year-old, Puerto Rican)

> "It's rare you find a White boy who's real hood, a thorough gangster. Most White boys are punks, they rather not fight. They don't really be standin' up for themselves except if it's a group of Aryan Nations. Latin Kings readily accept Blacks and Whites but the White boy gotta be double-checked they in it for the right reasons and not for protection. Blacks use White boys because the White boys get better jobs. Some Spanish people do that. But most Latinos show love and respect to everybody. Everybody that leaves I hope is replaced by a White or Puerto Rican. The last guy I want is a Black guy. Most is rude, ignorant, selfish, dirty troublemakers and is lazy. They put others at risk. By starting fights and not following rules. They jeopardize the whole unit. They disrespectful. Wanna be loud, rapping to the music. Especially the young ones—they the worst." (#37, 36-year-old, Puerto Rican)

> "[I couldn't] laugh or rib with my Black bunkie outside our room. [Black people are] selfish, grimy, greedy. We aren't savages. They will stab you in the back with no qualms. They rat out guys. Drop a slip. If you're White, you're an Aryan. If you're Black, you're banging. If you're Mexican, you're an illegal alien. Everything is based on appearance here." (#49, 38-year-old, White)

> "I believe racism has its power because people can be easily converted, especially in a prison setting because there's so much fear. The prison system also plays a part in the hostility. The gangbangers: when you separate me and mine

from them and those you're telling me to stay away from them. Maybe they're gonna jump me. Our minds gonna grow that way." (#38, 52-year-old, Black)

These quotes indicate that racial prejudice and stereotypes are alive and well within prison walls. Race still plays a very tangible role in prison life.

The influence of gangs

As noted earlier, the prison administration racially classifies all prisoners when they are processed upon entering the prison system. In today's prisons, however, where gangs have immense influence (Knox, 2005), one's gang identity can be seen as more important than one's race. According to #13, a 37-year-old with a Puerto Rican mother and a White father: "It's different in prison now. When I first started comin' to prison 20 years ago Blacks were with Blacks, Hispanics with Hispanics. Now, it's by gang. Gangs don't separate based on race." In fact, in terms of interacting with fellow inmates, gangs have taken some of the pressure off of having to identify racially and, instead, the pressure is to identify with a gang regardless of race (though gangs tend to be predominantly one race). As #11 explained: "Gangs just want numbers. It's different from when I first came to prison [20 years ago]." The focus of gangs on numbers, rather than race, is one example of increased signs of a color-blind perspective in prison.

Some prisoners report that it is even possible to join a gang traditionally regarded as race-based (like the Netas), regardless of your race. As #1, a 49-year-old Puerto Rican inmate, who is a Latin King, explains: "you can be Black, White, or Latino in the Latin Kings." A 21-year-old with a White and Puerto Rican mother and Puerto Rican father who speaks English and Spanish, #24 reported: "When it [Dios, Patrios y Libertad] first started, it was all-Spanish, now you grab anybody. It's all about numbers." A multigenerational multiracial with an African-American mother and a father who is both African-American and White, #17 agrees, saying: "In [this state], none of the gangs be about race. They just use them. Blacks and Spanish be extorting Whites. It's about numbers." A 24-year-old with a White mother and a Puerto Rican father, #53 echoes this thought: "Gangs are very diverse. Doesn't really matter about race with gangs in here." A 22-year-old with a Puerto Rican mother and a Black father, #43 also lends support to the idea that gang loyalty supersedes race: "Gang is more important than race. Because there's White Bloods. Not gonna be a race thing. If somethin' pops off, Bloods will be with him, not Whites." Respondent #36, a 33-year-old with a Black mother and an Italian and Black father, goes so far as to say that gang membership can actually obviate racial identity, declaring: "If you a White Blood you not White no more, you with your family—the Bloods."

These statements indicate that in order to recruit more members, gangs will act color-blind—as though race does not matter. However, there is rarely true equality when a person joins a gang in which he is a minority. White people who join Black gangs, for example, may find themselves being ill-used, as the following quotes indicate:

> "Blacks use White boys as stunt dummies [to do dangerous things]" (#37, 36-year-old, Puerto Rican)

> "Black Bloods call a White Blood their 'stunt dummy'" (#47, 24-year-old, Italian mother, Puerto Rican father)

> "Bloods and Crips have the White boys do the stupid stuff. They use them." (#52, 60-year-old, White)

So, while gang leaders may be open to taking people from races outside of the one traditionally associated with their gang in order to bolster their numbers, the status hierarchy within the gangs reveals that in prison gangs, just as in free society, race still matters. Moreover, research has found limited instances of White inmates belonging to traditionally Black gangs, but no cases of Black or Hispanic inmates in White prison gangs (Noll, 2012).

Race more of an issue in prison

A large majority of all respondents said that they thought prison was more racist than free society. Twelve of 18 (67%) participants with parents of different races, 16 of the 24 (67%) respondents with multigenerational multiracial heritage, and 22 of the 29 (76%) monoracial participants reported that they experienced more racial tension inside prison than out. Respondent #10, a 38-year-old with a Puerto Rican mother and a Black and Puerto Rican father, explained the difference this way: "In the hood, nobody hate nobody. In prison, I seen racists. Racist statements have been made to me. I just have to let it go." Respondent #14, a 26-year-old with a Puerto Rican mother and a Puerto Rican and Black father, echoed this, saying:

"A lot of Puerto Ricans be racist. Never seen that out there. Never knew that. Thought it was always between Black and White. I seen and learned a lot of new things. Not good things. Gangs and racism in here more than out on the street."

Likewise, #24, a 21-year-old with a White Puerto Rican mother and Puerto Rican father, portrayed prison in very racial terms: "In prison, it's all about race. The Spanish with the Spanish and the Black with the Black. On the streets, it's every race with each other. The Spanish are outnumbered so they stick together [in prison]." Respondent #32, a 44-year-old with an African-American and Native American mother and an African-American and West Indian father, described how correction officers (COs) regularly use racist language. He said: "They try and provoke you. I didn't experience that stuff out in society. It [racial prejudice] never affected me." In the bluntest of terms, #69, a 21-year-old with a White mother and Black father, called prison "the most racist place in the world." These quotes indicate that, while the color-blind ideology is evident in prison, especially among multiracial prisoners, it has not yet become as dominant as it now is in free society.

Conclusion

Our findings reveal that in prisons, as in the larger society, racial identity has become more fluid but the official racial categorizations of prison administrations have not yet adapted to these changes. Increasing numbers of people of multiracial backgrounds within, as well as outside, the prison system would like to identify themselves with more than one race—or no race at all. While we realize the necessity to identify people by race in the larger society and in prisons due to the need to track and address racism within both, prisons should adjust to the presence of more inmates who identify with multiple races. Prisons should conform with the racial classification systems used by the US Census to provide inmates with the opportunity to identify with more than one race, if they so choose.

The respondents with multiracial backgrounds do not indicate that the prison experience has impacted how they see themselves racially. This study, however, did not look at their racial self-identification before and after their prison experience, as did Saperstein and Penner (2010). Therefore, we cannot say for sure whether or not prison has an unconscious impact on the racial identity of our respondents.

Finally, most of the respondents of multiracial descent—but fewer of the monoracial ones—made statements indicating that they have been influenced by the color-blind ideology—and believe, to some extent, that race does not matter as much as it once did. Almost two thirds of multiracial- and close to one third of monoracial-descent respondents who fathered children with multiple mothers did so with women of various races. These findings provide some tangible evidence that interracial interactions, as well as racial identities, have become more fluid. Race policies in prison and in the larger society must adjust accordingly.

References

Beeman, A. (2015) Walk the walk but don't talk the talk: the strategic use of color-blind ideology in an interracial social movement organization. *Sociological Forum* 30(1): 127–47.

Bonilla-Silva, E. (2013) *Racism without racists: color-blind racism and the persistence of racial inequality in America*. Lanham, MD: Rowman and Littlefield.

Bratter, J. (2010) The "one drop rule" through a multiracial lens. In: K. Korgen (ed) *Multiracial Americans and social class*. London: Routledge, pp 184–204.

Brunsma, D. (ed) (2006) *Mixed messages: multiracial identities in the "color-blind" era*. Boulder, CO: Lynne Reinner Press.

Burke, R. and Kao, G. (2010) Stability and change in the racial identities of multiracial adolescents. In: K. Korgen (ed) *Multiracial Americans and social class*. London: Routledge, pp 39–50.

Campbell, M. (2010) Social class and multiracial groups: what can we learn from large surveys? In: K. Korgen (ed) *Multiracial Americans and social class*. London: Routledge, pp 165–83.

Daniel, G.R. (2002) *More than Black: multiracial identity and the new racial order*. Philadelphia, PA: Temple University Press.

Gallagher, C. (2007) New directions in race research. *Social Forces Special Section* 86(9): 1–9.

Goodman, P. (2008) "It's just Black, White, or Hispanic": an observational study of racializing moves in California's segregated prison reception centers. *Law & Society Review* 42(4): 735–70.

Harris, D.R. and Sim, J.J. (2002) Who is multiracial? Assessing the complexity of lived race. *American Sociological Review* 67(4): 614–27.

Helman, S. (2007) Obama shows an ability to transcend race. *The Boston Globe*, 10 August. Available at: http://www.boston.com/news/nation/articles/2007/08/19/obama_shows_an_ability_to_transcend_race/?page=full

Khanna, N. (2010) Country clubs and hip-hop thugs: examining the role of social class and culture in shaping racial identity. In: K. Korgen (ed) *Multiracial Americans and social class*. London: Routledge, pp 53–71.

Knox, G.W. (2005) The problem of gangs and security threat groups in American prisons today. Available at: http://www.ngcrc.com/ngcrc/corr2006.html

Noll, D. (2012) Building a new identity: race, gangs, and violence in California prisons. *University of Miami Law Review* 66: 847–78.

Pager, D., Western, B., and Sugie, N. (2009) Sequencing disadvantage: barriers to employment facing young Black and White men with criminal records. *Annals of the American Academy of Political and Social Science* 623: 195–213.

Project Race (2014) Project RACE. Available at: http://www.projectrace.com/about_us/our_history/project-race

Rockquemore, K.A. and Brunsma, D. (2002) *Beyond Black: biracial identity in America*. Thousand Oaks, CA: Sage.

Saperstein, A. and Penner, A.M. (2010) The race of a criminal record: how incarceration colors racial perceptions. *Social Problems* 57(1): 92–113.

Saperstein, A., Penner, A.M., and Kizer, J.M. (2014) The criminal justice system and the racialization of perceptions. *The Annals of the American Academy of Political and Social Sciences* 651: 104–21.

Spencer, R. (2006) *Challenging multiracial identity*. Boulder, CO: Lynne Rienner.

Wacquant, L. (2002) The curious eclipse of prison ethnography in the age of mass incarceration. *Ethnography* 3(4): 371–97.

Will, G. (2007) Obama transcends racial confinements. RealClearPolitics. Available at: http://www.realclearpolitics.com/articles/2007/12/obama_transcents_racial_confin.html

Williams, K. (2008) *Mark one or more: civil rights in multiracial America*. Ann Arbor, MI: University of Michigan.

ELEVEN

Multiraciality and the racial order: the good, the bad, and the ugly

Hephzibah V. Strmic-Pawl and David L. Brunsma

A recent Cheerios commercial featuring a Black–White biracial daughter along with her Black father and White mother incited a lot of debate about the implications of multiracial families (Elliot, 2014). Many multiracial families responded by posting their family photos to the "We Are The 15 Percent Tumblr," showing the beauty and strength, as well as positive change, that they represent. This Cheerios commercial and the consequent national conversation reflect a broader set of discussions about the implications of multiraciality, the resultant assemblage of meanings associated with and attached to the offspring of interracial sexual unions. Since its inception, the US has always been deeply engaged in conversations about race and racisms. As multiraciality continues to enter these debates, it is important to ask questions that force us to think about the various options that multiraciality presents and the potential impacts of these on the contemporary and future realities of race and racism.

Race is a human construction, one whose meanings are debated and defined by society. Thus, the meanings of multiraciality, as a racial category, also vary. Multiraciality is a complex and problematic notion because it both challenges and reifies the socially constructed, but experientially real, notion of race. On the one hand, it directly confronts the power of ascribed monoracial classifications, but, conversely, it still works within the language and ideologies of the racial classification system. We believe multiraciality is an important social and cultural barometer to watch.

Multiraciality within the matrix of race

To understand the importance of multiraciality in any society, one must analyze the relationship among: (1) racialization; (2) racial social structure; (3) racial ideologies and (4) racial policies. Racialization is a complex process—bound with domination, power, and politics—

whereby groups of people are ascribed racial identities and ranked within a society, its culture, and its institutions (Bashi, 1998). This ranking system comprises the racial social structure. Those in the top strata are conferred cultural, social, political, and economic benefits (Omi and Winant, 1991; Bonilla-Silva, 1997). The racialization process and changes in the racial social structure are guided by racial ideologies. In the contemporary US, the predominant racial ideologies are "color-blind" and "post-racial." The desire to be past our racial problems manifests itself in people thinking they do not *see* race. Race scholars, however, define color-blindness as a recent (post-1965) ideology that allows, largely, White people to ignore racism and believe that any persisting racial inequality is a consequence of socio-economic status, bad culture, and/or individual choices (Bonilla-Silva, 2003; Gallagher, 2003, 2006). Post-racialism acts in a similar manner in that it obscures the realities of racial discrimination, but does so by claiming that race and racism simply no longer exist (Vickerman, 2013). Living in a "color-blind" and "post-racial" racialized society is like putting on a special set of lenses that allows us to identify racial categories and talk about diversity but not recognize the realities of racism.

Racialization, racial social structure, and racial ideologies are tightly wound with the realm of policy regarding race. Racial policies can instigate institutional change and even modify racial categories, as well as the social and cultural meanings that we attach to a particular racial category. In doing so, they can fundamentally alter (or reproduce) the racial social structure. For example, the Immigration and Nationality Act 1965 abolished national origin quotas and put preference on immigrants' skills. As a result, between 1965 and 1985, four times more Asian immigrants entered the US than during the hundred-some years between the gold rush of 1849 and 1965 (Takaki, 1989). Such a racial policy led to a demographic change, which then led to a change in racial categories and their meanings. Prior to 1965, Asian-Americans were more commonly known as distinct ethnic categories, such as Japanese, Chinese, or Korean, and they experienced discrimination and negative stereotypes (Yoo, 2003). However, after 1965, the category of "Asian-American" emerged, along with the erroneous and prejudiced idea that Asian-Americans are "model minorities" who no longer experience discrimination (Chou and Feagin, 2008). We can learn from such moments in history that racial policies have the power to alter the future of multiraciality in the US.

Today, multiracial people have agency and many identify *as multiracial*; however, the ability to do so is tied to the larger racialization project of the US. In the US, the racialized social structure is White supremacy (as White is the dominant race), and the reigning racial ideologies are colorblindness and post-racialism. We use this framework to think through multiraciality and its perils and promises in contemporary US society. Will multiraciality create a positive window for racial reconciliation and bridge-building? Will multiraciality serve to reproduce or strengthen White dominance? We consider these and several other questions in order to assess the role of multiraciality in the US racial order. We close with some policy suggestions to help steer multiraciality in a positive direction.

The good: multiraciality moving racial reconciliation forward

Several positive implications and consequences of multiraciality in the US are already observable. In this section, we look at five: (1) the challenge to the "one-drop rule"; (2) a rise in people identifying with two or more races as part of an increasingly demographically diverse US; (3) society's cultural approval and even promotion of multiracial families; (4) a shift toward the acceptance of interracial relationships and multiracial children; and (5) the link between multiraciality and a more complex, yet accurate, view of racial identity as fluid and flexible. Multiraciality has changed the US demographically, ideologically, and culturally.

Social and cultural breakdown of the one-drop rule

The one-drop rule stated that if one had even one drop of Black blood, s/he was determined to be Black (Davis, 1991). This ruling was used to enforce the strict segregation of White people and Black people in all areas, including in marriage and family. Since the days of plantation slavery in colonial times up until the 1967 *Loving v. Virginia* Supreme Court decision, anti-miscegenation laws prohibited the "intermixing" of White people and Black people; this disdain for interracial coupling extended to their offspring. Mixed-race children were considered an abomination on society and any "mixed" children were considered Black because they were not "pure White" (Davis, 1991).

The long-standing power of the one-drop rule was successfully challenged when in the 1980s, there was a noticeable increase in mixed Black–White children choosing to identify as multiracial. These self-identifying multiracial children sent a strong message to society that their racial identification was a personal choice, not an ascribed one, *and* they constructed a new racial formula: no longer did "White +

Black = Black"; instead, "White + Black = biracial." There is really no overestimating the significance of this change in racial assignment for society's conceptions of racial categories and perceptions toward racial identity ascription.

"Browning of America": changing racial demographics

The "Browning of America" refers to the increased racial diversity of the US and the fact that, for the first time in the history of the nation, the majority of babies are of color. More than half of the growth in the US population between 2000 and 2010 was due to Hispanic population growth. The Asian population also saw a significant jump from 3.6% of the population to 4.8% in 2010. A part of this "Browning of America" is also the increase in people identifying with "two or more races," which saw a 32% increase between 2000 and 2010 (2.4% to 2.9% of the population). The choice to identify with White and Black was the largest multiple race combination (1.8 million people); one fifth of the "two or more races" population identified as White and Black/African-American. Other mixed-race populations also had significant population counts, with White and "some other race" at 1.7 million, White and Asian at 1.6 million, and White and American Indian/Alaska Native at 1.4 million (Humes et al, 2011).

The recent change in racial demographics was widely recognized by both scholars and the media. One example is Gibbs Leger's (2012) *Essence* article, entitled "Preparing for the browning of America," in which she states: "This coming change should also be an opportunity to continue to build the inter-ethnic coalitions we've seen across the country." Leger (2012) further suggests that increased racial diversity can be an asset to the stability and growth of the US as "with no one clear majority (economics aside), people of all races will have to work together to advance their common agendas." We can also continue to extrapolate out—and demographers have done so—to think through the possibilities of the next few decades. With the pressure of the US's rapid racial demographic changes, there may be corresponding shifts in the racialization processes, the racial social structure, and racial ideologies. Multiracial people, through resisting the single-box categories of the classic racial structure and claiming their preferred racial identity, greatly contribute to shifting both the demographic and cultural conversations around race.

The increasing popularity of multiraciality

The multiracial movement might have begun with a small group of families but the cultural popularity of multiraciality has spread. The Internet blogosphere and group chat options for self-identifying multiracial people are in the hundreds, with blogs such as Swirl, the Multiracial Network Blog, and Multiracial Asian Families. The Multiracial Network Blog alone averages 2,000 to 3,000 visitors a month. Multiraciality has also hit the art world with a range of programming, including National Public Radio's (NPR) Summer Blend Book Club, the Mixed Roots Festival, and Kip Fulbeck's The Hapa Project, which includes a book, traveling photographic exhibition, and online community forum (Lee, 2011; Fulbeck, 2014). The fascination with multiraciality is also apparent in marketing and consumer goods. The popular online companies CafePress and Zazzle sell a range of products, from Black and White biracial wedding invitations and "biracial pride" hoodies to products with more personalized slogans, such as "Italipino" (Italian and Filipino), "Blasian" (Black and Asian), and "Polarican" (Polish and Puerto Rican). Popular commercials also proudly use diverse characters; companies such as Apple and United Colors of Benetton use a multiracial cast of people and those deemed "ethnically ambiguous" in their marketing (La Ferla, 2003; DaCosta, 2006; Mueller, 2007).

DaCosta (2006) identifies the phenomenon of "multiracial marketing," wherein companies intentionally use a group known as "multiracial" and specifically distinguishes them from "monoracials" while also aiming for a message of racial harmony/blending. Companies including Cheerios, Swiffer, David's Bridal, and Honey Maid (graham crackers) increasingly use multiracial people and/or interracial families to sell their products (ProducerRobPerkins, 2012; Feloni, 2014; Highfill, 2014). Yet, well before Madison Avenue "celebrated" multiraciality through its marketing strategies, groups and communities around the country have celebrated various milestones of interraciality and multiraciality.

Every year, in many cities and towns across the US, a Loving Day celebration is held. This day of festivities commemorates the Supreme Court case *Loving v. Virginia* that banned anti-miscegenation laws. The Loving Day (2012) festival's stated goals are to: "Create a common connection between multicultural communities, groups and individuals, Build multicultural awareness, understanding, acceptance, and identity, Educate the public about the history of interracial relationships in order to fight prejudice." Such public and widespread celebrations of multiracial people, multiracial marketing, and the integration of multiracial people in art and popular culture bring multiraciality to the fore. Not only have people who self-identify as multiracial successfully proclaimed multiraciality for themselves, but their efforts have also been picked up and amplified through these other outlets.

Racial reconciliation

Multiracial people and multiraciality encourage a multicultural approach to race. Specifically, multiraciality is used as a tool to promote racial reconciliation. On a base level, multiracial families represent the union of diverse races. Interracial/interethnic heterosexual marriages grew 28% between 2000 and 2010. In 2010, 10% of heterosexual married couples were interracial, 18% of heterosexual unmarried partners were interracial, and 21% of same-sex unmarried partners were interracial (US Census Bureau, 2012). Many multiracial people also explicitly identify themselves as part of a racial reconciliation process (Strmic-Pawl, 2012). Strmic-Pawl notes that the multiracial people she interviewed often referred to a theme of "bridge-building." With a foot in each of two racial worlds, multiracial people feel that they can help racial groups understand one another and come together. For example, one participant who is White–Black, sees her role as biracial in an almost strategic manner:

> I was just always taught that the role of a biracial/multiethnic child is to bridge the gaps between Black and White or Asian and White and to help promote unity. It's pretty big. In this society, it's a huge marker, right?... So I think it's pretty big, identifying that [biraciality], so I can use it for whatever I need to use it for. (p 57)

As part of racial reconciliation and bridge-building strategies, Strmic-Pawl (2012) also finds that multiracial people identify themselves as occupying a special, unique status in that they feel that they represent the future of the US. One multiracial person, who is White–Korean, feels that more racial mixing should have a positive outcome for race relations: "Yeah—that has to reduce [racism] eventually. The more you come into contact with mixed races, the less you care about race, basically" (Strmic-Pawl, 2012, p 57). Kathryn, who is Filipino–White, also reflects a similar sentiment. She believes in the positive influence of multiraciality: "I hope more people are mixed and we can continue to be peace makers" (Strmic-Pawl, 2012, p 57).

Multiracial organizations and news commentators express similar messages about the potential of multiraciality to overcome racism. One multiracial advocacy organization, MAVIN (2014), states on its webpage:

> We see our work as part of a larger movement to end discrimination and inequality on individual and systemic levels. Ultimately, we see our work with mixed heritage issues as an important way to create supportive and inclusive communities for all people.

News outlets, likewise, discuss the positive future of race relations by noting the roles of President Obama and New York City Mayor De Blasio (who has a Black wife and two biracial children). An issue of *NY Magazine* entitled "Why the De Blasio family matters: meet the 'boring White guy' of the future" reviews how Obama and De Blasio, as important public figures, represent the future of the US, wherein biracial children and interracial families become not only accepted and the norm, but even perhaps desired (O'Connor, 2013).

The multiracial identity matrix

Multiraciality may also be leading to a broader and more holistically inclusive view of racial identities and identities more generally. Although racial identity is often described as an either/or choice, a recent paper by Brunsma, Delgado, and Rockquemore (2013) on multiracial identity theory points to the possibility that racial identity is *itself* multifaceted and that studying racial identity through the concept of the "identity matrix" is closer to the strategic and agentic formation, maintenance, and navigation of an identity for multiracial people. They argue that by exploring the *identities of multiracial people* rather than multiracial identity, we are beginning to more fully grasp the dizzying variation in individuals' identities. Such acknowledgment, should it become more of a reality on the ground, would indeed be a benefit—leading to higher potential for interracial or cross-racial interactions, friendships, and intimacies. As the reality of individuals' multiracial experiences within the matrix is acknowledged, the various hooks that connect people increase. Acknowledging that individuals have a plurality of identities (roles, political views, religious identities, etc) in addition to their master statuses (race/multiracial, gender, etc) allows for more points of connection among people.

The bad: multiracial as status quo

As discussed in the previous section, there are some openings for multiraciality to challenge the power of the racial hierarchy. Multiraciality, with informed policies and campaigns, can help shape more egalitarian racial ideologies and structures (see the suggestions at the end of the chapter). At the same time, it is possible that multiracial people can fit into the logic and structure of the existing racial order. Bonilla-Silva (1997: 469) contends that "in all racialized social systems the placement of people in racial categories involves some form of hierarchy that produces definite social relations between the races." For Bonilla-Silva, and similar scholars of race, including Bell (1992), Crenshaw (2011), and Feagin (2006), there is an inherent tie between the existence of race, the racial hierarchy, and racism. Despite hopes for attaining a color-blind or post-racial society in the 21st century, there is still a racial hierarchy in place. In this section, we discuss the ways in which multiraciality might support, rather than contest, a racial hierarchy.

Using boxes to deconstruct boxes

As mentioned in other chapters of this volume, early multiracial organizations accomplished one of their goals by convincing the government to change how the racial identity question is posed on federal forms. Prior to 1997, respondents checked one, and only one, box, but respondents are now permitted to mark multiple boxes. On the one hand, this change permits people to identify with as many boxes as they feel are true to themselves. Their options, however, are still restricted by boxes. The idea that race is a box that can be checked still constricts our conceptual ideas about the fluidity and flexibility of racial identity. Moreover, marking two boxes, rather than marking just one, does not do much to challenge the ideological power of race. Choosing two (or more) races, and identifying as multiracial, relies on the logic that there are "races" that can be mixed, thereby suggesting a biological reality to race. Thus, one negative implication of multiraciality is that it moves us outside one box but only to other boxes.

Multiracial people face status distinctions

The fundamental idea behind the push for multiracial identification is that there is something different and distinct about multiracial people in comparison to monoracial people. Following this logic, it is also presumed that there is a common experience among multiracial people, which is why they should share the same racial label. There are some commonalities among multiracial people (Strmic-Pawl, 2012), but there are at least three (interconnected) fundamental ways in which there are status distinctions among multiracial people: the type of racial "mix," skin tone, and class status.

Multiracial people can be a combination of any two or more races, yet using the term "multiracial" can gloss over significant differences in one's experience as multiracial. For example, Asian–White people, Asian–Latina/os, and Asian–Black people will have very different experiences as multiracial. Also, while those identifying as both Black and White are the fastest-growing "two or more races" group, they continue to face discrimination in ways that other multiracial groups do not. There are also distinctions regarding the skin tone of the multiracial individual. There are cultural expectations that mixed means having a light-brown skin tone; thus, multiracial individuals who are not part-White or do not look light are not as easily recognized as mixed. Moreover, "non-White" with "non-White" multiracial people are less numerically common and receive less attention as part of the multiracial community (for more information, see Chapter Two) (Strmic-Pawl, 2014).

Class status also shapes the experiences of mixed-race people. As class status influences culture, education, employment, and networking opportunities, it also shapes how multiracial people are received by society, as well as how they might self-identify. Those with a lower-class status may not identify as multiracial as they do not feel as much agency in their racial identity choices compared to those with a higher-class status (for more information on interactions between class and multiracial people, see Chapter Four; see also Korgen, 2010).

In all of these three interconnected status distinctions—type of racial mix, skin tone, and intersections with class—multiracial people face status distinctions that relegate them into a hierarchy. Intersections with other salient identities such as gender and sexual orientation can also support racial status distinctions among multiracial people. Thus, identifying as multiracial does not necessarily provide an escape from the racial structure.

The ugly: reification of the hierarchy and Whiteness

There is evidence which suggests that multiraciality not only fits within the current racial logic, but also helps to affirm and support it. Many multiracial people do better socio-economically in comparison to monoracial people of color in the racial hierarchy (as Campbell and Barron show in Chapter Two), and multiracial people can act as a "middleman" minority. Another way in which multiracial people are also at risk of upholding Whiteness is by adopting the racial logics of White people.

Multiracial people compete for a top spot

Some multiracial people do better than their monoracial counterparts. As multiraciality increasingly becomes en vogue, we see a push against those who are "just Black" or "just Asian," therefore reifying a hierarchical logic. For example, we see that Black–White people do better socio-economically than Black people, and Native American–White people do better than Native Americans. Also, the same push that we see in marketing multiracial people to achieve a more cosmopolitan look can also result in the implicit degradation of people of color who are not mixed (Beltran, 2005; Victorian, 2012).

Even worse, multiracial people can bolster a White-dominated racial hierarchy if they operate as a middleman buffer group between White people and other monoracial groups. Bonilla-Silva and Embrick (2006) suggest that the future hierarchy may have an "honorary White" status that includes many multiracial people who have light complexions. In this instance, multiracial people serve the purpose of maintaining the line between "White" and "other" by creating distance between White people and people of color and decreasing coalition possibilities among racial groups. Efforts to challenge the power of the racial structure and Whiteness are suppressed if multiracial people become more enticed by the rewards of a higher position in the hierarchy rather than contesting it (Bashi Treitler, 2013).

Upholding Whiteness

Multiracial people can support the White-dominated racial hierarchy by adopting the color-blind and post-racial ideologies commonly held by those at the top. Those who act as the buffer between White people and "others" tend to adopt the logics that will help them maintain that position. For example, in Strmic-Pawl's (2012) study, she finds that her Asian–White respondents adopt color-blind and/or post-racial ideologies and a "White privilege" logic. When asked about racialized policies such as school busing and affirmative action, they rejected such policies by relying on color-blind logics such as a belief in meritocracy and seeing failure as a result of bad culture. When asked about their racial identity, they also reflected ideas similar to "White privilege" by responding that they "feel normal" and stating that they were largely unaware of racism. In contrast, Black–White respondents were highly cognizant of racial differences and racial discrimination. This vast difference in understanding racial identity and the consequences of race exposes how some multiracial people, who have a higher status within the existing racial structure, can (unintentionally) bolster the racial structure and reinforce White dominance.

Moving multiraciality forward

Multiraciality is, without a doubt, breaking some racial boundaries in the US. From multiracial organizations, multiraciality in the media, and the choices of multiracial people themselves, we see changes in the racial social structure, the racial ideologies, the racialization process, and racial policies. As discussed in this chapter, these changes are evident in the weakening of the one-drop rule, changing racial demographics, improved portrayals of people of mixed-race descent in popular culture, movement toward racial reconciliation, and a significant turn toward understanding race and racial identity as more fluid and flexible. All of these changes are laudable and denote a marked improvement in how race, and multiraciality specifically, operates in the US.

Despite the positives that multiraciality brings, there is a bad and ugly side to the ways in which multiraciality operates. The logic of multiraciality is potentially locked within the racial social structure, racial ideologies, and racialization process of the US. First and foremost, multiraciality makes sense only because it uses racial boxes and a biological view of race. Multiracial is the "mixing" of races, yet one cannot be "half and half" when "races" do not exist in any biological reality. Thus, multiraciality dangerously relies upon and reinforces a biological idea of race and the social power of race.

People were labeled with racial categories in order to create a racial hierarchy, and this hierarchy is maintained through racism. This relationship between race and racism is why we see status distinctions among multiracial people and multiracial people becoming part of and participating in the racial social structure. From the ugliest perspective, it becomes clear that multiraciality should be condemned if it becomes a part of the racialization process of working toward Whiteness, becomes bound by the White supremacy racial social structure, and adheres to the color-blind and post-racial ideologies. Thus, the underlying question driving this chapter is: what policies might be instituted to steer multiraciality in the right direction?

We opened this chapter by briefly describing the relationship among racialization, racial social structure, racial ideologies, and the policies that can shape the interactions among these forces. To help multiraciality move toward the good, and away from the bad and the ugly, we put forth three policy suggestions for multiracial people and multiracial-affiliated organizations: (1) adopt a clear statement declaring the social construction of race; (2) develop broad cross-racial coalitions with other race-based organizations; and (3) create project goals that include not only the recognition of multiracial identity, but also programs that directly address the oppression of people of color (to be directed at any number of issues, such as inequality in wealth, residence, education, and criminal punishment).

The first suggestion reduces the likelihood of falling prey to the racialization process of Whiteness by reaffirming the socially constructed nature of race and inherent faulty logic of a "White race." The second suggestion of cross-racial coalitions challenges the White supremacy social structure by creating relationships across racial boundaries. Finally, the third suggestion to create projects that address racial oppression reminds people of the ongoing realities of racial discrimination, thereby debunking the color-blind and post-racial ideologies. If people promoting multiraciality can be aware of the possible pitfalls that come with promoting a new racial identity, then multiraciality might lend itself to positive racial change.

References

Beltrán, M.C. (2005) Only the fast, furious, (and multiracial) will survive. *Cinema Journal* 44(2): 50-67.

Bashi, V. (1998) Racial categories matter because racial hierarchies matter: a commentary. *Ethnic and Racial Studies* 21(5): 959–68.

Bashi Treitler, V. (2013) *The ethnic project: transforming racial fictions into ethnic factions.* Stanford, CA: Stanford University Press.

Bell, D. (1992) *Faces at the bottom of the well: the permanence of racism.* New York, NY: Basic Books.

Bonilla-Silva, E. (1997) Rethinking racism: toward a structural interpretation. *American Sociological Review* 62(3): 465–80.

Bonilla-Silva, E. (2003) *Racism without racists: color-blind racism and the persistence of racial inequality in the United States.* Lanham, MD: Rowman and Littlefield Publishers, Inc.

Bonilla-Silva, E. and Embrick, D.G. (2006) Black, honorary White, White: the future of race in the United States? In: D. Brunsma (ed) *Mixed messages: multiracial identities in the "color-blind" era.* Boulder, CO: Lynne Rienner Publishers, pp 33–48.

Brunsma, D.L., Delgado, D., and Rockquemore, K.A. (2013) Liminality in the multiracial experience: towards a concept of identity matrix. *Identities: Global Studies in Culture and Power* 20(5): 481–502.

Chou, R.S. and Feagin, J.R. (2008) *The myth of the model minority: Asian Americans facing racism.* Boulder, CO: Paradigm Publishers.

Crenshaw, K.W. (2011) Twenty years of critical race theory: looking back to move forward. *Connecticut Law Review* 43: 1253–352.

DaCosta, K. (2006) *Making multiracials: state, family, and market in the redrawing of the color line.* Stanford, CA: Stanford University Press.

Davis, J.F. (1991) *Who is Black? One nation's definition.* University Park, PA: Pennsylvania State University Press.

Elliot, S. (2014) An American family returns to the table. *The New York Times*, 28 January. Available at: http://www.nytimes.com/2014/01/29/business/media/an-american-family-returns-to-the-table.html?_r=1

Feagin, J. (2006) *Systemic racism: a theory of oppression.* New York, NY: Routledge.

Feloni, R. (2014) Swiffers' new ad features a real multiracial couple and an amputee dad who cleans the house. *Business Insider.* Available at: http://www.businessinsider.com/swiffer-ad-with-the-rukavina-family-2014-1

Fulbeck, K. (2014) About The Hapa Project. Available at: http://kipfulbeck.com/the-hapa-project/hapa-about/

Gallagher, C. (2003) Color-blind privilege: the social and political functions of erasing the color line in post race America. *Race, Gender & Class* 10(4): 1–17.

Gallagher, C. (2006) Color blindness: an obstacle to racial justice? In: D. Brunsma (ed) *Mixed messages: multiracial identities in the "color-blind" era.* Boulder, CO: Lynne Rienner Publishers, pp 103–17.

Gibbs Leger, D. (2012) Preparing for the browning of America. *Essence*, 23 May. Available at: http://www.essence.com/2012/05/22/preparing-for-the-browning-of-america/

Highfill, S. (2014) Honey Maid takes a stance for "Love" in new commercial—video. *Entertainment Weekly.* Available at: http://popwatch.ew.com/2014/04/04/honey-maid-commercial/

Humes, K.R., Jones, N.A., and Ramirez, R.R. (2011) Overview of race and Hispanic origin: 2010, 2010 Census Briefs. U.S. Census Bureau, C2010BR-02.

Korgen, K. (ed) (2010) *Multiracial Americans and social class: the influence of social class on racial identity.* New York, NY: Routledge.

La Ferla, R. (2003) Generation E.A.: ethnically ambiguous. *The New York Times*. Available at: http://www.nytimes.com/2003/12/28/style/generation-ea-ethnically-ambiguous.html

Lee, F. (2011) Pushing boundaries, mixed-race artists gain notice. *The New York Times*. Available at: http://www.nytimes.com/2011/07/06/arts/mixed-race-writers-and-artists-raise-their-profiles.html?

Loving Day (2012) About Loving Day. Available at: http://www.lovingday.org/about

MAVIN (2014) About—Purpose. Available at: http://www.mavinfoundation.org/new/purpose/

Mueller, B. (2007) *Communicating with the multicultural consumer: theoretical and practical perspectives.* New York, NY: Peter Lang Publishing, Inc.

O'Connor, M. (2013) *Why the De Blasio family matters: meet the "boring White guy" of the future.* New York: New York Media LLC. Available at: http://nymag.com/thecut/2013/09/why-the-de-blasio-family-matters.html

Omi, M. and Winant, H. (1991) *Racial formation in the United States: from the 1960s to the 1990s.* New York, NY: Routledge.

ProducerRobPerkins (2012) David's Bridal commercial. Online video. Available at: https://www.youtube.com/watch?v=KwptYWxk0U8

Strmic-Pawl, H.V. (2012) *"What are you?" Multiracial identity and the persistence of racism in a "post-racial" society.* Charlottesville, VA: University of Virginia.

Strmic-Pawl, H.V. (2014) The influences affecting and the influential effects of multiracials: multiraciality and stratification. *Sociology Compass* 8(1): 63–77.

Takaki, R.T. (1989) *Strangers from a different shore: a history of Asian Americans.* New York, NY: Penguin Books.

US Census Bureau (2012) *2010 Census shows interracial and interethnic married couples grew by 28 percent over decade.* Washington, DC: Census Bureau. Available at: http://www.census.gov/newsroom/releases/archives/2010_census/cb12-68.html

Vickerman, M. (2013) *The problem of post-racialism.* Hampshire: Palgrave Macmillan.

Victorian, B. (2012) Biracial chicks get no love in Hollywood? Juliette Fairley missed the mulatta is the new Black memo. *MadameNoire*. Available at: http://madamenoire.com/203047/biracial-chicks-get-no-love-in-hollywood-i-think- juliette-fairley-missed-the-mulatta-memo/

Yoo, D.K. (2003) Testing assumptions: IQ, Japanese Americans, and the model minority myth in the 1920s and 1930s. In: S. Chan (ed) *Remapping Asian American history*. Walnut Creek, CA: AltaMira Press, pp 69–85.

TWELVE

Multiracial identity and monoracial conflict: toward a new social justice framework

Andrew Jolivette

This chapter describes how the growth of the multiracial population is impacting traditionally monoracial organizations and efforts to impact public policy. As multiracial subjects increase their participation in monoracial or non-ethnic specific organizations, they can: (1) transform advocacy groups founded on traditional understandings of identity-based organizing; and (2) radically alter, disrupt, and destroy notions of ethnic and racial authenticity as fundamental qualifications for participation in social movements.

Through examining the merits of multi-issue organizing and the participation of multiracial people in four San Francisco Bay Area social justice organizations (Data Center for Research Justice; Speak Out—Institute for Democratic Education and Culture; the Native American Health Center's Circle of Healing program; and the African American Art and Cultural Complex [AAACC]), I show how multiracial people are transgressing social, economic, cultural, and political boundaries to produce meaningful social reforms in the areas of health, education, labor, and Lesbian, Gay, Bisexual, Transgender, Queer or Questioning (LGBTQ) rights.[1] The chapter concludes with a social justice framework for advocacy groups that will allow for the full civic engagement of multiracial people in the US and, in the process, make these organizations more effective.

Multi-issue organizing has a long history, dating back to community organizer Saul Alinsky's labor rights activism in the 1930s. Multi-issue organizing in the Alinsky tradition posits that when you organize people of different class and racial and ethnic backgrounds, you must create a political platform that a broad range of people and groups can buy into. You must also build power through addressing "winnable" issues. According to *Dissent Magazine*:

Organizers seek what Alinsky called "immediate, specific, and winnable issues." These are tools to build power that can subsequently address more deeply embedded problems. Success can be used to convince the skeptics on the sidelines to participate. When more people participate, more people power is built and more recalcitrant issues can be addressed. Multi-issue organizing is required because different people experience different problems with different degrees of intensity at different points in their lives. The single working mother without extended family supports is interested in childcare; the homemaker mom with teenagers is interested in the local middle or high school. The retiree who depends on public transportation has yet a different concern. The organization that wants to involve all of them has to offer the possibility of addressing all their concerns in the not-too-distant future. A believable picture of what people power can accomplish must be painted; the initial painter is a professional community organizer. (Miller, 2010)

In Alinsky's model of multi-issue organizing, it becomes clear that addressing a wide range of winnable issues can bring masses of people together to address problems of inequality.

Some three decades later, in 1974, African-American feminists reasserted the importance of multi-issue organizing across different sets of social and political identities with the publication of the Combahee River Collective Statement (see Circuitous.org, no date). The statement raised important issues relating to intersectionality and multi-issue organizing that had been a principle of Black feminists since the 1960s. The signatories declared their desire to fight "a whole range of oppressions" that intersect and reinforce one another, including, racism, sexism, heterosexism, and classism.

Despite over 80 years of research and writing on the need for organizing across differences and the need for the inclusion of different types of bodies and political issues in social justice movements, however, there continues to be a lack of focus on multi-issue organizing when it comes to different racial and ethnic groups. While many interracial solidarity organizations exist, the majority of organizations based on race or ethnicity are monoracial rather than multiracial or multi-ethnic in their mission and organizing practices. In this instance, I use both multiracial and multi-ethnic to refer to mixed-race people and to multiracial organizations with diverse population demographics. Critical Mixed Race Studies, as an emerging movement, attempts to build upon intersectional principles of social justice and policy reform by making strategic use of the experiences of mixed-race, biracial, and multiracial community organizers to bridge the divides between monoracial organizations and mixed-race/multiracial communities.

As other authors in this volume have noted, the multiracial population grew by more than 32% between 2000 and 2010 and continues to increase rapidly. However, multiracial people still tend to be ignored by non-profit and community-based organizations working with communities of color, which must often compete with one another for funding. For example, racial- or ethnic-specific LGBTQ and HIV/AIDS community-based organizations often compete for the same buckets of economic funding in order to maintain their operations. As this funding is often based on racial- or ethnic-specific community demographics, multiracial people and multi-issue organizing are often neglected or become peripheral issues.

Cathy Cohen (1999) addresses this tension in her book, *The boundaries of blackness*, with her description of consensus issues, cross-cutting issues, and secondary marginalization. According to Cohen, consensus issues are social problems and concerns that communities place at the center of their organizing agendas because they impact the "majority" of the members of that population. Cross-cutting issues are those issues that impact some members of the community but may not be of concern to the majority, so they are not given any priority in calls for policy reform. The pushing of these issues to the periphery creates a form of secondary marginalization, where the issues facing the most vulnerable members of a population (i.e, lesbian, gay, bisexual, and transgender [LGBT] people, women, immigrants, the formerly incarcerated, and people living with disabilities) are diminished not just by mainstream society, but by members of their own racial or ethnic groups. For multiracial people, working within and seeking services from monoracial organizations can set up difficult identity-based binaries, where singular issues and calls for racial authenticity can serve as impediments to healthy participation and development.

The election of President Barack Obama has had some impact on the public visibility of multiracial citizens, but despite the election of a biracial person to the presidency and the growth of the mixed-race population, there are still very few organizations dedicated to multiracial organizing and social justice. The impact of President Obama's biracial identity is also somewhat less significant, at least politically, as he identifies publicly as African-American and not mixed-race. As more monoracial and multiracial people adopt a critical mixed-race framework, however, there will be greater opportunities for multi-issue organizing within traditionally monoracial community-based organizations.

Research justice: the DataCenter and multiracial, multi-issue policy reform and advocacy

The DataCenter for Research Justice was founded in 1978 to establish a national clearinghouse for the collection of data and research by and for underserved communities and to influence policy impacting marginalized, often neglected, populations. Since its establishment, the organization has worked on issues ranging from health-care reform, rights for families of prisoners, and indigenous water rights, to immigrant rights. While the initial make-up of the staff and founders was primarily White, over time, many of the participants in and leaders of research projects have come from indigenous nations and communities of color.

One of the DataCenter's recent projects, "Voces del Canal," was a collaborative project between multiracial/multi-ethnic Latina/o community members in San Rafael, California, and members of the DataCenter staff, along with faculty members at Dominican University of California. A mixed-race people, Latinos are often placed into quasi-monoracial categories, but the social and cultural issues facing the residents of San Rafael demonstrate how their mixed-race identities impact their daily lives, from language to education—as well as racial misrepresentation. The community members who carried out the study presented their research in a public forum that included the San Rafael Mayor, members of Marin County's Board of Supervisors, and the San Rafael Chief of Police. They shared the concerns of the residents in the community, including the need for "a better quality education and after-school programming for their children, more parent resources, and improved coordination and delivery of family services" (DataCenter for Research Justice, 2014c: 3).

The "Voces del Canal" project demonstrates a principle of Alinsky's organizing approach: when you focus on multiple issues, you can draw in people from different racial and ethnic backgrounds, gain people power, and create positive change. The residents of the Canal community in San Rafael—an ethnically diverse area—found that when they collaborate and work together, they can gain strength and influence policies affecting their community. The results of their efforts led to a greater focus by elected and appointed officials on their community and collaborations across racial and linguistic differences.

The DataCenter's model is important for multiracial, mixed-race organizing because of the group's focus on including all voices in a community-based, participatory approach. In many other organizations, people of mixed descent find their voices rendered mute, and rather than finding collaboration, they are forced to fall within a one-dimensional, often monoracial, framework. The DataCenter describes its participatory research methods model this way:

> When we conduct grassroots research [on our communities] through surveys, oral histories and other projects, we counter the belief that there is only one side to the story.... Part of oppression is keeping information and knowledge in the hands of the powerful. When we reclaim research, we walk one step closer to achieving liberation. (DataCenter for Research Justice, 2014b)

The DataCenter works with community members—of all races and ethnicities—to help them document and understand their experiences as they build social justice campaigns and movements.

In addition to focusing on policy reform, the DataCenter also utilizes a robust programming mechanism that speaks directly to the power of multi-issue organizing by and among multiracial people. Several of the current and previous board members and staff at the DataCenter are themselves from multiracial/ethnic backgrounds, and in 2013 and 2014, these individuals played key roles in the organization of international community events that highlighted the importance of what the DataCenter terms "research justice." The forthcoming anthology, *The research justice handbook: envisioning sacred methodologies*, defines research justice in the following way:

> Research Justice (RJ) is a strategic framework and methodological intervention that seeks to transform structural inequities in research. RJ centralizes community voices and leadership in an effort to facilitate genuine, lasting social change and seeks to foster critical engagement with communities of color, indigenous peoples, and other marginalized groups to use research as an empowering intervention and active disruption of colonial policies and institutional practices that contribute to the (re) production of social inequalities in research and public policy. DataCenter believes that research justice is achieved when marginalized communities are recognized as experts,

and reclaim, own and wield *all* forms of knowledge and information. (Jolivette, 2015: emphasis in original)

We must, as the research justice paradigm embraced by the DataCenter suggests, recognize that cultural and experiential knowledge can be attained when marginalized communities are recognized as experts. We must see multiracial people as policy experts in their own right who should not be shut out of monoracially dominated organizing

Multiracial people must be involved in the process of telling their story. As Linda Smith (2015) explains:

> Sometimes we tend to think what we know is so special that it's sacred, perhaps it is. But sometimes its sacredness comes from putting the pieces of knowledge together collectively.... What makes that knowledge sacred is not that a few people know it, but that it is known by many. That's where I would start.... A community [needs] to believe that what it knows about itself is unique and is a story that needs to be told, but [also] that it is a story that only they can tell.

The DataCenter places the experiences of people of mixed descent at the center of many of their important projects and campaigns by soliciting the feedback and guidance of multiracial people both from the communities they work with and from the members of their board of directors. Other Bay Area organizations are also seeing a rise in the participation of multiracial leaders who simultaneously seek increased visibility for ethnic-specific groups and for multiracial people.

Circle of Healing: multiracial Native American identity, voice, and public visibility as a strategy for policy reform

Native Americans and organizations with a focus on the rights of indigenous peoples are an important marker for measuring multiracial political participation in the shaping of public policies. As the ethnic group with the highest percentage of interracial marriage (50%) and racially mixed people (more than 70%), Native American are fighting to maintain ethnic-specific identities (US Census Bureau, 2010). It is within this context, that the Native American Health Center (NAHC) in the San Francisco/Oakland, California area launched its Circle of Healing program in 2011. The mission of Circle of Healing focuses on culturally diverse and inclusive services for those living with or at high risk of HIV infection:

> Circle of Healing is a culturally diverse staff of the Native American Health Center that serves the Bay Area community. We are open to all with a focus on serving the Native community. We provide prevention & HIV/ AIDS and HCV services in a caring, supportive, culturally rich, and community-focused environment. Our goal is to offer a spectrum of service from prevention into treatment, which includes education, practical support, coordination of services & advocacy. (Native American Health Center, no date)

Circle of Healing's success is in large part due to its massive public visibility campaigns around knowing one's HIV status. As the Native American populations have such a high degree of racial mixing, many mainstream health-care facilities and hospitals often misidentify members of this community as belonging to another racial group. Due to this issue, Circle of Healing launched a twofold media campaign back in 2011.

The media campaign makes use of community posters with images of elders, youth, and adults with varying phenotypes to demonstrate the physical and cultural diversity of the Native American population. In addition to the media photo campaign, the group also incorporates a digital storytelling component that traces and documents the life stories of people of Native descent who also self-identify as lesbian, gay, bisexual, transgender, two-spirit,[2] and queer. This multi-identity approach, like that of the DataCenter, is inclusive and represents an approach that brings greater visibility to the experiences of multiracial people as change agents in campaigns for policy reform in public health.

Circle of Healing has initiated several important programs and campaigns that impact policies at the Native American Health Center. The digital storytelling project has brought together mixed-race indigenous peoples across different generations to tell their stories of survival, coming out as LGBTQ, addressing HIV/AIDS disparities, relocation, and battles against assimilation. This program allows more Native women, children, and men to relate to one another and to share their stories with city officials and organizations working to improve public health and wellness within urban Native American communities. The Circle of Healing program's "I know" campaign uses social media outlets such as Twitter, Instagram, and Facebook, as well as print media, to encourage Native people of various phenotypes and racially mixed backgrounds to learn their HIV status by getting tested.

The "I know" campaign includes elders, youth, and adults and uses photographs of members of the community to create effective advertisement campaigns targeting individuals who may not know their status or who, because of their mixed-race background, may not be identified as Native American. This project is important in terms of its policy implications because there is a history of miscategorizing and underreporting HIV cases among Native people. This is due, in part, to racial mixing and stereotypes about what Native Americans look like in contemporary society. Presentations by Circle of Healing to the Mayor of San Francisco's Office, federal public health agencies, and community-based organizations influence beliefs, attitudes, and perceptions of mixed-race identity and encourage the recognition of more Native Americans regardless of their phenotypical features or enrollment status.

Like the DataCenter, Circle of Healing serves as an excellent example of how many community-based organizations recognize the growing numbers of multiracial people and are reaching out to them. They are making an effort to ensure that when it comes to issues like public health-care access, prevention, and treatment, mixed-race individuals are included and not left on the margins.

Speak Out—The Institute for Democratic Education and Culture as a model for multiracial engagement and resistance among college students and university administrators

The Institute for Democratic Education and Culture (also known as Speak Out) is the nation's only not-for-profit agency for progressive speakers and artists. For more than 20 years, Speak Out has sent orators and artists to college campuses, governmental agencies, and national conferences to deliver messages that inspire social change and policy reform. Speak Out has also sent speakers to major university conferences such as the National Conference on Race and Ethnicity, the American Association of Collegiate Registrars and Admissions Officials, the National Association of Student Personnel Administrators, and the American College Personnel Association to bring issues of mixed-race identity and changing population demographics to the forefront of higher education policies. Over the past decade, several hundred presentations, including films, workshops, and lectures, have been delivered across the nation on issues ranging from multiracial identity and mental health to mixed-race identity and social movements in the arts and political arena.

Although Speak Out does not have a direct services program, as do the DataCenter and Circle of Healing, it reaches large numbers of students, educators, policymakers, and community organizers. More than a million people have been impacted by the work of the speakers and artists. By giving visibility to multiracial topics, speakers, issues, and research, Speak Out is helping to create a national dialogue on the multiracial experience. For example, for many years during the 1990s, it sponsored a traveling photo exhibit of multiracial families. The exhibit included both monoracial and mixed-race parents with mixed-race, multi-ethnic children. The exhibit worked to shift attitudes about the rights of people of mixed ancestry to claim their dual heritages without implying a denial of political allegiance to any of the multiple groups to which they belong.

What is missing, however, from Speak Out, Circle of Healing, and even the DataCenter is a, multi-organizational space where multiple groups can come together to address social justice issues. As the next section highlights, the AAACC in San Francisco is creating a collaborative space where African-American, LGBTQ, Native American, multiracial, and other groups can gather collectively to produce programs and services that will reduce social inequities within traditionally marginalized populations.

The AAACC: innovations in multi-community arts organizing

Founded in 1989, the AAACC is a space where all residents of San Francisco can find creative and innovative ways to produce social and cultural change. Intrinsic to the mission of AAACC is the importance of multi-community organizing aimed at ameliorating ethnic, racial, religious, and sociocultural disparities—particularly through Afro-centric artistic initiatives. The AAACC mission clearly identifies collaboration as a central feature of its mission and objective:

> The African American Art and Culture Complex (AAACC) is a community based, 501 (c)3 arts and cultural organization. Our mission is to empower our community through Afro-centric artistic and cultural expression, mediums, education and programming. We are dedicated to inspiring children and youth to serve as agents of change, cultivating their leadership skills and fostering a commitment to community

service and activism. In addition, we encourage, support and promote the work of young, aspiring Bay Area artists. We also strive to develop partnerships with organizations that are similarly committed to our mission, and offer our space to the community for special events. (AAACC, no date)

In the past, ethnic and cultural group boundaries often made it difficult, if not impossible, to bring together diverse populations into the same space for potential social, cultural, and political organizing efforts.

As the interim director of the AAACC, I am actively working to build a multiracial space at the complex. I was recruited to the board of the AAACC because of my mixed African-American, Native American, and European background and my ties to multiple ethnic communities and the LGBT population in the Bay Area. The shift of the focus of this monoracial organization to reflect a multiracial, multi-issue framework reflects a growing trend in political organizing across the US. Increasingly, mixed-race people are serving in important leadership roles within ethnic- or racial-specific non-profit organizations and making important policy changes for all communities. For example, the new director of the AAACC identifies as mixed-race/multi-ethnic, African-American, Native American, and European.

As at the DataCenter, Circle of Healing, and Speak Out, multiracial staff, board members, and key community stakeholders are at the heart of these changes. It is no coincidence that the multi-issue organizing of these organizations began to come about after some of their leadership positions began to be filled with people who identify as multiracial. In the past, multiracial people have often sacrificed their dual or multiple heritages in order to develop social justice and policy reform approaches with which monoracial leaders were traditionally comfortable. Organizations like the AAACC serve as important examples of the ways in which mixed-race people, who identify as multiracial rather than monoracial in increasing numbers, are shifting the once-strict boundaries of organizing among racially identified groups.

Multiracial organizing and monoracial solidarity as a new social justice framework for policy reform in the US

The multiracial organizations that continue to thrive following the 2000 decision to allow people to check off more than one racial category on the US Census, such as MAVIN, the Association for MultiEthnic Americans, and SWIRL, tend to be those that focus on multi-issue organizing. The takeaways from this fact and from successful organizations like the DataCenter, Circle of Healing, Speak Out, and the AAACC is that when we organize around our multiple issues rather than just our identities, we have more success. As we continue to organize for social justice reforms, we should pay careful attention to organizations that work to bring visibility to multiracial concerns by linking these issues to other broad, coalitional issues that other communities of color can relate to as important for societal reform

Today, multi-issue organizing goes hand in hand with multiracial organizing. However, while advocacy groups using Alinsky's model of multi-issue organizing often include multiracial people as part of their overall broad-based organizing efforts, they do not tend to have a specific focus on multiracial and multi-ethnic organizing. In recent years, other organizations have created programs that speak directly to both multi-issue, multiracial, and multi-ethnic organizing. For example, in 2005, iPride launched the Fusion summer program for mixed-heritage youth and transracially adopted kids in San Francisco, California. A few years ago, the program moved to Oakland, where it brought together multiracial organizations to develop important curriculum changes impacting youth from broad socio-economic, racial, ethnic, and cultural backgrounds. As Williams and Chilungu note in Chapter Seven, multiracial students are still largely ignored in kindergarten through 12th grade (K-12) school curricula. As a result of the work of Fusion, however, several hundred families from different mixed racial and social class backgrounds in the Bay Area come together in an educational environment where the mixed-race experience is a central theme in their daily learning.

A new social justice framework

In 1995, philosopher and mixed-race theorist Naomi Zack suggested that the ability of Black and White mixed-race people to self-select an ancestry that would include both groups would have significant and far-reaching policy implications. The chapters in this book show the prescience of her prediction. Now that multiracial people have greater visibility across the US and an increasing level of civic engagement in monoracial organizations, the future of public policy must necessarily turn to issues related to multiracial Americans. In the case of each of the four organizations discussed in this chapter we see a specific and intentional focus on multiracial people as subjects rather than objects

The earlier we involve young people in organizing across different forms of identity, including multiracial and multi-ethnic identities, the better. As the numbers of people identifying with two or more races grows and the overall demographic make-up becomes more diverse, with numbers of Latinos and Asian-Americans also rising, organizing across racial and ethnic lines becomes increasingly important. Many of the same issues facing other marginalized people of color impact mixed-race people. Education, immigration, prison reform, and health care, especially mental health, are all public policy topics that concern monoracial and multiracial people of all races. As we continue to acknowledge critical mixed-race activism, we have to embrace the membership of multiracial people in many different communities.

A new social justice framework outlined in the following—and exhibited by the work of the DataCenter, Circle of Healing, Speak Out, and AAACC—ensures ongoing cross-racial and cross-ethnic coalition-building and policy reform among mixed-race and monoracial groups:

1. *Public Visibility.* Media (social, print, and otherwise) must proactively and comprehensively include the experiences of both monoracial and multiracial population demographics in the US in order to sustain the public visibility of the shared, yet distinct, ways in which discrimination and oppression impact minority populations.
2. *Multi-Issue Organizing.* To avoid the trappings of ethnic-, racial-, gender-, and sexuality-based conflicts, multiracial leaders who advocate for policy reforms must always create agendas that are multi-issue, rather than single issue. This will produce higher levels of societal buy-in and an increase in the likely success of any reform measures. Multi-issue organizing also attacks the Western compartmentalization of various aspects of human identity by approaching social problems from a holistic approach, where all aspects of each person are equally considered.
3. *Shared Ethnic Leadership.* Shared leadership between multiracial and monoracial individuals in non-ethnic-specific, monoracial, and multiracial organizations is not only important for issues of inclusivity and equity, but also crucial for a varied and complex view of the many different routes through which reform can take place.
4. *Transformational Programming.* Programs and research projects (such as those discussed in this chapter) must seek to transform society, now bifurcated among Black–White, male–female, rich–poor, and so on. Transformational programming seeks to shift the cultural, as well the ideological, foundations of US policies and to produce racial and ethnic equality not just for one group, but for all groups.

Moving forward, these four steps may serve as a potential roadmap for monoracial and multiracial organizations and organizers seeking social justice in the coming decades. The time for organizing across single issues and with monoracial- or multiracial-only constituencies will necessarily become an obsolete phenomenon as the racial and ethnic demographics of the nation continue to shift, bringing ever-greater levels of interracial contact, cooperation, and ideological pluralism.[2]

Notes

[1] "Two-spirit" refers to a contemporary term coined by First Nations community organizers and tribal members from Canada in the late 1980s/early 1990s to refer to a historic tradition with indigenous, Native American, Alaskan Native, and First Nations communities where people who identified with more than one gender identity and/or engaged in same-sex relations were generally accepted prior to colonial contact. For more information on the term "two-spirit," see Jacobs (1997).

[2] A note of disclosure. I have worked closely with each of the organizations discussed in this chapter as a board, advisory board member, or speaker over the past decade.

References

AAACC (African American Art and Culture Complex) (no date) Mission & vision. Available at: http://www.aaacc.org/mission-vision.php (accessed 11 August 2014).

Circuitous.org (no date) Combahee River Collective Statement. Available at: http://circuitous.org/scraps/combahee.html (accessed 11 August 2014).

Cohen, C. (1999) *The boundaries of blackness: AIDS and the breakdown of Black politics*. Chicago, IL: University of Chicago Press.

DataCenter for Research Justice (2014a) Building safe communities through strong partnerships in the canal. Available at: http://www.datacenter.org/wp-content/uploads/VDC_Report_Final_Draft_ENGLISH_WEB.pdf

DataCenter for Research Justice (2014b) 11 Participatory Research Tips for Creating a Survey. 29 July. Available at: http://www.datacenter.org/11-participatory-research-tips-survey/ (accessed 11 August 2014).

Jacobs, S.-E., Thomas, W. and Lang, S. (1997) *Two spirit people: Native American gender identity, sexuality, and spirituality*. Chicago, IL: University of Illinois Press.

Jolivette, A. (2015) Research justice: radical love as a strategy for social transformation. In Andrew J. Jolivette (ed) *The research justice handbook: methodologies for social change*. Bristol: The Policy Press.

Miller, M. (2010) Alinsky for the Left: the politics of community organizing. *Dissent Magazine*. Available at: http://www. dissentmagazine.org/article/alinsky-for-the-left-the-politics-of-community-organizing (accessed 30 October 2014).

Native American Health Center (no date) Circle of Healing program. Available at: http://www.nativehealth.org/content/circle-healing-hiv-and-hcv-services (accessed 11 August 2014).

Smith, T.L. (2015) Decolonizing knowledge: towards a critical research justice praxis with Dr. Linda Tuhiwai Smith. In: A. Jolivette (ed) *Research Justice: Methodologies for social change*, Bristol: Policy Press.

US Census Bureau (2010) Homepage. Available at: http://www.census.gov/ (accessed 11 August 2014).

Zack, N. (1995) Mixed Black and White race and public policy. *Hypatia* 10(1): 120-132.

Conclusion: Policies for a racially just society

Kathleen Odell Korgen

Race policies are a vital part of efforts to promote racial justice. At the most basic level, race policies that require keeping race-based data are invaluable resources in the fight for racial justice. Without such policies, we would not be able to prove or, in some cases, even notice patterns of racial discrimination. If we are not aware of such patterns, we cannot address them.

Without data to prove a pattern, it is common for the American public to ignore or brush off experiences of racial discrimination as isolated or unusual cases. In contrast, social protests sparked by the deaths of Michael Brown and Eric Garner in the summer of 2014 helped bring the killings of unarmed Black men by police officers to the consciousness of the US public. However, it would be impossible to make the case that they are examples of a social pattern of racial discrimination without race policies that require tracking the treatment of different racial groups by the police. With the evidence provided by such tracking, we can *show* that these episodes are part of a pattern of racial discrimination in the US criminal justice system that must be addressed (Alexander, 2010; The Sentencing Project, 2014).

Why must race policy include multiracial Americans? As the chapters in this book demonstrate, more Americans than ever before now identify with more than one race, and their numbers will continue to grow rapidly. We need race policies that will help us better understand the various multiracial populations and measure and address the racial discrimination they face. The very existence of growing numbers of people who identify as multiracial indicates that racial lines are not as stark as they once were. However, they do not imply the end of racial disparities and racism. We may have a Black President (of multiracial descent), but we do not live in a color-blind and post-racial society. When unarmed Black men can be killed by police officers without penalty and the unemployment rate for Black people remains persistently double that of White people, race still matters (Somashekhar et al, 2015; Bureau of Labor Statistics, US Department of Labor, 2015).

As Campbell and Barron show in Chapter Two, the incomes of multiracial groups tend to "follow patterns that resemble the racial inequality experiences of the single-race groups to which they are connected." According to the US Bureau of the Census, the median household income in 2012 for Asian-Americans was $68,636, and for White, non-Hispanic Americans it was $57,009, but it was just $33,321 for Black and $39,005 for Hispanic Americans (DeNavas-Walt et al, 2013). Wealth, which requires time to accumulate, reveals even starker disparities between White Americans and Black and Hispanic Americans. The average White American has 13 times the wealth of the average Black American and 10 times that of the average Latino American (Kochhar and Fry, 2014).

We know that these differences in income and wealth relate to both past and *current* practices of racial discrimination. For example, because we can track groups by race, we know that Black people and Latinos still face racial discrimination when seeking employment (Pager et al, 2009) and applying for a mortgage (Rothstein, 2012). Racial discrimination against people who identify as multiracial should also be recorded and addressed.

Reasonable people can debate the pros and cons of a stand-alone multiracial category. However, the need to somehow attain more data on those who fall under the multiracial umbrella is clear. As the chapters in this book reveal, we still have a relative dearth of information about multiracial people in the US. For example, as Bratter and Mason point out, we do not yet have systematic means to collect data on multiracial people from health-care providers. Utilizing the limited available data, Bratter and Mason show that the health status of multiracial people does not match those of monoracial people. However, we do not yet have enough data to effectively shape health policy directed at specific multiracial demographic groups.

Likewise, we do not have the data we need to ascertain the extent to which multiracial Americans face racial discrimination in housing, attaining loans, retail shopping, schools, and so on. In order to create effective race policies, we need better means of collecting data about the various multiracial groups. Furthermore, as Campbell and Barron note, we also need to be able to distinguish among the various types of multiracial persons. A single multiracial category conceals wide variations in socio-economic status among the different combinations of multiracial people.

Together, the authors of this book have provided much-needed information on the various multiracial populations and the social policy issues related to the increasing numbers of Americans who identify as multiracial. These new (multi)racial demographics have helped bring about an opportunity for constructive change that scholars should help guide, as well as study. Critical race and critical mixed-race (CMR) scholars recognize that both racial categories and hierarchies are social constructions. They also note that what is socially constructed can be reconstructed. The authors in this book reveal the need for policy changes in such areas as health care, discrimination and affirmative action policies, education, prisons, and social justice organizations. Key policy suggestions include the following:

- The US Census should replace the separate Hispanic/Latino ethnicity and race questions and adopt a unified race and origin question for the Census 2020 that allows people to choose their "race/origin" from a single list that includes "Hispanic/Latino."
- US antidiscrimination law should provide multiracial Americans the status of a "suspect class" with a history of facing discrimination, or recognize multiracial as an established racial identity.
- Colleges and universities ought to prioritize enrolling low socio-economic status monoracial and multiracial applicants. Doing so requires accurately compiling the racial identification of the applicants, including the various racial combinations of multiracial applicants.
- Government agencies should track discrimination against people who identify as multiracial and include analysis of the extent to which different multiracial groups face discrimination based on their multiracial background, rather than their perceived identity as a member of a monoracial minority racial group. This data collection would also provide useful information for determining how multiracial people should be covered under affirmative action programs.
- Teacher training should cover issues related to multiracial students, and the history of multiracial Americans should be properly recognized and incorporated into curricula.
- Institutions of higher education should make conscious and systematic efforts to include and recognize multiracial students in curricular, extra-curricular, and co-curricular programming.
- Government agencies and health providers should track the health of multiracial patients and include information on the type of multiracial background and on how health providers identify patients racially.

- Prisons should follow Census racial categorization policies and allow inmates to racially self-identify and identify with more than one racial category, if they choose to do so.
- Organizations working for social justice should, whenever possible, find common cause across monoracial and multiracial lines and welcome the input of those who identify with more than one racial category.

These race policies would recognize the right to identify with more than one racial group and the reality that multiracial Americans can face discrimination for being multiracial, as well as being of a particular minority group. We need such policies to create a just society for Americans of *every* race—and multiple races.

In our increasingly diverse and unequal society, race still matters and affects the lives of all Americans—including multiracial Americans. We must resist efforts to abolish race policies and protect the status quo of White privilege in the process, as advocates of the color-blind ideology suggest we do. In addition, we must revise existing race policies to effectively measure and curb the racial discrimination faced by both monoracial and multiracial Americans. To do so, we need to work across lines of all types of identity (e.g., racial, ethnic, class, gender, sexual identity, disability, etc) to create a society where social justice prevails for all. As Strmic-Pawl and Brunsma state, together we can create "a positive window for racial reconciliation and bridge-building." Working across traditional boundaries and following Jolivette's inclusive social justice framework, we can foster "coalition-building and policy reform among mixed-race and monoracial groups." It is time for race policy in the US to catch up to the nation's new demographics and work for a racially just society for all. The authors in this book have helped pave a path toward that goal.

References

Alexander, M. (2010) *The new Jim Crow*. New York, NY: The New Press.

Bureau of Labor Statistics, US Department of Labor (2015) The employment situation: March 2015. Available at: http://www.bls.gov/news.release/empsit.nr0.htm

DeNavas-Walt, C., Proctor, B.D., and Smith, J.C. (2013) Income, poverty, and health insurance coverage in the United States: 2012. September. Available at: https://www.census.gov/prod/2013pubs/p60-245.pdf

Kochhar, R. and Fry, R. (2014) Wealth inequality has widened along racial, ethnic lines since end of Great Recession. Pew Research Center. Available at: http://www.pewresearch.org/fact-tank/2014/12/12/racial-wealth-gaps-great-recession/

Pager, D., Western, B., and Sugie, N. (2009) Sequencing disadvantage: barriers to employment facing young Black and White men with criminal records. *Annals of the American Academy of Political and Social Sciences* 623(May): 195–213.

Rothstein, R. (2012) A comment on Bank of America/Countrywide's discriminatory mortgage lending and its implications for racial segregation. Economic Policy Institute, 23 January. Available at: http://www.epi.org/publication/bp335-boa-countrywide-discriminatory-lending/

The Sentencing Project (2014) Statement of The Sentencing Project to the Senate Judiciary Committee, subcommittee on the constitution, civil rights and human rights hearing on "The state of civil and human rights in the United States." 9 December. Available at: http://sentencingproject.org/doc/publications/rd_Statement_for_SJC_Hearing_on_Civil_and_Human_Rights_in_the_U.S._Dec_2014.pdf

Index

Note: page numbers in *italic* type refer to Figures; those in **bold** refer to Tables.

Asian or Pacific Islander (racial category) 4, 22, 71
Asian-American people 192
  demographics 194
  health issues **160,** 161
  social class and racial identity 68
Asian-Some Other Race (racial category); socio-economic profiles 31–2, 33, **34,** 35, **36,** 37, 118
assimilation *see* racial assimilation

B

Barron, Jessica M. 6, 29–49, 118, 222
Beeman, Angie 173
Behavioral Risk Factor Surveillance Scheme 157–8
bilingualism, of multiracial groups **34,** 35, **36,** 37, 41–2, *42, 43*
biological races, belief in 86–7, 92–3, 95
birth certificates, and racial categorization 23
Black people:
  health issues 155, **160,** 161, 164
  killing of by police officers 221
  and residential racial segregation 44–5
Black Seminoles 15–16
Black-American Indian Alaskan Native (racial category); socio-economic profiles 31, 33, **34,** 35, **36,** 37
Black-Asian (racial category); socio-economic profiles 32, **34,** 35, **36,** 44, 45, 46–7
Black-White multiracial people
  social class and racial identity 68, 69, 70, 194
  see also White-Black (racial category)
Black/African American (racial category) 4, 22, 60
  demographics 194
  in higher education 113, 114, 115, 141
  in prison 176, **177, 178,** 179, 180, 181
  socioeconomic profiles 222
  see also African American people; Black-American Indian Alaskan Native (racial category); Black-Asian (racial category); Black/African American (racial category); Latina/o-Black-Some Other Race (racial category); White-Black (racial category); White-Black-American Indian Alaskan Native (racial category)
blood quantum system of racial categorization 16
Bonilla-Silva, E. 73, 198, 200
Botts, Tina Fernandes 6–7, 81–100
Bratter, Jenifer L. 8, 155–71, 180, 222
bridge-building 196

Brown University 147
Brown v. Board of Education 22, 56, 103
Brown, Michael 221
Browning of America 194
Brunsma, David L. 4, 8, 29, 68, 69, 143, 191–205, 197, 224
Bryn Mawr College 115
Buckner, J. 146–7

C

Campbell, Mary E. 6, 29–49, 72, 118, 222
Chavez, G. 156–7
Cheerios advertisement 129, 132, 191, 195
Chicago; socio-economic profiles of multiracial groups 38, *38,* 39, *40, 41, 42, 43, 44*
Chilungu, E. Namisi 7, 123–37, 217
Chinese-Hawaiians 18–20
Circle of Healing program, Native American Health Center 212–14
Cisneros v. Corpus Christi Independent School District 56
Civil Rights Act, 1866 88
Civil Rights Act, 1964 22, 89, 103
civil rights movement 103, 109
Clark, T.T. 157
CMR (critical mixed race) studies 1–2, 4, 140–1, 208–9, 223
Cohen, Cathy 209
colleges *see* higher education
color-blind ideology 7, 9, 73–4, 76, 102, 104, 173, 192, 193, 200
  in prisons 175, 182–3, 187, 188
colorism 129–30
Columbus, Christopher 131
Common Application 115, 117
Common Core Curriculum 132–3
community-based health initiatives 163–4
Connerly, Ward 74, 102
consensus issues, in social justice 209
crisis management, in the Nixon administration 105
critical race studies 4, 223
cross-cutting issues, in social justice 209
Cuba 54
cultural resource centers, in higher education 146–7
curriculum issues, and multiracial students 130–3

D

DaCosta, K. 195
DataCenter for Research Justice 207, 210–12